Bring Me Home!

DOGS make GREAT PETS

W9-BYK-782

Bring Me Home!

DOGS make GREAT PETS

Margaret H. Bonham

Howell
Book House™

Howell Book House
Published by Wiley Publishing, Inc., Hoboken, New Jersey

All color insert photos by Kent Dannen.

The publisher and the author make no representations or warranties with respect to the accuracy or completeness of the contents of this work and specifically disclaim all warranties, including without limitation warranties of fitness for a particular purpose. No warranty may be created or extended by sales or promotional materials. The advice and strategies contained herein may not be suitable for every situation. This work is sold with the understanding that the publisher is not engaged in rendering legal, accounting, or other professional services. If professional assistance is required, the services of a competent professional person should be sought. Neither the publisher nor the author shall be liable for damages arising here from. The fact that an organization or Website is referred to in this work as a citation and/or a potential source of further information does not mean that the author or the publisher endorses the information the organization or Website may provide or recommendations it may make. Further, readers should be aware that Internet Websites listed in this work may have changed or disappeared between when this work was written and when it is read.

For general information on our other products and services or to obtain technical support please contact our Customer Care Department within the U.S. at (800) 762-2974, outside the U.S. at (317) 572-3993 or fax (317) 572-4002.

Wiley also publishes its books in a variety of electronic formats. Some content that appears in print may not be available in electronic books. For more information about Wiley products, please visit our web site at www.wiley.com.

Library of Congress Control Number: 2005926635

ISBN-13 978-0-7645-8831-0

ISBN-10 0-7645-8831-1

Printed in the United States of America

10 9 8 7 6 5 4 3 2

Book design by Melissa Auciello-Brogan
Cover design by Suzanne Sunwoo
Book production by Wiley Publishing, Inc. Composition Services

Table of Contents

SPOT

To Larry, as always.

Acknowledgments

I wish to thank those who made this book possible:

Jessica Faust of Bookends
The Howell team: Roxane Cerda, Cindy Kitchel, Christina Stambaugh, Kathy Nebenhaus, and Kitty Jarrett

And special thanks to Larry, who has been through this more than once.

Introduction

So you want to own a dog? Dogs are the second most popular pets (after cats)—but they're not for everyone. How do you decide whether to get a dog? And if you decide to get one, how do you decide what type of dog to get, and how do you take care of your new dog? This book will help you answer these questions.

In this book, you'll learn all about the basics of dog ownership and what you need to do to find a well-adjusted and healthy pet and what you need to do to make your new dog a vital part of your family. Unlike many books that focus on simple dog ownership, this one focuses on how a dog will fit into *your* family and *your* life.

This book includes checklists, tips, and worksheets that will help you decide what to do when choosing, caring for, and training your dog. These tools help you really think about the important issues in owning a dog; you should use them to assess your family's—and your dog's—particular situation. Here are a few examples:

- Worksheets that help you decide if a dog is right for you, give you some key interview questions to ask a breeder, and help you find a veterinarian
- Information that helps you find the right dog
- Checklists that guide you through dog-proofing your house and purchasing items for your dog
- Step-by-step instructions that teach you how to train your dog on a number of common commands

This book is intended to be an interactive resource that you can turn to again and again to help with your decision making and organization. Each chapter opens and closes with a bulleted list that guides you through the chapter at a glance.

In the very back of this book is an appendix titled "Useful Resources." I encourage you to photocopy its forms, use a three-hole punch, and put them in a notebook labeled "dog stuff," so you can keep vital records and information about your dog handy at all times. The appendix also includes chore lists that you can post on the refrigerator and refer to at any time. As your dog becomes a part of your family, you'll find that you'll refer to the notebook constantly. When were his last shots? How did he do with the pet sitter? Do you remember when he got his Canine Good Citizen? All of these things and more make up your dog's life and should be noted in your notebook. This will enhance your pet ownership experience.

With the help of the tools in this book, I hope you have a more pleasurable experience in dog ownership.

Chapter 1

Are You Ready to Get a Dog?

What's Inside...

- Learn whether owning a dog is a good choice for you and your family.
- Learn what time constraints a dog will put on your lifestyle.
- Learn the time and financial costs of dog ownership.
- Learn whether your living situation warrants owning a dog.

A dog. The word may conjure up Lassie going to rescue Timmy yet again. Or Ol' Yeller, who served his family so faithfully. Or perhaps Pongo of *101 Dalmatians,* Benji, or some other dog superstar has caught your eye. Maybe you always wanted a dog, but your parents didn't let you have one. Or maybe you've grown up with dogs and are looking for another one. Maybe you have a family now and you want your family to enjoy a pet.

If you're interested in getting a dog, you're in good company. There are approximately 63 million dogs in the United States alone. About 45 million U.S. households have dogs. You can get a dog in almost any shape, size, or color imaginable (at least those found in nature), and the variety of dog breeds is staggering. If you want a purebred, you have 154 American Kennel Club (AKC) breeds, as well as more than 150 other breeds, to choose from, or you might opt for a one-of-a-kind mixed-breed dog.

Dogs offer companionship, protection, and, in some cases, services. Most people know about dogs who help visually impaired people, but there are also dogs who hear for those who are deaf and those who can help quadriplegics. Likewise, dogs work as sled dogs, tracking dogs, hunting dogs, herding dogs, search-and-rescue dogs, and a variety of other jobs for humans. No other domesticated animal is so versatile and so bonded to humans.

Whatever the reason, you want a dog. You're ready for one now.

Or are you?

Responsible Pet Ownership

We hear a lot about "pet overpopulation" and unwanted pets. It's been estimated that about five million pets are euthanized every year in the United States. The reasons are varied, but many dogs are given up because their former owners brought home pets without understanding the responsibilities of pet ownership. By picking up this book, you've taken the first step toward responsible pet ownership.

Owning a dog is a big responsibility, both in time and in cost. Every year millions of dogs make their way into shelters and rescues because people thought that they would like a dog but weren't prepared for the responsibility of having one.

Even if you're dead-set on getting a dog, don't jump to chapter 2 and ignore my warnings. It's important that you understand the responsibilities of pet ownership.

Time Commitments and Inconveniences of Owning a Dog

Dogs are pretty unique critters. They offer their owners companionship, love, and humor, but in return, dogs require time and can be inconvenient. In most cases, dogs are dependent on their owners for attention (no, they don't amuse themselves—or if they do, it's usually with something you don't want them to amuse themselves with), and they require training, exercise, and attention every day.

Every day? Yes. *Every* day.

Dogs are pack animals, meaning that they require companionship from their pack. That means you. So owning a dog involves a commitment in a relationship.

Owning a dog is a ten- to fifteen-year commitment to that relationship. That means you have to be there to let her out to relieve herself at least every four hours as a puppy and every nine hours as an adult. You have to feed her two (or three, if a puppy) times a day. You have to provide fresh water. And you have to train and exercise her.

If you get a dog or puppy, she's going to be dependent on you for attention. A lot of attention. Depending on the type of dog you have, you may have a dog who clings to you like Velcro. (In fact, Shadow is a very popular name for dogs.) One person described certain breeds by saying, "You'll never go to the bathroom alone again." That sums up many dog breeds. If you don't want a dog hounding you at every step (pun intended), don't get a dog. Granted, there *are* independent-minded critters out there, such as some of the hounds and dogs that come from the northern breeds, including Alaskan Malamutes, Siberian Huskies, and Samoyeds.

So, with a dog, you have an animal who clings to you and who is looking for your guidance and interaction. But dogs also get into a tremendous amount of trouble when they're not looking for your attention. The roast on the counter is enticing; so is the garbage you put in the pail just under the counter. The chair legs are yummy. You have to spend time watching to make sure your new dog or puppy isn't getting into things she shouldn't. This takes away from the time you have for other things.

You're going to have to consider your dog instead of going out to dinner with your coworkers right after work or otherwise spending a long day away from home. Your dog will need to be let out, played with, exercised, and fed. And at least for a while after you bring her home, you're going to need to spend time watching your dog to make sure she doesn't get into trouble.

How long do you need to spend training and exercising your dog? Well, that depends on the dog, how old she is, what breed she is, and other factors. If you live in an apartment, you can expect that you're going to have to take your dog outside a minimum of four to five times a day to eliminate (and take her on one long walk of twenty minutes or more). If you have a fenced-in backyard, you'll have to let your dog out several times each day, and you're going to have to take her for at least one long walk every day or at least two or three times a week, depending on the breed.

Think about your current lifestyle. Taking off for a spontaneous weekend at the beach is out of the question if you can't bring your dog with you or you don't have a pet sitter or boarding kennel lined up. You must come home every day to care for your dog. You must walk her daily (or at least several times a week). Training is a must—dogs (especially puppies) don't come housetrained, and basic commands don't come easily to all dogs.

Training takes time. You'll need to start training classes, whether your dog is a puppy or an adult. If you're getting a puppy, consider taking five or six hour-long puppy kindergarten classes and then hour-long weekly obdience classes for eight to twelve weeks. An adult dog will only need the obedience course. During the obedience course and afterward, you need to work at home on training your dog. These sessions need to last ten to twenty minutes a day to keep her training fresh.

If you get a puppy (or an adult dog who isn't housetrained), you can count on spending some time housetraining her. If your dog is a puppy, it may take some time to housebreak her—from two or three months all the way up to one year. Some puppies catch on fast; others do not. Housetraining an older dog is easier, as most older dogs usually have some experience with housetraining already. If you stick with a schedule and crate your dog when you can't watch her, a few times of teaching her to eliminate outside is usually all that's needed.

Grooming takes time. Most dogs require some sort of grooming, whether it's combing and brushing or clipping, once a week. If you're doing it yourself, plan on taking an hour or so each week for grooming. If you're not planning on doing it yourself, consider the cost in having a groomer do it for you.

If you have small children and are planning on getting a dog, think of the dog as adding one more small child to the mix. Only this child doesn't understand English and certainly doesn't wear diapers. Most new parents have their hands full with a child. A new puppy or dog usually is too much on top of all that.

Dogs will do the darnedest things to waylay your best plans. Plan on going to a big interview for a new job, and your dog will have chewed your $300 shoes. Need to get a good night's sleep for tomorrow's big presentation? Your dog will be up all night, puking up something that she ate the day before. What about that special holiday dinner? If you're not careful, your dog will snatch the roast off the counter (and, again, you can expect that she's going to be up all night puking). To fix all this takes time. Whether you're washing off the roast after grabbing it from your dog, going shopping for another pair of shoes, or taking the time to prevent these problems from happening in the first place, you're looking at a fair amount of time. Early on as a dog owner, I came home from a trip to find that my dog sitter had let my dogs run loose, and they had trashed the entire house. It took nearly a whole day to clean up.

Dog owners have to have a sense of humor when it comes to dog ownership and time constraints. If you're the type of person who can never find enough time in a day, don't own a dog. If you travel a lot, don't own a dog. If you're never home except to go to sleep, don't own a dog. And if you don't have a sense of humor, consider a very serious breed that is easily trained.

How much time will having a dog take? Again, that depends on the age, breed, and activity level of the dog. Between care, attention, exercise, playtime, and snuggling on the sofa, for puppies and young dogs, you can expect to spend about four to six hours each day; for older dogs, expect to spend three to four hours each day. Arguably, you can spend less, but then why bother owning a dog? Of course, this time can be split up between different family members, but someone must oversee the care to make sure that the dog is being properly cared for.

Financial Commitments of Dog Ownership

There is no such thing as a free dog. Nor does the cost of a dog stop at her purchase or adoption price. All dogs require adequate food, supplies, and veterinary care. Depending on the size of your dog, she may eat a little or quite a bit. Expect to buy a twenty-pound bag of premium food for a small dog and a forty-pound bag of premium food for a large dog once a month, plus canned meat and treats.

Your puppy will need a series of four to six vaccinations (usually a distemper-parvovirus combo and rabies). She'll need to be dewormed, tested for heartworm, and given heartworm-preventive medication. And if she's not already spayed or neutered, your dog will have to be spayed or neutered before the age of 6 months.

How Much Does a Dog Cost?

The cost of a dog doesn't end at her purchase or adoption price. If you decide to buy a puppy, you can expect certain costs the first year. The following is a list of potential costs you might face the first year:

Item	Cost	Total
Veterinary Care		
Distempter-parvo combo vaccination	$10–$50 each	$40–$200 (four times)
Rabies vaccination	$10–$30 each	$10–$30
Lyme disease vaccination	$30–$75 each	$60–$150 (two times)
Bordetella vaccination	$20–$40 each	$40–$80 (two times)
Giardia vaccination	$30–$75 each	$60–$150 (two times)
Office visit	$10–$30 each	$40–$120 (four times)
Spay/neuter	$25–$200	$20–$200
Deworming	$20–$50 each	$40–$100 (two times)
Heartworm test	$10–$50 each	$10–$50
Heartworm medicine	$4–$8 per dose	$50–$100
Supplies		
Crate	$20–$200 each	$20–$200
Bowls	$5–$10 each	$10–$20
Food	$10–$50 per month	$120–$600
Treats	$1–$5 per week	$52–$260
Toys	$3–$15 each	$9–$45
Grooming supplies	$20–$50	$20–$50
Collars, leashes, etc.	$10–$30	$30–$90
Miscellaneous supplies (bedding, etc.)	$10–$100	$10–$100
Services		
Grooming	$25–$75 per visit	$300–$900
Boarding	$10–$40 per day	$140–$480
Training	$80–$300 per 8-week class	$160–$600
Yard cleanup	$25–$50	$350–$600

Most puppies are expensive for the first year of life because of the required vaccinations, supplies, and veterinary checkups. (If you get an adult dog, you can still expect to have increased costs the first year, although they won't likely be as high as those for a puppy.) The cost usually decreases or remains steady during the dog's adult life (assuming no serious injury or illness) and then rises again as the dog passes 7 years of age and becomes a senior citizen. Problems such as cancer, arthritis, and other age-related diseases may crop up after that time.

But there are other costs to owning a dog, too. Most municipalities require that you license your dog. Some insurance companies raise homeowner insurance rates if you own a dog of a certain breed. It's a good idea to go through professional training sessions with your dog, so the dog learns basic manners and obedience commands. If you're not the type who will groom your dog yourself, you can expect to pay groomers' bills, too. Other costs can include treats, toys, crates, car seat belts, beds, and cleaners and cleaning appliances.

Environmental Requirements of Owning a Dog

So far, I've talked about the time and monetary requirements of owning a dog. Another requirement has to do with you and your lifestyle. Dogs are very adaptable creatures, but there are situations that just aren't conducive to owning a dog.

First, your dog must be safe and secure. That means you can't let your dog run loose in the neighborhood, whether you're in the country with "room to roam" or in the city. If you aren't planning on taking your dog for walks several times a day, you need a kennel run or a fenced-in yard where your dog can relieve herself and get some exercise.

If you rent, keep in mind that not all places are "dog friendly." Talk with your landlord about bringing in a dog.

Dogs are social creatures and want to be with their owners. If you're planning on having an "outdoor only" pet, think again. Leaving a dog outside all the time with no interaction is not fair to the dog.

Room to Roam?

Many people have the notion that dogs need room to run around. The problem with this thinking is that dogs can get into a lot of trouble running around free, whether in the country or in the city. A game warden or rancher can usually shoot a dog legally if she's caught harassing either wildlife or livestock. A hunter or trapper may accidentally hurt or kill a dog. A dog who runs loose risks being prey to coyotes and other predators, even in cities. Dogs aren't savvy about cars, and many are hit by them. And, of course, dogs can get into trouble with porcupines, snakes, skunks, trash cans, and rotting carcasses. When your dog is outside, she should be on leash or in a fenced area.

Certain breeds of dogs can do well in an apartment, provided that the owner is committed to exercising the dog throughout the day. As I said earlier, a dog requires the chance to relieve herself at least every nine hours (fours hours, for a puppy).

If you have kids, you may be thinking that getting a dog is a good way to teach your children about responsibilities. This is fine; however, an adult in your household must be responsible for the dog. While children can help with the daily tasks, dog ownership requires a responsible adult to oversee the dog's care. You really can't expect a young child to be responsible for a living, sentient creature. You can give children tasks to do (and follow up on them) as a responsibility, but most children can't care for a dog properly.

Whether your child can care for a dog depends largely on the maturity of the child. I've known some very smart and responsible 12-year-olds whom I would think could care for a dog *with parental supervision,* and I've known teenagers I wouldn't trust caring for a houseplant. If you get a dog "for the kids," be aware that if your kids can't properly care for the dog, you've added a burden on yourself.

Am I Ready for a Dog?
Questions to Ask Yourself

Consider the following questions when getting ready to adopt or purchase a dog or puppy:

A dog is a ten- to fifteen-year commitment. Are you willing to rearrange your life for ten to fifteen years to care for a dog?

_____

_____

How long will the dog be alone during the day? (You should leave a puppy alone for no more than four hours at a time and an adult dog for no more than nine hours.)

_____

_____

continues

Can you be home at appropriate times every day or make arrangements so that your dog can eat, drink, exercise, and relieve herself?

_____

_____

If you live in an apartment, does your landlord allow dogs?

_____

_____

If you live in an apartment, are you willing to take your dog for brief walks three to four times every day and for one long walk (over twenty minutes) every day?

_____

_____

Do you have a fenced-in backyard suitable for the type of dog you want to get? (Small to medium dogs require a four-foot fence; medium to large dogs require a six-foot fence.) Are there no holes, and can you make it dig-proof and climb-proof?

_____

_____

Does your homeowners' association allow you to fence in your backyard or have a kennel run?

_____

_____

Which adult will be responsible for the care of the dog? (Children can't be expected to take responsibility for a dog. A dog must be the responsibility of an adult in the household.)

_____

_____

Are you willing to clean up after accidents and dog vomit? (Puppies have accidents, and even adult dogs may from time to time.)

_____

_____

How would you feel if your puppy chewed up something important or valuable? Puppies and adult dogs may chew inappropriate items.

_____

_____

Are you willing to housetrain your dog using a crate?

_____

_____

Are you willing to groom your dog as required? Some breeds and mixes require more grooming than others do, but all dogs need a good brushing at least once a week. Dogs with double coats shed profusely. Some dogs need periodic clipping.

_____

_____

Can you spend time training your dog ten to fifteen minutes every day so she understands your house rules and is enjoyable and fun to be around?

_____

_____

Can you spend an hour a week for six to eight weeks to socialize your puppy?

_____

_____

Can you spend an hour a week for ten weeks to train your dog properly?

_____

_____

Are you willing to pick up after your dog? Many cities have ordinances requiring that dog owners clean up after their dogs defecate. Even in cities that don't have such ordinances, picking up after your dog is a good, neighborly habit to be in.

_____

_____

continues

How do you feel about dog hair on everything and in everything, including food? (Yes, dog hair goes everywhere.)

_____

_____

How do you feel about muddy footprints on your clean clothes, or clothing that's been chewed?

_____

_____

Is anyone in your family allergic to dogs? If so, you might want to reconsider getting a dog. Who is allergic? Do you have an allergist who is willing to work with you on having a dog?

_____

_____

Does everyone in your family want a dog? Everyone must agree on wanting a dog.

_____

_____

Are you willing to exercise your dog every day? Activity levels of dogs differ considerably. A dog from a working breed is going to have a much different activity level than, say, a toy breed.

_____

_____

There is no such thing as a free or low-cost dog. You must buy dog food, bowls, dog beds, dog toys, and grooming items. You must pay for routine veterinary care and other care when the medical need arises. Can you pay for these items?

_____

_____

What will you do with your dog in a family emergency? Who can take care of her?

_____

_____

Do you have enough money (or credit) to pay for a veterinary emergency? These can run several thousands of dollars. Could you afford pet insurance?

_____

_____

If you've answered these questions positively, you're ready to consider owning a dog.

Why You *Should* Get a Dog

Now that I've sounded terribly discouraging, the truth is that having a dog is a wonderful thing. The problem is that many dog owners aren't prepared for all the inconveniences associated with having a dog. If you know about all these things, then you probably have a good idea why you want a dog and why you should get a dog.

Dogs provide companionship and, to a certain extent, security. You're never truly alone when your dog is with you. Dogs are great for people who live alone, providing both friendship and security. Most dogs will alert you to unusual things or people coming around. In many cases, just the sight or sound of a dog thwarts many people bent on doing harm. Even a small dog can be a deterrent.

According to studies, dogs are great for your health, too. Many studies suggest that pet owners live longer than those who do not have pets. Something about pets tends to make us healthier. Maybe it's the interaction or the need to take the dog for a walk. (Walking is great exercise for your dog and for you, too!) Your dog is likely to get you off the couch and outside a bit more for at least a walk or a game of fetch.

What about that unconditional love you hear about? Despite some cynics, many dog experts agree that dogs do love us. Your dog will love you for who you are, even when it feels like the rest of the world is against you. When you're feeling down, your dog will be happy to cheer you up. Dogs do goofy things and make you laugh. Even if your date has dumped you, your dog will watch that sappy romantic comedy and will be happy to share the ice cream and pizza you bought for dinner.

Many dogs are good with kids if both the kids and the dogs are properly trained and socialized. Having a dog is a great way to get kids away from the computer or video games and go outside to have fun. Having a dog is a great way to get your kids exercise, too (someone has to walk and play with the dog).

But dogs are more than just companions. Don't know how to meet other people? Get a dog. Dog lovers abound, and when you're looking to meet people, your ambassador is at the end of the leash. Get involved in various canine activities—even walks around your neighborhood—and you will meet people and make friends.

Dogs are great companions for those who like the outdoors, too. Plenty of dogs are ready to go on hikes, ride in a boat, and go swimming, jogging, biking, and plenty of other wonderful activities.

Whatever your own reasons for getting a dog, you should weigh them carefully against the responsibility of dog ownership.

What You Now Know...

- Dogs require a commitment of lots of your time. You should reconsider getting a dog if you have very young children, are constantly busy, are constantly traveling, or are unable to care for a dog or make the time commitment necessary.
- You need to be prepared for all the expenses that come along with dog ownership.
- You must provide a safe and secure environment for your dog.
- Having a dog provides a world of great benefits, from companionship to great fun!

Chapter 2

A Good Match— What Dog Is Right for You?

What's Inside . . .

- Learn what breeds of dogs are appropriate in various situations.
- Learn the advantages and disadvantages of purebreds and mixed breeds.
- Learn what size and sex of dog is right for you.
- Learn some general characteristics of different dog breeds to help decide what type of dog is a good match for your family.

You're ready for dog ownership, but now you have decisions to make: What kind of dog do you want? Mixed breed or purebred? Puppy or adult? Male or female? And would you like to supersize that?

A Good Match?

Let me say right up front that the guidelines in this chapter are generalities and that no one dog or breed is perfect. Dogs are as individual as humans are, and it is nearly impossible to guarantee that a particular dog will show all the attributes espoused by the breed club, experts, or, for that matter, this book. When I suggest that a dog breed is good for X or Y, I'm speaking in generalities. There are many factors associated with an individual dog, including genetics, socialization, health issues, training, former owners (or breeder), environmental stresses, and personality.

When you find the right dog, everything is wonderful. You and that dog just click, and you can work through housetraining, the chewed shoes, and even the dog puke without a second thought. But finding the match can be difficult if you don't really think about your situation.

Not all dogs are right for everyone. Even if you have the best intentions, sometimes you and a particular dog just don't click. Many people are surprised to learn that there are differences between the dog breeds. It's not just a matter of size or hair or color, but a question of personality and activity level, too. No matter how appealing a dog may be, if his personality doesn't fit your lifestyle, it won't work, and the dog is most likely the loser in this relation-ship. So think carefully about what's required to have a successful relationship.

Consider the following when deciding whether a particular dog is right for you:

- Children can hurt small dogs; large, boisterous dogs can hurt children accidentally by knocking them down. If you have children, be sure that they're old enough and the dog is appropriate for their age.
- Apartment dwellers are often limited to smaller dogs. Check with your landlord.
- Some dogs are not suited to apartments, no matter how good an owner you are. They may need lots of exercise, or they may bark a lot when left alone.
- Some dogs require a lot of grooming. If you don't have the time or interest for this, con-sider a dog who doesn't need much grooming.
- If you are elderly, a large, strong dog who can knock you over or drag you around might not be a good thing. Consider a smaller, calmer dog.
- Some dogs are easier to train than others. If you prefer a dog who is very trainable, con-sider a breed that has that reputation, and opt for the least dominant individual.
- If you have allergies, be aware that there is no such thing as a "hypoallergenic dog." There are dogs who have double coats (who shed) and those who have single coats (like human hair). Single-coat breeds *tend* to cause fewer problems for certain allergy suf-ferers, but that doesn't guarantee that you won't be allergic to them.
- Many breeds shed profusely. You will have dog hair on your clothes, woven into your carpet, and even in your food. Some pet owners joke about dog hair as being a condi-ment. If you can't stand the thought of all that mess, consider a dog who won't shed too much.
- Dogs can be very destructive. They often chew things you don't want them to and may make messes inside the house. Dogs cannot differentiate between a leather rawhide toy and your best leather shoes. They have to be taught the house rules.
- Expect to have dirt tracked in and maybe muddy paw prints on your floors and even your clothing, all of which can be avoided through simple training. For example, you can use the commands "Wait" while you wipe off his feet and "Off" to prevent jumping up.

Let's look at some of the issues surrounding what people are looking for when they look for a dog.

Dogs Who Are Good with Babies

I have bad news for you: No dogs can be trusted entirely with babies. Sorry. This doesn't mean you can't have a dog. It means you should never allow the dog to interact with the

baby because even a friendly and well-adjusted dog can unintention-ally hurt a baby. Large dogs can accidentally knock down a baby. When babies poke and prod dogs, they can cause pain and encour-age a dog to snap or bite. Babies and young children can often incite a prey instinct in dogs who don't look on children as humans. Small children play with small toys, which dogs can easily swallow, requiring surgery to remove. Not all dogs tolerate a baby or toddler on ground level—that's the dog's turf.

A dog of any breed can be good with babies or young children. However, not all dogs of *any* breed are good with babies and young children. Although most dogs of a certain breed might be tolerant or fond of kids, some dogs of that breed may for some reason not be patient with them. The best dogs for children of all ages, regardless of breed, have these characteristics:

- They are obedience trained and well socialized.
- They are spayed or neutered.
- They are kept in a family environment and not chained outside or left outside in the yard.
- They are medium to large sized (but be aware that they may knock down toddlers).
- They do not have the words *aloof* or *reserved* in their description or American Kennel Club (AKC) breed standard.
- They do not have flattened faces (brachycephalic heads) because dogs with these types of heads can't run around the way kids like to and often overheat.
- They can be physically active and are not upset by children's active play.
- They are not so small that they can be hurt underfoot.

If you're looking for a specific breed that's always "good with kids" you won't find one. However, you can look at medium to large dogs of Sporting Breeds, Hound Breeds, and Non-Sporting Breeds for candidates. Avoid any dogs with aggressive and guarding histories. Likewise, Herding Dogs have a propensity to nip at heels. Chris Walkowicz, in *Choosing a Dog For Dummies* (Wiley), recommends Golden Retrievers, Labrador Retrievers, Springer Spaniels, and English Cocker Spaniels, among many others, as being good with kids.

Dog Bites and Kids

Sadly, according to the American Veterinary Medical Association, every year some 4.7 million people are bitten by dogs. Of those, 800,000 people are bitten so badly that they require medical attention, and about half of those are children. Children are often bitten in the face and require plastic surgery. Between 10 and 35 people are killed every year by dogs.

In a report published in 2001 by the Centers for Disease Control and Prevention (CDC), within one year, 333,700 (out of that 4.7 million) people were admitted to emergency rooms for dog bites, and of those, 154,625 children 14 years and under were bitten seriously.

If you have children, it is *your* responsibility to keep your kids safe. Never, ever leave a child alone with a dog and never keep an aggressive dog. Any dog may bite—even those who are normally considered gentle.

Dogs Who Are Better with Young Children

As with babies, most dogs aren't good with young children. The reasons are varied but come down to the facts that most young children don't respect dogs as living creatures who can feel pain, and some dogs don't recognize children as humans. You should never leave a young child alone with a dog. This doesn't mean that you can't h   a   v   e a dog, but you must watch the interaction carefully. See chapter 7, "Educating Your Whole Family," for guidelines on how children should interact with a dog.

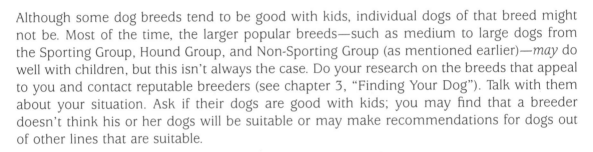

Although some dog breeds tend to be good with kids, individual dogs of that breed might not be. Most of the time, the larger popular breeds—such as medium to large dogs from the Sporting Group, Hound Group, and Non-Sporting Group (as mentioned earlier)—*may* do well with children, but this isn't always the case. Do your research on the breeds that appeal to you and contact reputable breeders (see chapter 3, "Finding Your Dog"). Talk with them about your situation. Ask if their dogs are good with kids; you may find that a breeder doesn't think his or her dogs will be suitable or may make recommendations for dogs out of other lines that are suitable.

Dogs Who Are Better with Older Children

Many dogs can do well with older, considerate children, but again, you must never leave a child alone with a dog. When looking for the right dog, talk to breeders about their dogs. Have your children meet these dogs and see how the dog reacts. Most dogs can be good with older, considerate children, provided that they have been properly trained and socialized with children.

Dogs Who Do Well in Apartments

If you're looking for an apartment dog, your first consideration should be whether the landlord allows dogs. A second consideration should be whether there is a size restriction (many apartments do have them). In the case of a size restriction, consider dogs from the Toy Group (later in this chapter). Other dogs that may do well in apartments include:

> Golden Retrievers (but not field dogs)
> Labrador Retrievers (but not field dogs)
> Greyhounds
> Smaller terriers (Terrier Group), but watch out for barkers
> Dogs from the Non-Sporting Group
> German Shepherd Dogs
> Shetland Sheepdogs (can be yappy, but with training, you can fix this)
> Standard Schnauzers

Biting Dog Study

An interesting study on biting dogs was done in Denver, Colorado, and published in *Pediatrics* in June 1994. The common denominators of the biting dogs were being owned by a family with one or more children who kept the dog chained up in the yard, being intact (not neutered), and being untrained and unsocialized. The authors of the study felt that the chaining attribute was due to the dog's antisocial and aggressive behavior and may not have been a factor in the bites themselves.

This study found that the most common biters were (according to predominance of breed in the dog):

1. German Shepherd Dogs
2. Chow Chows
3. Unknown
4. Labrador Retrievers
5. Cocker Spaniels (tie)
6. Collies (tie)
7. Doberman Pinschers
8. Akitas
9. Standard Poodles
10. Scottish Terriers
11. Shetland Sheepdogs (tie)
12. Chihuahuas (tie)
13. Golden Retrievers (tie)

Other breeds made up for over 25 percent of the bites experienced—more than any single breed.

What's the reason for giving you these statistics? To make sure you understand that *any* dog may bite, and even dogs considered "good with kids" can and do bite. The biggest problem isn't the dog, but the owner and the dog's training (or lack thereof).

Dogs Who Do Well with Other Pets

There isn't a hard-and-fast rule about finding a dog who will do well with other pets. You should never allow a dog to interact with any of the "pocket pets," such as rodents, rabbits, reptiles, birds, and other pets that might be mistaken for prey items—or serious tragedy could befall them.

However, you can find a dog who can tolerate cats well. Most puppies raised with cats can do very well with them. Occasionally, you'll find a dog such as those from the Terrier Group,

the northern breeds (Alaskan Malamutes, Siberian Huskies, Samoyeds, and so on), or the sighthounds (Greyhounds, Salukis, Borzois, Whippets, and so on) whose natural tendency to chase and attack prey overwhelms training. For this reason, you should avoid leaving your family cat unsupervised with your dog when he is uncrated, even if your dog has been raised with cats.

Good Traveling Dogs

Most dogs travel well by car if exposed at an early age. When traveling in a car with a dog, you must be constantly aware of the temperature outside, in the crate, and in the car because dogs can overheat very quickly. *Never leave a dog alone in the car for any length of time during a warm or sunny day, even with the windows rolled down.*

If you're looking for a dog who will fit under the seat in most airliners and travel with you with ease in a specially designed carry on, check out these dogs:

> Any of the dogs from the Toy Group
> Small terriers such as West Highland White Terriers, Cairn Terriers, Parson Russell Terriers, Standard Manchester Terriers, and Norwich and Norfolk Terriers
> Bichon Frises

For more on traveling with your dog, see "Traveling Together" in chapter 15, "Your Dog as Part of the Family."

Dogs Who Are Good for Neat-Freaks

The best dog for neat-freaks is a stuffed animal that they can vacuum every day. In lieu of that, the neat-freak might prefer a dog who doesn't shed quite as much as others. These dogs are dogs who have single coats (that is, no undercoats) and do not shed the way most dogs shed. A few double-coated dogs also don't shed much. However, the owner will still have to care for the coat frequently, including trimming, brushing, and combing. There's no such thing as a shed-free dog, but these dogs are about as close as you can get:

Bedlington Terriers	Chinese Cresteds
Kerry Blue Terriers	English Toy Spaniels
Sealyham Terriers	Japanese Chin
Soft Coated Wheaten Terriers	Poodles (all varieties)
Welsh Terriers	Miniature Schnauzers
Cavalier King Charles Spaniels	Papillons
Chihuahuas	Silky Terriers

Dogs Who Are Great for Really Active Families

Plenty of dogs are great for active families. Usually working dogs, such as northern breeds, and sporting dogs, such as Labrador Retrievers, Pointers, and Spaniels, are active enough to keep up with an athletic family.

Dogs Who Work Well with Older Family Members/Senior Citizens

Seniors often have problems controlling stronger and heavier dogs. For this reason, I recommend dogs who were bred to be companions, such as those in the Non-Sporting Group or the Toy Group. These dogs are generally less active and are often small enough to not be dangerous to senior dog owners.

Dogs for People with Allergies

There is no such thing as a hypoallergenic dog. If you have allergies and are very allergic to dogs, it's unlikely that you're going to find a dog you can tolerate for any length of time. This is because the allergy is not necessarily due to the hair or even the dander—often allergies occur due to the saliva of the dog.

However, there are dogs some allergy sufferers are able to tolerate. These dogs are normally the breeds with single coats, such as Poodles, some terriers, and some toy breeds. Check out the list of dogs under "Dogs Who Are Good for Neat-Freaks," on page 20. But before you get a dog, visit the breeder and spend some time with the dogs to see if the dogs affect your allergies.

Dogs Who Are Truly Trainable

The perfectly trainable dog sounds like a dream come true. The truth is that all dogs are trainable to some degree, but some "get it" faster than others. Regardless of what dog you get, you still have to put the work in and train him. Dogs who are more easily trainable include the following:

Dogs from the Herding Group (Shetland Sheepdogs, Australian Shepherds, German Shepherd Dogs, Corgis)
Dogs from the Non-Sporting Group (Keeshonden, American Eskimo Dogs, Poodles)
Golden Retrievers
Labrador Retrievers
Other retrievers

Designer Dogs

A designer dog is a dog that is a crossbreed of two different purebreds. You may have heard of Cockapoos, Peekapoos, Labradoodles, and others. These dogs may be first-generation or multigeneration, and while they're not breeds, some of these dogs are coming close to being breeds. Most designer dogs are very expensive, some costing over $2,000. They are, however, not recognized breeds by the AKC.

Mutt vs. Purebred

Mixed breed or purebred? If you're looking for a pet, you may not care whether your dog is purebred or a mixed breed. After all, there are millions of wonderful mutts out there, many looking for homes. What could be more lovable than the mutt—an all-American dog? On the other hand, you might want a purebred if you want some consistency of size, temperament, and looks.

Mutts, or Mixed Breeds

Mutts have both positives and negatives. The biggest negative for many is that they can't participate in the AKC shows and performance events. However, mutts can earn performance titles through the United Kennel Club (UKC), all other agility organizations, flyball, and other performance organizations. Mutts can even earn Canine Good Citizen titles through the AKC. If pedigrees and dog shows aren't your thing, then a mutt may be for you.

Mutts can be a surprise package—both good and bad. You may get a different personality than you expected with a mixed breed—usually a blending of the breeds within the mutt. You usually get a unique look, and many mutts are smart and make great pets. You usually save a life when you adopt a mixed breed and usually don't pay quite as much up-front on the purchase price (or adoption fee). On the negative side, you don't usually know what genetic problems might be lurking in a mixed breed. This can be an issue if your mutt has hip dysplasia or one of many genetic diseases. You may get a surprise about how your dog will look and what's in his background, but if you want a pet as unique as yourself, get a mutt.

Purebreds

Purebreds, too, have positives and negatives. With a purebred, you get a distinctive look and can usually rely on the type of personality. A purebred won't have as many surprises in size or looks, which means that if you know what the parents look like, you can guess the puppies will look similar. Purebreds can compete in AKC conformation dog shows and can compete in performance events within the AKC.

On the negative side, purebreds can have genetic diseases that exist within certain lines or even within the breed. However, mutts aren't free from genetic diseases, and many mixed breeds with unknown ancestry may carry the same genes that cause hereditary diseases in purebreds. Both mixed-breed and purebred dogs can have hip dysplasia, elbow dysplasia, eye diseases, and allergies, to name a few.

Most purebreds tend to be costly as puppies. You can expect to pay $300 or more for a purebred puppy, and well-bred purebred puppies can cost almost $1,000. Mixed-breed puppies are usually inexpensive, except for the "designer" crossbreeds, which can cost over $1,000. Purebred adults are usually lower-cost—about half or less what you expect to pay for a puppy—if you get them from a shelter or a breed rescue organization. Breeders often place older dogs no longer being shown or used for breeding at a reasonable price.

Reasons for Getting a Mutt or a Purebred

Mutt

- ☐ I don't want to pay a lot for my dog.
- ☐ I don't necessarily want a special look.
- ☐ I want a nice companion who will primarily be a pet.
- ☐ I want to save a dog's life.
- ☐ I will neuter my dog.

Purebred

- ☐ I want a dog with a specific temperament and look.
- ☐ I like a particular breed and that is the best breed for me.
- ☐ I don't mind paying a fair amount of money to have the type of dog I want.
- ☐ I want a specific type of dog for a specific job, such as guarding, police work, search and rescue, agility, sled dog racing, or some other function that requires the dog to have been bred for the job.
- ☐ I want to show a dog in conformation dog shows.

Which is better, mutts or purebreds? It's really a matter of opinion. I've owned plenty of mixed breeds and purebreds, and both have made outstanding pets.

Small, Medium, or Large?

Size does matter when it comes to dogs. You probably already have a preference. But before you decide on a particular size, consider the following:

- Small and medium-sized dogs tend to be good for apartment dwellers or people with limited strength or lower activity levels. They're also good for people with small yards.
- Medium-sized and large dogs can be intimidating to strangers but may make a person living alone feel more secure.
- Medium and large dogs generally need fenced-in yards and more exercise than smaller breeds.
- Large dogs are good for people who live athletic lifestyles or need athletic dogs.
- Medium-sized dogs often offer a compromise between large and small dogs.

There are caveats to these rules. For example, many terrier and terrier-mixed dogs can be very active (Parson Russell Terriers and their mixes, for example) and would not necessarily be suited to a home that requires a low activity level. Some large dogs, such as retired Greyhounds, can live in an apartment because of their couch-potato temperaments.

Male or Female?

After deciding on size, your next choice is whether to choose a male or female dog. For the most part, this is a personal preference as both males and females make excellent pets. If you're a first-time dog owner, a female may be a better choice because they are less likely to test you.

In some breeds, females tend to be more dependent (that is, more likely to be attached to you emotionally, preferring to sit in your lap or eager to go places with you) and males more independent (favoring the floor or content to watch you walk away). In other breeds, the exact reverse is true. It really depends on the breed. With mixed breeds, you can't make these assumptions, so be ready to rely on personality tests to determine which puppy or dog is right for you.

Females will come into estrus (season, or heat) twice a year, if left intact. The estrus usually lasts about three weeks, and during this time, you need to protect her from unwanted male dogs. During estrus, the female will have a light bloody discharge that will be extremely attractive to male dogs for three weeks. If she's bred anytime during that period, she may have puppies. During this time, the female goes through personality changes because of the hormones involved. Most people find this very inconvenient because they can't exercise their female dogs and may attract suitors who will go to great lengths to breed her. However, if you spay her, this will not be a problem.

If you are getting a dog who will be a pet, you should spay or neuter the dog, regardless of whether he is a purebred or mixed breed. Spaying—that is, removing the female's reproductive organs—generally costs more than neutering—that is, castrating a male dog—and is a major surgery compared to neutering. However, a good veterinarian who has performed spays routinely should not have any problems spaying your dog. There are also many spay/neuter clinics that spay or neuter a dog for a very low cost.

Neutering is a less involved surgical procedure than spaying, where the male dog is castrated under anesthesia. Both spaying and neutering have many health benefits. (See chapter 8, "Keeping Your Dog Healthy.")

Puppy or Adult?

Do you want to get a puppy or an adult? Well, there's nothing more adorable than a puppy. One look into a puppy's soulful eyes, and you're gone. Who, except those with the strongest will, can resist a puppy?

There's something to be said for a puppy. If you get a puppy younger than 4 months, it is like starting with a clean slate. The puppy hasn't had time to learn bad habits. You can train your puppy right the first time—if you know how to train properly. You also get the joy of seeing your puppy grow into an adult dog.

Puppies vs. Adult Dogs

	Pros	Cons
Puppies	Cute factor	Not housebroken
	Training can start at young age	Fewer available for adoption
	You can watch them grow	
	Several available for adoption	
Adults	Usually housebroken	Potential existing behavior problems
	More mellow and you can usually get the dog's attention more easily	Potential existing health problems

But before you rush out and pick your ball of fluffy fur, sit back and think a moment. Do you have the time to take care of a puppy? Puppies don't come housebroken, and many take weeks, if not months, to housebreak. They don't "know the rules" and will chew inappropriate items. They require more attention than an adult dog and need more socialization, training, and exercise. If no one is around during the day, you might wish to reconsider your desire to own a puppy. If you're considering a mixed breed, you may be in for a surprise as your puppy grows. ("Wow! I didn't know he would be this big!")

Adult and adolescent dogs are usually housebroken (or can be housebroken easily) and may know some commands. An adult dog will have settled down a bit and won't need all the attention and exercise a puppy requires. There aren't too many surprises with an adult dog—what you see is what you get. However, an adult dog may have picked up bad habits from previous owners or may have been traumatized during his life. Training and socialization are important for these dogs.

Adult dogs generally aren't as adoptable as puppies. If you're looking to rescue a dog from a shelter or breed rescue group, get an adult dog; they are the most needy ones.

Breed Overview

The AKC has divided the breeds into seven groups: Sporting, Hound, Working, Terrier, Toy, Non-Sporting, and Herding. While the AKC isn't the only breed club in existence (nor does it recognize every breed), it recognizes 154 breeds, including the most popular breeds, as of this writing.

When looking at each group, be aware that the temperaments of all breeds vary widely. For example, the temperament of a Saluki will be vastly different than that of a Bloodhound, even though they both belong to the Hound Group. You should consult a breed book or *The Complete Dog Book* (Howell Book House) for information on the characteristics of various breeds.

Let's look at the breed groups and the breeds that comprise them.

The Sporting Group

The Sporting Group consists of dogs who were bred to hunt waterfowl and other game birds. These dogs tend to be people oriented because when hunting, they had to take commands from their owners. The types of work these dogs did varied according to the type of birds the sportsmen hunted. Some dogs were required to point out game birds; others were bred to flush the birds from the bushes so the hunter could shoot them. Others were bred to retrieve the bird after it was shot. Still others could do some or all of these tasks.

While many of these dogs are still used for hunting, many more have been discovered to make fine pets because of their friendliness and their eagerness to work with people.

The Sporting Group includes the following breeds:

American Water Spaniel
Brittany
Chesapeake Bay Retriever
Clumber Spaniel
Cocker Spaniel
Curly-Coated Retriever
English Cocker Spaniel
English Setter
English Springer Spaniel
Field Spaniel
Flat-Coated Retriever
German Shorthaired Pointer
German Wirehaired Pointer
Golden Retriever
Gordon Setter
Irish Setter
Irish Water Spaniel
Labrador Retriever
Nova Scotia Duck Tolling Retriever
Pointer
Spinone Italiano
Sussex Spaniel
Vizsla
Weimaraner
Welsh Springer Spaniel
Wirehaired Pointing Griffon

The Hound Group

The Hound Group consists of dogs who were bred to hunt game by sight (sighthounds) or by scent (scenthounds). These dogs tend to be independent, bred to follow a scent or course game for miles while the hunters followed along either on foot or on horseback. Some of these dogs hunted in a pack; some hunted alone. Sighthounds hunt game (whether a rabbit, deer, or even wolves) by sight rather than scent and are prone to chase creatures that flee from them. Scenthounds pick up their quarry's scent on the ground and in the air and may bay as they run, tracking their prey as they do so.

Although some dogs from the Hound Group are still used for hunting, hounds are favorites among pet owners because they are good-natured. Harder to train than some breeds, hounds are still a lot of fun.

The Hound Group includes the following breeds:

Afghan Hound	Harrier
American Foxhound	Ibizan Hound
Basenji	Irish Wolfhound
Basset Hound	Norwegian Elkhound
Beagle	Otterhound
Black and Tan Coonhound	Petit Basset Griffon Vendéen
Bloodhound	Pharaoh Hound
Borzoi	Rhodesian Ridgeback
Dachshund	Saluki
English Foxhound	Scottish Deerhound
Greyhound	Whippet

The Working Group

The Working Group consists of dogs who were bred for a variety of tasks, including sledding, guarding, carting, and other jobs that do not fall under the hunting and herding categories. This encompasses a wide range of dogs with different temperaments, from dogs who are independent but friendly to dogs who are good with commands to those who are aloof with strangers. These dogs are as varied as their tasks. Some, like the Mastiff and Rottweiler, were bred for guarding; others, like the Samoyed and Alaskan Malamute, were bred for pulling sledges. Others, like Saint Bernards and Newfoundlands, were used for rescue. Some of these dogs still work, but many have become fine pets.

A Golden Retriever in a Husky Suit?

A common mistaken idea many new dog owners have is that all dogs have the same temperament, but in basically different wrappings. But just as people aren't the same, neither are dogs. Don't think you're going to get a Golden Retriever temperament when you see a Siberian Husky!

How do you determine a dog's temperament? First, you need to do research on each individual breed you're interested in (the dog breed books in the Your Happy Healthy Pet series, by Howell Book House, are an excellent resource; you can also talk with owners and breeders of these dogs) and determine whether the temperament of the breed is right for you. As you look at individual dogs, you'll need to perform the basic puppy tests and temperament tests included in chapter 3 to see if the dog is right for you and your family.

Internet Resources for Finding the Right Breed

The AKC has a wonderful breakdown of breeds on its Web site, at www.akc.org. On the AKC's Web site, you can get an overview of each breed in question plus the breed standard—that is, the set of rules that makes a breed a particular breed. The AKC also has links to the home page for each national breed club and e-mail addresses and phone numbers for breeder referral and breed rescue organizations.

The Eukanuba Web site, www.eukanuba.com, provides a fun tool called the Dog Breed Selector. You select factors such as size, coat, and look of dog; how much time you want to spend on training and exercising your dog; and what type of activities you'd like to do with your dog. The tool then gives you a list of breeds that are likely to be good matches for you. To get to the Dog Breed Selector, go to www.eukanuba.com, click New Puppy, and then click What Breed of Dog Might Be Right for You?

The Pedigree Web site (www.pedigree.com) has a similar tool, called Select-a-Dog. To get to it, go to the Pedigree site, click The Pedigree Center, and then click Select-a-Dog. Answer a few key questions, and the tool gives you a list of the ten best matches for your criteria. Using one of these tools is a good place to start in choosing a breed.

The Working Group includes the following breeds:

Akita	Greater Swiss Mountain Dog
Alaskan Malamute	Komondor
Anatolian Shepherd	Kuvasz
Bernese Mountain Dog	Mastiff
Black Russian Terrier	Neapolitan Mastiff
Boxer	Newfoundland
Bullmastiff	Portuguese Water Dog
Doberman Pinscher	Rottweiler
German Pinscher	Saint Bernard
Giant Schnauzer	Samoyed
Great Dane	Siberian Husky
Great Pyrenees	Standard Schnauzer

The Terrier Group

The Terrier Group consists of dogs who were bred to hunt vermin such as rats and woodchucks. These dogs often have a frisky temperament, are quick and agile, and are very intelligent. They seldom tolerate other dogs or other animals and are quick to chase smaller creatures and argue with larger ones. The largest terrier is the Airedale; however, most terriers, such as the Parson Russell Terrier, are small.

Terriers can be a handful even though they are trainable and clever. While they're seldom employed for getting rid of vermin, there are earthdog tests designed to prove their worthiness as ratters.

The Terrier Group includes the following breeds:

Airedale Terrier
American Staffordshire Terrier
Australian Terrier
Bedlington Terrier
Border Terrier
Bull Terrier
Cairn Terrier
Dandie Dinmont Terrier
Glen of Imaal Terrier
Irish Terrier
Kerry Blue Terrier
Lakeland Terrier
Manchester Terrier (Standard)
Miniature Bull Terrier

Miniature Schnauzer
Norfolk Terrier
Norwich Terrier
Parson Russell Terrier
Scottish Terrier
Sealyham Terrier
Skye Terrier
Smooth Fox Terrier
Soft Coated Wheaten Terrier
Staffordshire Bull Terrier
Welsh Terrier
West Highland White Terrier
Wire Fox Terrier

The Toy Group

The Toy Group consists of dogs who were bred to be small companion dogs. These dogs are often very intelligent and trainable. In most cases, toy dogs are a good size for apartment dwellers and for people who don't have a lot of arm strength. However, toy breeds can be harmed by small children, and great care should be taken by parents to ensure their dog's safety.

Most toy dogs are trainable, but they can be spoiled rotten if their owners do not bother to train them. They respond well to positive training techniques.

The Toy Group includes the following breeds:

Affenpinscher
Brussels Griffon
Cavalier King Charles Spaniel
Chihuahua
Chinese Crested
English Toy Spaniel
Havanese
Italian Greyhound
Japanese Chin
Maltese

Manchester Terrier (Toy)
Miniature Pinscher
Papillon
Pekingese
Pomeranian
Pug
Shih Tzu
Silky Terrier
Toy Fox Terrier
Yorkshire Terrier

Toy Dogs and Kids

Toy dogs aren't usually good pets for young children, who may not understand the difference between a stuffed toy and a real dog. If you're looking for a dog and have a child younger than 5 years, choose a medium to large-sized dog.

The Non-Sporting Group

The Non-Sporting Group is a catchall group for dogs who were bred to be companion dogs or who no longer do the work they were originally bred to do. For example, the Bulldog is no longer associated with bull-baiting, and the Poodle no longer hunts. These dogs are often very intelligent and trainable. They make great companion dogs.

Like the toy dogs, the non-sporting dogs need obedience training and respond well to positive training techniques.

The Non-Sporting Group includes the following breeds:

American Eskimo Dog	Keeshond
Bichon Frise	Lhasa Apso
Boston Terrier	Löwchen
Bulldog	Poodle
Chinese Shar-pei	Schipperke
Chow Chow	Shiba Inu
Dalmatian	Tibetan Spaniel
Finnish Spitz	Tibetan Terrier
French Bulldog	

The Herding Group

The Herding Group includes the brainy dogs who were bred to herd livestock. While some of the herding dogs (such as the German Shepherd Dog) were bred to guard as well as herd,

others, like the Border Collie, were bred to obey commands from a distance and had to be very good at following orders but still had to be intuitive enough to know what to do in unusual situations.

Herding dogs are often quite active and require mental stimulation. Many owners find some types of herders to be intense workers who need jobs. Other herding dogs make fine pets.

The Herding Group includes the following breeds:

Australian Cattle Dog	Canaan Dog
Australian Shepherd	Cardigan Welsh Corgi
Bearded Collie	Collie
Belgian Malinois	German Shepherd Dog
Belgian Sheepdog	Old English Sheepdog
Belgian Tervuren	Pembroke Welsh Corgi
Border Collie	Polish Lowland Sheepdog
Bouvier des Flandres	Puli
Briard	Shetland Sheepdog

What You Now Know . . .

- You should familiarize yourself with general characteristics of different dog breeds to help decide what type of dog is a good match for your family.
- There are advantages and disadvantages to both purebreds and mixed breeds.
- You need to consider a number of choices when choosing the right dog.
- The AKC has seven major groups—Sporting, Hounds, Working, Terriers, Toys, Non-Sporting, and Herding—each with unique characteristics.

Chapter 3

Finding Your Dog

What's Inside...
- Learn how to find reputable breeders.
- Learn where to get the very best dog.
- Learn how to choose the very best dog for your family.

There are plenty of choices to make when looking for a dog. But once you decide what you want, there's an even more important choice ahead—choosing where to get your new pet. Many people don't know where to look, and the avenues they choose often aren't the best ones. If you're planning on buying a dog, be sure that you get the best dog for your money.

Where to Find Your Dog

Where do your find the perfect dog for you and your family? Look in the newspaper? Visit a shelter? Go to a pet store? Look on the Internet? Ask your neighbor?

You can get a dog just about anywhere. Walking down the street, you might even see a kid handing out free puppies, but is such a dog right for you? Where you get your dog is important and, especially if you're going to spend a fair amount of money on a dog, shouldn't you get the very best dog for your money?

Often the easiest avenues for getting a dog aren't the best. For example, puppy mills—that is, commercial breeders that breed solely for profit—often have "puppies always available." Generally, you shouldn't buy from any place that mass-produces puppies. Most puppies from these sources are of poor quality, and their parents have no health certifications.

You may have heard about genetic diseases in purebred dogs. All purebred dogs have genetic diseases that the breeder should screen for. Anyone who buys a puppy should buy one from a breeder who screens for genetic diseases and breeds dogs to improve the breed.

Checklist for Finding a Reputable Source for Dogs

☐ Source breeds only one or two dog breeds.

☐ All dogs are offered with health guarantees.

☐ Source will take back the dog at any time in the dog's life.

☐ All puppies' parents are certified through the Orthopedic Foundation for Animals (OFA) and/or PennHIP and the Canine Eye Registration Foundation (CERF). OptiGen and VetGen registries are optional.

☐ Puppies' parents are screened for genetic diseases.

☐ The dogs bred are registered through the American Kennel Club (AKC), the United Kennel Club (UKC), the Canadian Kennel Club, or a legitimate international registry.

☐ Dogs bred have conformation, obedience, agility, tracking, herding, hunting, or other titles.

☐ Dogs are bred to improve the breed, not just to produce puppies.

☐ Source breeds on average no more than three litters a year.

☐ Puppies are not always available.

☐ Source will not sell puppies just before Christmas or other holidays.

☐ No puppy is taken away from her mother before 8 weeks of age.

☐ Puppies are dewormed, vet-checked, and vaccinated.

☐ Source offers a contract that stipulates all guarantees.

Reputable Breeders

It's important to look for reputable and responsible breeder when purchasing a purebred dog or puppy. But what exactly does a reputable breeder do that's so different from the others?

First and foremost, reputable breeders don't breed purebreds for the money. As hokey as it might sound, they've fallen in love with their breed and want to improve the breed by adhering to the breed standard (the "blueprint") in order to produce the best dogs possible.

Responsible breeders are totally devoted to their breed. Crazy as it seems, they're fanatics. They have books of photos of their dogs; trophies and ribbons line their walls. They'll talk about puppies they placed like they were their grandkids and tell you about all their accomplishments. "Mitzy is the daughter of Cindy here, and she has her UDX and is going for her OTCH." "Chet just got his MACH—the fifth Samoyed to get it." And so on. Your eyes will cross, looking at all the photos these breeders show you.

Responsible breeders know their breed's standard and don't breed just to have puppies, but to improve the breed. They don't always have puppies available. Most reputable breeders have a waiting list for their puppies and screen their buyers rigorously.

Quite often, puppies from reputable breeders will cost the same as puppies from backyard breeders, pet stores, or puppy mills. When you purchase a puppy from a reputable breeder,

What's a "Puppy Mill"?

Those who breed dogs for profit only are commercial breeders who are often called "puppy mills." A puppy mill's sole purpose is to produce a dog for profit. Some puppy mills have sub-standard conditions, with dogs kept in row after row of kennels or cages, where they aren't allowed to socialize and there's very little interaction with humans. Little thought is given to genetic diseases or breeding for temperament, and most dogs bred in puppy mills are not quality specimens of the breed.

you purchase a quality puppy with a known history. The breeder will offer you help and advice in training issues and will take an active interest in your pet. You are not on your own if you have training difficulties or health problems.

It's not hard to find a reputable breeder, but it may be hard to pass their criteria when you do. Reputable breeders want to be sure that your home is as good as their own. They want to be sure that the puppies match with their new owners' lifestyles and personalities. And if they don't and there's a problem, the reputable breeder will take the puppy back. Reputable breeders will guarantee the health of their dogs and refund money or offer a replacement should there be a problem.

Reputable breeders screen for genetic diseases. They want to ensure that the puppies they're breeding are the healthiest they can be. Reputable breeders also will tell you everything about the breed you're considering—both the positives *and* the negatives. They won't try to press you into buying a puppy right on the spot.

Steps for Finding a Reputable Breeder

1. Go to www.akc.org and find the national breed club or breeder referral (if listed) on the AKC Web site. If no breeder referral is listed with the AKC, go to the breed club's Web site and look for a breeder referral contact or contact the secretary of the breed club.
2. Contact the breeder referral person for the location of breeders in your area.
3. Call the breeders in your area to find out if they will have puppies in the near future or if they currently have dogs available.
4. If the breeder has puppies available or soon will have, take the time to qualify the breeder. ***Do not skip this step—this is important!*** Ask the questions in the worksheet "Is This a Responsible Breeder? Breeder Interview Questions" on page 36.
5. Visit the breeder to see the facilities and to meet the breeder.
6. Ask to see appropriate paperwork and make sure everything is in order before putting a deposit down on a puppy or dog.

Is This a Responsible Breeder?
Breeder Interview Questions

Do you belong to the national breed club or at least a local breed club?
Responsible answer: Yes.

_____

_____

Do you show your breed in conformation or in performance events?
Responsible answer: Yes (and names what events).

_____

_____

How long have you been a breeder with this breed?
Responsible answer: Varies, but a more established breeder is usually reputable. Backyard breeders—that is, those who don't have the experience to improve the breed—usually are first- or second-time breeders.

_____

_____

How many breeds do you show/breed?
Responsible answer: One or two.

_____

_____

Do the puppies' parents have conformation, obedience, hunting, herding, lure coursing, or agility titles?
Responsible answer: Yes (and shows you what titles or tells you what the dogs are working toward).

_____

_____

How did you choose the stud dog?
Responsible answer: I searched for the right dog to breed to this female. I looked for a dog that would improve the conformation and bloodline of my stock.

_____

_____

Do you have photographs and information concerning the parents, grandparents, great-grandparents, uncles, aunts, and cousins of the puppies?
Responsible answer: Yes (and shows you the photos and pedigrees).

_____

_____

Do you have OFA (or PennHIP) and CERF certification on both parents (if applicable to the breed)?
Responsible answer: Yes (and shows you the certificates). OFA must be GOOD or EXCELLENT. CERF must be PASS.

_____

_____

Why did you breed these two dogs?
Responsible answer: To produce puppies that will improve the breed.

_____

_____

How old are the puppies' parents?
Responsible answer: Two years or older.

_____

_____

Have the puppies been wormed and vaccinated?
Responsible answer: Yes (and specifies dates).

_____

_____

continues

How old must the puppy be before I take her home?
Responsible answer: Eight weeks old or older. No exceptions.

_____

_____

Do you have a contract? May I see it?
Responsible answer: Yes (and shows the contract).

_____

_____

Do you guarantee your puppies? If so, for what?
Responsible answer: Yes. (Should guarantee puppy free from hip dysplasia, eye diseases, and other genetic diseases found in that particular breed. Also should guarantee the health of the puppy on leaving the kennel. Should offer refund or replacement of puppy. There is usually a time limit on the guarantee—usually two to four years.)

_____

_____

Will you take back the dog under any circumstance?
Responsible answer: Yes (and shows you where in the contract he or she guarantees this).

_____

_____

Are these dogs AKC or UKC registered (if they are registered purebreds)?
Responsible answer: Yes (and shows the certificates).

_____

_____

What items will you provide at the time of sale?
Responsible answer: Information on raising and training your dog, the buyer's contract, AKC registration papers, copies of the parents' OFA and CERF certification (if applicable), startup supply of the puppy's food, record of vaccinations and worming (health checkup record from veterinarian if vaccinations and deworming were done by breeder), vaccination schedule, and pedigree.

_____

_____

Do you have references?
Responsible answer: Yes. (The breeder should be able to provide you with names and phone numbers of other members of his or her national or local club and people who have bought puppies who will gladly vouch for this breeder.)

_____

_____

Shelters and Rescues

If you're planning on getting a mixed breed, the first place you might think to look is the local pound, animal shelter, or rescue. Three-quarters of all dogs brought to shelters are mixed breeds. That includes crossbreeds such as Labrador Retriever and Australian Shepherd mixes and dogs that aren't any discernable breed. However, there are plenty of purebreds there, too. Indeed, some shelters may actually call certain dogs "mixes" even though they are purebred because they do not have any actual papers proving their pedigrees. Rescues specialize in particular purebred breeds; you can find the national rescues through www.akc.org and find the contact info either on the AKC Web site or on the breed's national club's Web site.

If you go to a shelter or rescue, you probably don't care if your dog has papers or not. In this case, whether your dog is purebred or not shouldn't make a difference. However, if you're planning on doing some type of performance sport with your dog, you can obtain Indefinite Listing Privilege (ILP) numbers from the AKC, which will allow your dog to compete in performance sports such as obedience and agility if she is a purebred but has no papers.

Regardless of whether you go to a shelter or a rescue, your main concern should be how the animals there are treated. Quite often, small shelters and rescues are run on a shoestring and don't have the facilities for all the animals present. Even so, each animal should be housed alone or maybe with one other animal, and the animals and their cages should be clean and well cared for. There should be no presence of diseased animals—all should appear healthy and energetic.

There are two types of shelters: no-kill and kill shelters. No-kill shelters do not euthanize animals brought to them, but because of this, they frequently turn down pets while trying to find homes for the ones they already have. Depending on their policies, they may or many not have what are considered "unadoptable animals"—that is, dogs who are too old or may have serious medical conditions that would preclude them from being adopted.

 Kill shelters, as the term implies, euthanize pets after a certain amount of time. Depending on how busy a shelter is, or what the local law dictates, this could be anywhere from a day to a few weeks.

Pet Supply Store Adoptions

Some pet supply stores partner with local shelters and rescues to offer adoptable animals to their clientele. These stores generally have one or two days a week, usually on weekends, when adoptable pets are in the store so potential owners can get to know them.

Rescues are another place to look for dogs. Most rescues are for purebreds, but some rescues have mixed breeds as well. Volunteers through organizations such as a parent breed club typically run rescues. Rescues are usually understaffed and their workers overworked, and they usually need money and volunteers. A rescue is not necessarily one place, like a shelter, but may actually be several volunteers who foster dogs in their homes.

Adoption procedures vary greatly in shelters and rescues. Most shelters and rescues require that you have the dog spayed or neutered—or do that for you—before you bring the dog home. Most shelters and rescues screen applicants to avoid having the dog returned to them or putting the dog in a situation that would be worse than her current one. Some won't allow dogs to be adopted outside a state or specific region.

Usually you can find dogs in all age ranges at shelters and rescues, but most dogs are between 6 months and 5 years old. Generally, puppies and kittens are most popular, followed by young adolescent animals, adults, and, finally, older pets. Purebreds tend to be a bit more popular than mixed breeds, so if you're looking simply to give a dog a second chance, you should go for a dog with the lowest chance of placement: an older, mixed-breed dog.

Shelters and rescues usually offer adoptable animals—that is, dogs that appear to be healthy and well adjusted. Dogs who are sick with incurable diseases, are aggressive, or have other problems are usually euthanized. However, don't assume that this is the case. If you look at a dog in a shelter or rescue, ask about the background of the dog. Why was she turned in? What is her history? Sometimes, but not always, the shelter or rescue can tell you about the dog. If the dog was turned in for aggression or serious health problems, you should probably reconsider your choice.

Pet Shops

People often go to pet shops when looking for pets, but they're not necessarily the best places to look. Pet shops usually buy from commercial breeders and occasionally from backyard breeders. They are unlikely to have puppies from reputable breeders because reputable breeders want to be involved in where their puppies are placed. Pet shops usually sell to whoever comes in with the right amount of money (often a lot of money—pet shop dogs generally have a hefty price tag). If you buy from a pet shop, you may be supporting the commercial pet industry and may not get the best pet for your money.

When a Dog Comes to You

Sometimes you become a dog owner when you least expect it. Maybe a coworker or friend tells you he's taking his dog to the pound, or maybe you are driving home one night and find a dog running loose in your area, and you stop to pick her up. Maybe you're a sucker for that kid giving away puppies. Whatever the reason, it seems that the dog comes to you. Let's look at each situation.

Want a Free Dog?

One way people become dog owners is that a coworker or neighbor decides that she doesn't want her dog anymore and tells the person that "it's off to the pound if I don't find a home." If you're a kindhearted person, you may take the dog (perhaps against your better judgment). Another way people become dog owners is that they see an ad in the newspaper for a "free to good home" dog.

Dog owners give away their pets for various reasons. One common excuse—often given because the owner doesn't want to go into lengthy explanations—is allergies. While some dog owners suddenly become allergic, many can tolerate their pets with medication. In fact, one study suggests that children with allergies who grow up in homes with pets are actually more resistant to allergens than those who grow up without pets.

Often, people take home puppies without understanding the true commitment required. Without proper discipline, their pups grow into adolescent terrors. The owners then give up the dogs because of bad habits. You can easily find out if a dog is being given up because of bad habits: Ask the owner what commands the dog knows and if she is housetrained. No training or minimal training is indicative of a dog who needs training and possibly needs to have bad habits broken. Where the dog sleeps is also a good indication of where the dog is in the family. If the dog sleeps outside, in the garage, or in the basement, the family has very little attachment to the dog. A dog can be cured of her bad habits, but doing so will take some work. Also, you need to find out if she is aggressive and avoid this dog if she is.

Other reasons (not necessarily good ones) for giving away or selling a dog include:

- Change of lifestyle or income for the owner.
- The owner died.
- The owner is moving overseas (although this isn't really an excuse, some people sell or give away their dogs when moving).
- The family dog had puppies.
- The dog didn't get along with other pets.
- The family had a child.

Strays

You might become a dog owner by picking up a stray. Strays are definitely a risky proposition, but I've done it with success, and others have, too. In many instances, strays are "dumped dogs"—that is, the owner was too afraid to take the dog to a shelter and instead decided

to give the dog "the long car ride." Sadly, these people dump the dogs off in the country or a wilderness area, thinking that someone will take them in or the dogs will manage to fend for themselves. The truth is, this is like dumping a 5-year-old child in the middle of nowhere and telling him to fend for himself. The prospect for survival is grim.

But not all strays are abandoned dogs. Indeed, some are lost dogs looking for their owners. Others are dogs whose owners have the mistaken notion that dogs should run loose. This is why when you find a stray, you should make a reasonable attempt to find the owner. Many newspapers offer free found ads for people who attempt to locate a dog's owner.

When you find a stray, the first thing you should do is check her for identification. Look for a collar and tags, tattoos, and microchips. Tattoos are located on the inside of the thigh, on the loin, or in an ear. (You may have to part the fur to find a tattoo.) If you find a tattoo, you should contact National Dog Registry, Tattoo-A-Pet, AKC Companion Animal Recovery (see the sidebar "Animal Registry and Recovery Services" on page 193), and other national registries to have them search their databases for the dog's ID. Microchips can only be read with a scanner. Veterinarians and shelters may have scanners to check for chips, but not all scanners can read all chips. Again, when you figure out what type of chip a dog has, you must contact the registry for information regarding the dog. Contact a local veterinarian to scan for a chip and to contact the appropriate registry. If there's a license, the local animal control can usually help you track down the owners. You can also run a found ad in a local paper.

Strays can have a multitude of health problems. Many have worms, fleas, mange, or other parasites, and they may have been starved. Strays often mistrust humans because of the injustice done to them. They may have been shot at or had things thrown at them. They may be fearful and cringing. Health problems such as parasites and malnutrition can be corrected. The emotional trauma may take some time to heal—if it ever does. But strays can become happy members of your family with patience and love. I have taken in two strays with great success—one of whom had suffered abuse—which shows how resilient dogs actually are.

Oops—Puppies!

Many owners of intact female dogs are surprised when their dogs have puppies. Despite campaigns for spaying and neutering pets, many owners don't spay their female dogs, who get out while in season. Sixty-three days later—puppies!

Purebred owners sometimes keep their females intact because they mistakenly think that their females should be bred because they are purebred. One litter of puppies usually con-

vinces an owner to get a female dog spayed, but that owner has already added to the pet overpopulation problem. While there are still many puppies with more than two breeds in them, most "accidents" are the product of crossbreeding.

A downside of puppies who result from accidental breeding is that quite often, the father is unknown, and the parents were never screened for genetic diseases such as hip dysplasia or eye diseases. If you choose a puppy from an accidental breeding, you are taking a risk on the puppy's being genetically healthy. (However, this is a problem with all mixed breeds because most have never been screened for possible genetic health problems.)

Picking Out Your Dog

Should you bring your family when you look for a dog? The answer is a qualified yes. When you go to a breeder or shelter, it may be very hard to say no when your children are pleading with you to get a puppy right then and there. However, if you can resist that urge, bring your family along because doing so will enable you to see how your prospective dog or puppy will react to your family. These are the people with whom your dog is going to interact on a daily basis. You're not going to want a dog who hates kids.

If you want to visit a number of breeders or shelters, it might be better to go it alone at first. If you find a prospective dog or puppy that you're pretty sure you want, ask if the breeder or shelter will hold the dog (most will do so for twenty-four hours) until your family can see the dog. When you've narrowed down your selection, bring the family to meet the potential new addition. Bring in one family member at a time and observe your potential dog's reaction. After she has met one family member, have that person leave and another one come in. Excitement is expected, but growling or snapping is not.

Choosing the Right Puppy

Depending on where you go to find a puppy, you may or may not have much background to go on when you look at the puppies. If you visit someone whose dog has had an accidental litter, you'll know the mother's breed, but you may not know the father's breed, unless the owners have the dog or unless the owner is sure which neighbor's dog bred her. In many cases, it's a matter of guessing. If the dog is purebred or the breeding was intentional, you might be able to meet both parents.

No matter how adorable those puppies are, do not take a puppy away from her mother before she is 8 weeks old. (In some states, it is against the law.) A puppy needs to spend time with her mother and siblings for socialization and to develop her own personality. If you take a puppy away from her mother much earlier, you run the risk of problems that will plague that dog throughout her life because she did not have a chance to learn how to be a dog or how to "read" other dogs.

As you look for a puppy, consider the following:

- **Health:** You need to consider the health of the puppies. Are they bright-eyed, eager, and alert? Are they clean, and are their coats shiny? They shouldn't be too fat or thin, nor should they have a potbelly—indicative of worms. They might be sleepy if they just woke from a nap, but they shouldn't be sluggish or unresponsive. Avoid puppies who cry or act unhappy—there's usually an underlying problem with them.

Check for blindness and deafness. If there are toys available, roll a ball in front of the puppy. She should chase it or at least watch it as it rolls. Look at her eyes for cloudiness or murkiness, which may indicate juvenile cataracts. Clap your hands behind her head to see if she reacts to the sound. You will want a puppy who can hear and see. Some breeds, such as Dalmatians and Australian Shepherds, have congenital deafness in their lines that can show up in mixed breeds as well.

- **Dominance:** When you visit a litter of puppies, kneel down and clap your hands. Some puppies may seem interested in you; others may ignore you. The ones who ignore you are usually the independent ones. The puppy who comes over first may be an alpha—that is, a dominant personality. While alpha puppies are great for those who are used to that personality, if you've never had an alpha dog, consider a puppy who is less dominant. Alphas will tend to "rule the roost" and will try to challenge you at every opportunity.

  Most alpha puppies will not accept being gently put on their back and held there, whereas most nondominant puppies will accept it after a slight fuss. An overly submissive dog will lie without a struggle. Neither an overly dominant nor an overly submissive dog is good for the average family.

- **Trainability:** Determining trainability in young puppies is difficult. You will have to rely on knowing the breed or what breeds are in the puppy's background to make a determination on how trainable the puppy will be. Certainly, intelligence plays a role in a puppy's trainability, but not all smart dogs are highly trainable. Indeed, some very intelligent dogs have an independent streak—they know what you want, but they just don't feel it is in their best interest to do what you want.

- **Appearance and size:** If the puppy is a purebred, you have a pretty good idea what the puppy is going to look like. However, if the puppy is a mixed breed, it's anyone's guess. You can make an educated guess if you know what at least one of her parents looked like or know what breeds they were. If the puppy is a crossbreed of larger and smaller dog breeds, you can guess that her size will be somewhere in between the two. If the puppy is truly a mix, not just a crossbreed, you may be in for a surprise. You can judge somewhat by her size at 8 weeks, but she may still surprise you.

- **Temperament:** Pick out your prospective puppy and separate her from her littermates. She should be a little apprehensive at first, but then with petting and encouragement, she should accept you cheerfully. If she cringes or acts submissive or becomes aggressive or hyper, consider another puppy.

Twice the Fun?

You may be tempted to get two dogs or puppies at once. This may not be a good idea, especially if you've never had a pet before. Two dogs or puppies can be quite a handful, and most pet owners agree that two puppies are at least four times the work of one puppy.

Choosing the Right Adult Dog

Selecting an adult or adolescent dog is a little less of a mystery than choosing a puppy. If the dog is an adult, what you see is what you get. There are no size surprises, and the dog will look the way she's going to look. Her personality is set, too; if she's a nondominant sweetie, she's likely to stay that way unless there's an underlying health concern. Adult dogs are usually housebroken, or can be housebroken more easily than puppies. An adult dog may know a few commands and may have learned a few tricks.

Adolescent dogs are generally big puppies who have hit the obnoxious phase of their life. Like human adolescents, they can be a challenging handful or sweet tempered. They usually have a case of the "uglies"—they're gangly and clumsy now. Their hair sticks out in all directions. They're all feet. They'll turn into a handsome adult someday, but the puppy cuteness has worn off, and the obnoxious behavior may have begun. If she has a rebellious streak, her attitude is "make me." Adolescent dogs are also a lot of fun.

As you look for an adult or adolescent dog, consider the following:

- **Background:** Find out all you can about the adult dog before you meet her. Why did the owner give up this dog or why is the owner looking for a new home? Remember that the word *allergies* is often a way for people to avoid talking about the real issue, which may be behavioral. Don't be confrontational, but sometimes when you ask about what training the dog does have, the owner may admit to certain behavioral problems. ("She isn't housebroken." "She barks all night when we leave her outside.") When looking at adopting from a shelter, you may have little to go on, but the shelter workers may be able to give you information about and their impressions of the dog ("Her owners were moving" "She's very sweet, but pulls on a leash when you walk her."). They may also have some health information.
- **Health:** Look at the overall health of the dog. Are her eyes clear and bright? Is her coat healthy? If she's been in the shelter some time, her coat may not be as clean as you might like. She should look healthy and be free from serious health problems. If she will let you examine her, do so gently. Look at her ears and teeth if she will let you. Her ears should be clean, and her gums should be free of redness and swelling. She should walk without a limp. In many cases, shelters will give you a health guarantee, but you must have a veterinarian examine your dog within a certain amount of time. If you are adopting or buying your dog from a private party, ask for a written guarantee stating that the owner will take back the dog if a veterinarian finds her to be unhealthy within seventy-two hours. Then, take the dog to the veterinarian.
- **Dominance:** Dominance tests are harder with adult dogs than with puppies. Unlike puppies, adult dogs may take serious exception to being rolled over. (Most adult dogs consider this an aggressive behavior and most likely will bite if you try it.) Instead, approach an adult dog in a gentle and nonthreatening manner. When you meet the dog, kneel down to greet her. Watch her behavior toward you. Is she happy to meet

Meeting with the Dog Separately

When you meet your potential dog, see if you can take her someplace where you can meet her separately. (Most shelters have meeting rooms for prospective owners to meet with pets.) When you meet with an adult dog in a shelter, remember that the shelter is a very stressful place for dogs, and you may not see the dog's true personality there. Still, you'll be able to meet a dog while under stress, and if she does well in this environment, you might be able to assume that she would do well in a calmer one.

you, or cringing and fearful? If she is happy and friendly, you can introduce yourself; if the dog is cringing and fearful, don't push! This could result in a quick fear-bite.

Avoid any dog who is aggressive or fearful. Remember, there are plenty of well-adjusted dogs in need of good homes. Don't try to force a dog to accept your petting or your touch. Look for another dog.

- **Training:** Once you've gotten on good terms with the dog, you can take her for a walk and perhaps see if she knows any commands. If the dog knows commands, walk her on a leash and practice the commands. Don't be surprised if she pulls on a leash—this is very common when dogs are excited. Offer her a dog biscuit whenever she performs a command correctly.
- **Friendliness:** If the dog you're considering is friendly, offer your hand for her to sniff. Be calm and relaxed, not stiff, when offering your hand. Rigidity is a sure sign of challenge to a dog, and many become fearful or aggressive if you tense up. Likewise, don't try to pet the dog on top of the head because that is a very dominant, sometimes frightening, move. Instead, the dog may accept an underhand chin tickle.
- **Independence:** Call the dog to you and clap your hands. She should show interest at the sound of a friendly voice, but she may show some independence and may not come immediately or may not come at all without food to lure her. Watch for any unusual behavior; if the dog behaves differently than what you expect, look elsewhere.

What You Now Know...

- ➤ You should purchase a dog from a reputable breeder or adopt from a shelter or rescue.
- ➤ It's important to make sure everyone in your family wants a dog.
- ➤ Your new dog should have a temperament that fits with your family, and your whole family should like the dog you choose.

Chapter 4

Preparing for Your Dog

What's Inside...
- Decide where your new dog should stay.
- Learn what supplies are right for your dog.
- Learn how to choose the best veterinarian for your dog and how you can protect your dog's health with pet insurance.

Now that you have a plan for getting a dog, the next step is to prepare for your dog. In this chapter and the next, we discuss making those preparations for the big day when you bring your new puppy or dog home.

If you plan now, bringing your new dog home won't be so hectic. If you have created a place for your dog to stay, purchased dog supplies, found a veterinarian, and dog-proofed your house ahead of time, you'll be able to focus on adapting to your new dog when you bring him home for the first time.

Where Should Your Dog Stay?

Before you bring your dog home, you should have a good idea where he is going to stay. Most pets should be indoor dogs. If your dog is physically capable of being outside for more than an hour at a time and you have a fenced-in yard and enough shelter to protect your pet from inclement weather, he may be able to be an indoor/outdoor dog. But no pet should be an outdoor-only dog. An outdoor-only dog won't get the same attention as a pet who is allowed inside. When you have a dog who is alone and has no job other than to be a pet, relegating him to the backyard is like sending a child to his room and never letting him out. Your dog needs companionship, socialization, and training. He's a new member of the family. If you're planning on having just an outside dog, rethink your decision to get a dog.

So, your dog needs to be inside the house, but where? You can specify areas in your house where your dog can and can't go, but you need to be careful about it. When you choose places where your dog can go and where he can't, be sure that the places he can go are

Creating a Safe Place

You may want to cordon off one or two rooms when you first get a puppy, not only to minimize the accidents and destructiveness but also to create a safe place for your dog. Then, as your dog becomes more trustworthy, you can allow him in other parts of the house.

It's a good idea to choose a room with tile or other flooring that is easy to clean. For this reason, the kitchen is often the best choice. If you don't have a room like that, you'll have to consider a carpeted area and expect to clean up there. Other features of the safe room include:

- Electrical and window-blind cords should be hidden or removed entirely.
- Nothing should be in the room that could fall on the puppy or otherwise injure him.
- No knickknacks or craft items should be in the room where the dog can get to them.
- The rooms should contain minimal furniture, and you should be prepared for that furniture to be chewed on.
- Install childproof cabinet latches and childproof outlet plug covers.
- Make sure there are no tight places for a puppy or dog to hide or get trapped in.
- Remove trash and garbage containers. A curious dog or puppy can open even so-called secure lids.

where your family spends time often enough and be sure that you can cordon off the areas with pet gates; otherwise, your dog won't understand the boundaries. Some homes have open floor plans that make this nearly impossible.

If you do have an open floor plan, the best thing to do is to purchase an exercise pen (or X-pen, as they're commonly referred to), which you can buy through an Internet pet supply store, a pet catalog, or a pet supply retailer. These pens come in a variety of sizes, and most can be linked together to form bigger pens. However, many puppies (and adults) become Houdinis pretty fast as they're growing up, and they learn to scale these pens with ease. Therefore, it will be important to have a crate for when you can't watch your new dog.

A puppy-friendly space is usually a smaller room with easy-to-clean floors and nothing that a puppy can chew or destroy or injure himself with.

Another consideration is where your dog will sleep. You will bond much more closely with your dog if you have him sleep in your bedroom in a crate than if you stick him alone in a room far away from you. (More on crates in chapter 11, "Crate Training and Housetraining Your Dog.") It's not a good idea for a dog to sleep in bed with you because of possible behavior problems, but he should sleep in his own bed in your bedroom or perhaps in a child's bedroom. This does two things: It helps bond your dog with you with hardly any effort on your part and it helps comfort your dog and reduces possible whining and crying.

Stocking Up on Dog Supplies

When it comes to dog supplies, you have quite a choice. In 2004, pet owners were projected to spend an estimated $34.3 billion on pet supplies, according to a 2003/2004 national pet owner's survey. That's a lot of toys and kibble. You may think that buying things for your dog would be a simple enough task, but there's a lot of junk in this market, as well as useful items.

Where to Buy

One way to avoid the hype and overpaying for items is to purchase your dog's supplies before you bring him home so that you won't scramble to buy things at the last minute. Last-minute purchases usually result in poor-quality and expensive supplies.

If you have a few weeks to plan, you may be able to save some money by purchasing your pet equipment from a catalog or an Internet site. Many good mail-order pet supply companies provide inexpensive, reliable service—but be wary of the shipping charges! It won't help you much if the dollars you save are eaten up by shipping and handling.

There are downsides of ordering online or from catalogs. If you need your order now or within a few days, you may be able to receive expedited shipping, but the higher cost may cancel out your savings. You also cannot examine the products closely to determine whether they are really what you want. Finally, be sure to buy from a reputable source because there are unreliable merchants on the Internet.

Large pet supply stores sometimes offer discounted items, but sometimes their items are more expensive than they might be at another store. Shop around if you can. You can usually go to various warehouse clubs (or "big box" stores) and look for discounted items as well. When buying something at a warehouse club, take into account the materials and whether the item is strong enough to handle the rigors of a puppy. Not everything available is of good enough quality, even if it's labeled for pets.

What to Buy

So, what supplies do you really need for your new dog? Let's take a look.

For Your Home

You'll need some supplies for your home. Most of these have to do with making sure that your dog doesn't get into mischief while you're not home. Let's look at each of them:

- **Training crate:** The training crate can be either wire or the plastic airline variety, but be certain it has a good latching system. (Many Houdini dogs have slipped out of crates that have poor latches.) You will need this crate for housetraining and for keeping your dog in a safe place when you are unable to watch him. Depending on your dog's age, you may have to purchase a smaller one when he is a puppy and a larger one when he

reaches his full size. The crate should be large enough for your dog to stand up, turn around, and lie down comfortably when full-grown. If you decide to buy only one crate, you'll have to block off a portion at the back of the crate until your dog gets large enough, or the crate will be useless as a housetraining tool (see "Crate Training 101" in chapter 11). There are fabric crates available, but they are only for competitive obedience-trained dogs, which yours is most likely not (yet!), and not meant to be used for any length of time.

- **Bed for the crate:** Just as you don't like sleeping on the hard floor, neither will your dog. You can fit a bed inside the dog's crate; it should be soft and comfy but have a washable cover that can zip off and be tossed in the laundry. The material inside should be nontoxic, in case your dog decides to chew the bedding. However, if your dog decides the bed is just another chew toy, you may have to forgo it altogether.

- **Fencing, outdoor kennel, or outdoor containment system:** As important as keeping your dog safe in the house is keeping your dog contained while he is outside. You will need appropriate fencing for your dog. Toy and small dogs can usually do well behind a four-foot-high fence; larger dogs need a six-foot-high fence. If you can't afford a fence or don't want to have your entire yard fenced in, a kennel run (portable-panel runs are sold at large hardware stores) may be a good alternative. In places where you can't have kennels or fencing, invisible fencing is an option, but it requires training, and a determined dog can get through an invisible fence. (See the sidebar "Physical or Electronic Fencing?" on page 51.)

- **Enzymatic cleaner for accidents:** You'll need something to clean up accidents when they occur (and they will!). Enzymatic cleaners made for pet messes are designed to break down the urine and feces into more basic components and thereby eliminate the smell. You still have to clean up after your dog, but the smell won't linger and won't attract your dog back to the spot.

Your Dog's Wardrobe

Although your dog probably thinks he's gorgeous in just his coat, he needs some accessories to complete his wardrobe. Let's look at each of them:

- **Flat or buckle collar:** Your dog will need a flat or buckle collar for everyday wear. The idea behind this is that you need a handle on your dog if you need to hold him, you have something to hook a leash to when you walk him, and you have something to affix tags to. The collar can be plain or fancy; nylon, cloth, or leather; plain or with a pattern for the holidays, for fun, or your favorite sports team. The main thing is that the collar needs to be fixed so that it doesn't act like a choke chain or training collar, which can pull tight and choke your dog if caught on something. *Never use a training collar as your dog's everyday collar!*

- **ID tags with your name, address, and phone numbers:** ID tags are mandatory in order to get your dog back if he ever gets lost. There's no excuse for not having up-to-date tags—ever. You can buy tags through Internet supply stores, through mail-order, through your veterinarian, and through many major pet supply retailers. Some stores have engraving machines to make tags right there while you shop for your dog's kibble.

Physical or Electronic Fencing?

You may have heard about electronic, invisible, or radio fences and may be wondering if they're something you should consider when getting a dog. The answer is complex, but in most cases, you should use a real fence.

How most invisible fences work is that you must either lay a wire along the perimeter where your dog should not go, put up boundary posts, or plug in a unit with a certain range. The dog must wear a collar that emits a shock when the dog attempts to cross the boundary. In the case of the broadcast units, anyplace outside the range of the transmitter causes the collar to emit a shock. In the case of the wire fences, getting close to and crossing the wire causes a shock. The theory is that once the dog receives the unpleasant shock, he learns to not cross the line.

The reality of invisible fencing is a bit different. Most of the companies that make them agree that you can't just put in an invisible fence and stick the dog in there—you have to train the dog to learn boundaries, and the invisible fence acts as a negative reinforcement. Some dogs learn it very quickly and do just fine with an invisible fence; others are constantly testing the boundaries. If the batteries wear down in the collar, it's likely that the dog will figure this out pretty quickly. Likewise, if your dog sees something he wants to chase—let's say a squirrel across the street—he may forget the boundary, take the shock, and go after the squirrel anyway. Now, he's outside the yard and can't get back in because the fence will shock him if he approaches it!

Perhaps the most compelling reason to stay with a real fence is that while invisible fencing may keep your dog in, it won't keep other dogs and other menaces *out.*

- **Training collar:** A training collar is necessary for training your dog. While there are many types of training collars, you should consider only a slip collar for right now. A slip collar is often misnamed as a "choke chain" (it isn't supposed to choke and, quite often, it's not made of chain but of nylon cord). Regardless of the material, the collar should be just big enough to fit around your dog's neck without excess hanging down.
- **Six-foot leather leash:** A six-foot leather leash is important for training. A leather leash is easier on your hands than a nylon leash when your dog pulls on it. While the cost seems extravagant, it's not. Use a leather leash where you can.
- **Six-foot nylon leash:** I usually steer people away from nylon leashes, but they do have their uses. A nylon leash is good if you have a puppy who likes to bite and pull at the leash. However, they're not Kevlar, and I've seen puppies saw through nylon leashes like a hot knife through butter. But they are a bit more resistant to a puppy's chewing than leather. Purchase a six-foot nylon leash in your favorite color or design, but expect that you'll be using the leather one once your puppy becomes strong (especially if he's from one of the larger breeds).

Tags Tip

I've seen plenty of dogs without tags or with tags that were totally illegible. Don't be one of those heartbroken owners who won't get their dogs returned to them because they don't have proper tags. Twice a year (when you change the clocks for daylight saving time is a good time—folks in Arizona and Indiana are out of luck!), look at your dog's tags. If they're worn, illegible, or look like they're about ready to fall off, get new ones made! Also, check the information on them. Addresses and phone numbers change, yet many people forget to change that on their dog's ID.

You should also consider having a permanent form of ID on your dog. See chapter 15, "Your Dog as Part of the Family," for more information.

Food Items

It's important to consider what your dog will be eating and chewing on. He'll need various yummy items and things to hold his food. Let's look at each of them:

- **Food and water bowls:** You'll need food and water bowls for your dog. These don't have to be fancy, but stainless steel bowls are the best because they will last and they are easy to clean. You can purchase cheaper plastic bowls, but some dogs are allergic to the plastic, which may actually cause acne or blister-like lumps around their mouths. (Switching to stainless steel bowls cures the problem.) If you choose ceramic bowls, be sure that the glaze isn't lead based because lead is as toxic to dogs as it is to humans.
- **Premium dog or puppy food:** You'll need to purchase dog or puppy food for your dog. While the breeder may provide an amount of food to start you off, you'll want to have enough on hand for a week or so. You should purchase a premium dog food made for a puppy if you're getting a puppy or for an adult dog, if your dog is an adult. More on selecting dog food in "Feeding Your Dog" in chapter 8, "Keeping Your Dog Healthy."
- **Training treats and dog biscuits:** Training treats (and regular treats) are vital for your dog, especially when it comes to training. While cute shapes appeal to people, be sure to get healthy treats that your dog likes. There are now many training treats that are specially made small so you can feed a bunch without interfering with your dog's diet. Treats that don't have colors and only have natural preservatives are best.
- **Various chew items and toys:** Chewing is a natural instinct, and your dog will need chews, especially if you have a puppy who is teething. For more information, see "Bones, Chews, and Other Edible Items," later in this chapter.

Grooming Items

When it comes to items for grooming your dog, fancy isn't necessary, but the better quality an item is, the more likely it's going to last. The necessary grooming items are described below:

- **Slicker brush or soft brush, depending on your dog's coat:** Depending on your dog's coat, you'll need to get either a slicker brush or a soft brush. A slicker brush is a brush with many thin wire bristles that looks a little like a pincushion. These brushes work for double-coated breeds. The thicker the coat, the larger and deeper you want the slicker brush so that it collects more hair. Soft brushes are preferable for dogs with short coats and for dogs with sensitive skin.

- **Flea comb:** Unless you live in a flea-free area (they do exist and are the best-kept secrets of the universe!), you'll need a way to comb out those pests. Flea combs are combs with very fine teeth that are made to catch fleas. (See chapter 8 for information on treatments for preventing fleas.)

- **Comb:** You'll need a standard dog comb. Most are metal and have long teeth—about ¾ to 1½ inches. Choose a comb with teeth long enough to handle the length of your dog's coat. Combs that have both fine- and medium-spaced teeth are especially good for longer coats that mat.

- **Nail clippers:** Nail clippers come in two varieties—a scissors type and a guillotine type. Both work very well. The guillotine type is more prevalent, and when the blade is dull, you replace it. (Kits are available.) The scissors type requires sharpening (groomers can do this for you).

Dog Supply Checklist

- ☑ Training crate
- ☑ Bed and/or bedding material
- ☑ Fencing, outdoor kennel, or some other outdoor containment system
- ☑ Enzymatic cleaner for accidents
- ☑ Flat or buckle collar
- ☑ ID tags with your name, address, and phone numbers
- ☑ Training collar
- ☐ Six-foot leather leash
- ☑ Six-foot nylon leash
- ☑ Food and water bowls
- ☑ Premium dog or puppy food
- ☐ Training treats and dog biscuits
- ☑ Various chew items and toys
- ☑ Slicker brush or soft brush, depending on your dog's coat
- ☐ Flea comb
- ☐ Comb
- ☐ Nail clippers
- ☑ Shampoo and conditioner made for dogs
- ☐ Toothbrush and toothpaste made for dogs

- **Shampoo and conditioner made for dogs:** It's a good idea to get shampoo and conditioner made for dogs. While you can occasionally use baby shampoo in a pinch, the shampoo and conditioners that are made for dogs are pH balanced for your dog's skin and coat. If you must bathe your dog frequently, dog shampoos and conditioners will keep your dog's skin and coat healthy, not dry or greasy.
- **Toothbrush and toothpaste made for dogs:** You need a toothbrush and toothpaste for dogs. (Human toothpaste is poisonous to dogs—do not use!) Toothpaste comes in a variety of doggy-pleasing flavors, such as chicken and malt.

Bones, Chews, and Other Edible Items

Controversy abounds when it comes to what is safe to give your dog. If you believe all the contradictory statements made among pet owners, on the Internet, and in books such as this one, you're likely to never give your dog a bone or chew again. The problem is that nothing is 100 percent safe for your dog to chew, and if there were something completely safe, he probably wouldn't like it anyway.

But dogs need to chew. And if you don't give your dog something appropriate to chew, he'll find something to chew on his own, and I guarantee it'll be less safe and you won't be happy with the results.

So, what do you do? Use common sense when purchasing items for your dog until you learn what his chewing habits are. Give your dog items that won't splinter and that he won't be able to break apart and swallow.

What about bones? Well, most bones are *not* safe. Don't give your dog poultry, fish, pork, steak, or any other sharp bones. These bones can lodge in the throat and present a choking hazard or can perforate an intestine. Even large bones can cause trouble if they splinter.

Are Raw Bones Safe?

You may hear about raw diets where you feed your dog raw meat and bones. Proponents claim these bones are safer raw than cooked. Consider the following:

- Raw bones can still splinter and become a choking, obstruction, or perforation hazard.
- Raw bones can carry bacteria that can be transmitted to you or your kids, such as *Salmonella*, *Campylobacter*, and *E. coli*.
- Feeding raw bones may cause diarrhea or constipation, depending on how the dog is affected (either through the bacteria or the excessive calcium).
- In extreme instances, raw bones can cause imbalances in minerals due to calcium interfering with other vital nutrients.

Rules for Picking Out Bones and Toys

Until you're absolutely sure about your dog's chewing habits, you will have to purchase tough toys, large chews, and items that are made for aggressive chewers. A few hints on finding the right toys:

- Choose bones, chews, and toys that are too large for your dog to completely get his jaws around. This will prevent him from bringing the full power of his jaws on the toy in question, and he'll have to really work at chewing it.
- Think heavy-duty rubber, large marrow bones or knuckle bones, large nylon bones, and other items made for aggressive chewers.
- Stay away from soft latex or things that can be torn apart or chewed to pieces and swallowed.
- Never give your dog a toy meant for children.
- Always watch your dog while he plays with his toys or chews. Don't leave him alone with them.
- If your dog starts to tear off pieces or rip apart the toy, chew, or bone, it's time to throw it away.

The "safer" bones are knuckle bones and large marrow bones, but there is controversy surrounding their safety because they harbor bacteria and can cause intestinal obstructions, and dogs can break teeth on them. Freezing them tends to make them tougher, but some veterinarians recommend boiling them. Again, experts dispute the right course of action. If you do give bones to your dog, only do it while you can watch him. If he chews off a piece or splinters the bone, take it and the pieces away from him. Some pet suppliers offer prebasted, precooked bones, but again, that's your choice if you feel it is safer. Some prebasted bones can stain carpet and upholstery.

Rawhides tend to be a favorite with many dogs, but if your dog is an aggressive chewer, you should watch him carefully. Too much rawhide can cause an intestinal blockage. If you do decide to give your dog rawhide, choose rawhide made in the United States to avoid the possibility of disease and poor handling.

Toys

No matter how optional you think toys are, I'll guarantee that your dog thinks they're mighty important. Dogs love toys to play with, cuddle, chew on, tug on, chase and retrieve, and have a great time with. Problem is, there is no such thing as a totally indestructible toy, and like bones and chews, toys are a must for a dog.

Look for items that can't be torn apart easily, and always supervise your dog while he is chewing on the toy until it is obvious that he can't easily chew it apart and swallow large pieces, which can present a choking or blockage hazard. Safer toys are usually made from hard rubber or flavored nylon, but tough chewers can snap pieces off or wear them down to nubs.

Let's look at the various toys.

Hard Rubber Toys

Hard rubber toys are probably the safest toys out there, provided that your dog can't get his jaws fully around them. (I had a Malamute who sawed the top off a toy made for aggressive chewers that was for medium-sized dogs.) Even so, if your dog is a very aggressive chewer, a hard rubber toy might get torn apart if your dog sets his mind (and teeth) to it.

These toys used to be somewhat boring to dogs, but manufacturers have made them so that you can hide treats inside them, thus making them more interesting.

Soft Toys

Soft toys are usually fleece or fabric, which collects the dog's scent and makes him feel more secure. Most dogs really love these toys, especially the ones with squeakers. The downside to these toys is that they can be chewed up easily, and swallowed fabric or stuffing can cause a blockage. If you give your dog one of these toys, do it only under your supervision.

Rope Toys

Some dogs really enjoy rope toys. These are braided or twisted rope that's soft enough so a dog can chew it. Sometimes the manufacturers put rubber chew toys or cow hooves on the rope to make it more interesting. Some dogs really love these; others couldn't care less. Rope toys can be chewed apart and swallowed, so you should only allow your dog to chew them while you supervise him.

Nylon Toys

Nylon toys are made in a variety of different shapes and sizes (bones, dinosaurs, etc.). They're very tough and can be impregnated with scents dogs love. However, many dogs don't find these toys interesting unless you play with the dog with them. Nylon toys are very tough, but if you buy toys that are too small or if your dog is an aggressive chewer, they can be dangerous. Manufacturers usually have a warning on the package that says when to discard the toy (usually when the ends are gnawed down).

Puzzle Toys

Puzzle toys, which are relatively new on the dog-toy scene, allow the dog to interact with the toy to get treats. You fill the toy with treats or food and hand it to the dog to play with. The dog bumps and rolls the toy around, and it dispenses treats, depending on how the dog rolls it. Food-oriented dogs usually have fun with these toys. Puzzle toys are good for dogs while you're away, but you should first learn your dog's chewing habits before leaving your dog alone with these toys.

Puzzle Toys

- **Buster Cube:** This is a plastic food cube that is a puzzle. It has different levels of difficulty that you can set. You fill all the Buster Cube's compartments with food and show your dog that by pushing the cube around with his nose in certain ways, he can get a treat. www.bustercube.com.
- **Crazy Ball:** This toy is based on a similar principle to the Buster Cube; the dog must push the ball around to obtain treats. www.nylabone.com.
- **Kong Ball and Planet Kong:** A Kong Ball is a treat ball made out of tough rubber material that dispenses treats. A Planet Kong allows you to hide treats in the "spaceship" toy and have your dog work to pull them out. www.kongcompany.com.
- **Busy Buddy Twist 'n Treat, The Groove Thing, Biscuit Bouncer, The Chuckle, and The Waggle:** These are all food-oriented toys that allow you to hide and dispense treats to your dog. www.busybuddytoys.com.
- **Talk to Me Treatball:** This toy allows you to record a fifteen-second message for your dog, which activates when the dog rolls the treatball and dispenses a treat. www.talktometreatball.com.

Other Toys

Soft latex toys with squeakers (often in the shapes of hamburgers, newspapers, etc.) are usually too flimsy to hold up to a dog's chewing. When looking at a toy, keep an eye out for things that can be chewed off, broken apart, or pulled apart. Always consider your dog's chewing habits before giving new toys to your dog.

There are also soft toys to play catch with. These toys are intended to not harm teeth. Don't leave these toys alone with your dog, or he may chew them up.

Optional Items (but You'll Wonder How You Managed without Them)

A number of not-so-necessary items may actually make you wonder how you did without them for so long. The items in the previous section are the basics; these items will make your life easier and, in many cases, may be essential for your dog's comfort:

- **Sweaters:** Don't laugh! If you have a short-coated dog or one with a single coat that requires clipping, a sweater will help keep him warm on cold winter days. Choose washable acrylic sweaters that won't shrink and that fit your dog well.
- **Seat belt harness:** This type of harness is good for keeping your dog safely strapped in for rides around town or farther.
- **Pooper scoopers:** These work better than a shovel to pick up dog poop. Choose the size that is appropriate for your dog.
- **Poop bags:** You can use plastic grocery-store bags to pick up after your larger dog on walks, but they can be flimsy and may have holes in them. Premade poop bags are self-sealing and very strong. Regular sandwich bags are fine for smaller dogs.

- **Clippers and grooming shears:** These items are essential for touch-ups on single-coated breeds, but it is imperative that you learn how to use them properly, or you may injure your dog. Ask a groomer for ones he or she recommends for your particular dog.
- **Nail grinders:** Some dogs who can't tolerate having their nails clipped will handle electric nail grinders just fine.
- **Grooming table:** If you have room for one, a grooming table will save your back by saving you from bending over all the time. Even if you have a large dog, these are essential for grooming. Most owners teach their medium to large dogs to jump up on the table on command. Whichever table you choose, be sure it is steady. A dog who's up off the ground is much easier to groom.
- **Pet gates:** These gates are essential for cordoning off areas that are off limits to your dog or retaining the dog in his confined area. Choose sturdy gates that won't be knocked over easily. Some gates actually have a door that allows you to walk through instead of having to step over.
- **X-pens:** You can use an X-pen (exercise pen) to confine your dog when you can't watch him. X-pens are portable, so you can bring them with you. Be sure you get one that's tall enough so your dog can't jump or climb out. Again, choose a sturdy X-pen; otherwise, your dog will bend the metal.
- **Blow dryer for dogs:** After you wash your dog, drying him so he doesn't get cold is important. Human hair dryers are too hot for a dog's sensitive skin and may burn him. Choose one that has a fair amount of drying power—you don't want to spend all day drying your dog.
- **Retractable leash:** Most owners of small and medium-sized dogs swear by these leashes for walking. Use them when you have learned how they work, and only with a well-behaved dog.
- **Litter box and doggy litter:** If you live in an apartment in the city, you may choose to litter train your small to medium-sized dog.

Choosing a Veterinarian

After you, the most important person in your dog's life should be his veterinarian. It only makes sense that you find the right vet for your dog. Your dog's vet can offer guidance on how to care for your dog and what to do when he's sick.

When you look for a vet, you should look for one who is compatible with you. This may sound strange, but whether you get along with your vet will affect whether you're willing to follow his or her directions. Your dog can't tell you how he feels or what's wrong, so good communication between you and your vet is essential.

Because there are a lot of vets to choose from, you can afford to be a bit picky. Although most vets offer similar services, not all vets offer the same services. For example, vets may offer mobile services (they come to you), emergency services, boarding, grooming, or other specialized care. When looking for a vet, consider what services you're looking for. Price shouldn't be the only consideration.

Veterinary Facilities

Veterinarians work at a variety of facilities. These include:

- **Animal hospitals:** These hospitals usually employ a large number of vets and may have specialists. They may have their own testing facilities that a smaller clinic can't afford. They may handle complex surgeries and emergencies that can't be treated anywhere else.
- **Veterinary clinics:** Vet clinics may have as few as one or as many as five or more vets. These clinics have office hours and may or may not handle emergencies.
- **Emergency clinics:** These vet clinics are for emergencies only. These clinics usually handle after-hours calls and tend to be expensive.
- **Low-cost clinics:** A relatively new type of vet clinic. The purpose behind most low-cost clinics is to provide routine services (vaccinations, heartworm tests, spay/neuters) at a low cost. These clinics make up in volume for their lower prices. They generally don't have the facilities to handle emergencies or complex diagnoses.
- **Mobile clinics:** Mobile clinics are usually associated with animal hospitals or veterinary clinics. They offer convenience to the pet owner but do not offer all the services of a stationary office, such as diagnostics, surgery, ICU, and other services.
- **University clinics:** These clinics are usually state-of-the-art when it comes to treating pets with unusual conditions or serious diseases, such as cancer. You may need a referral from your vet, but some university clinics do allow you to schedule regular appointments.

Locating a Vet

Finding the best dog doc in your neighborhood might be just a call away. Ask your dog-owning friends and neighbors whom they use as a vet. A glowing recommendation is worth its weight in gold. The good vets don't need to advertise; most get their clients through word of mouth.

But what if you can't find any good recommendations? In that case, you can contact your dog's breeder to see if he or she has suggestions. Even if the breeder doesn't live near you, he or she can ask other breeders in your area whom they take their dogs to. Other people to contact might be trainers and groomers in your area.

If you're stuck, you can contact the American Animal Hospital Association for a list of vets near you. Or you can look through the Yellow Pages under veterinarians and make a list of vets in your area.

When you have a list of vets, call their offices and ask questions. These questions will help narrow down your choices for a veterinarian. There are no right or wrong answers to these questions. Some questions may be more important to you than others.

Finding a Vet: Interview Questions

What hours is your clinic open? Do you offer after-hours services?

_____

_____

Do you handle emergencies or are you affiliated with a clinic that handles emergencies? Are the vets on call, and do they have on-call pagers? (This is important if your dog becomes sick after hours.)

_____

_____

Do any of the vets in the practice specialize in a particular area, such as allergies, neurology, or holistic treatments? (Some people like to have a specialist on hand if a problem arises. Many veterinarians also consider alternative therapies when conventional methods don't work. It's nice to have the option available.)

_____

_____

Do you offer an on-site groomer or boarding? (Having a groomer or boarding facility at the veterinary clinic means that your vet is likely to be the groomer or the boarding kennel you take your dog to if there is a problem. It's also a matter of convenience.)

_____

_____

What is the cost for vaccinations, office visits, and other routine services?

_____

_____

Do you offer a multipet discount?

_____

_____

Do you take pet insurance? (Some vets take pet insurance; others require that you file your own claims. Check with the insurance company.)

_____

_____

Do you make house calls? Under what circumstances? (House calls are important for people with several pets or for pets who are very old or stressed by the vet's office.)

_____

_____

How many dogs of [your dog's] breed do you see? (A vet who is very familiar with your breed is apt to know and recognize certain conditions your dog may be experiencing due to genetic problems or congenital problems seen in the breed. Some breeds are predisposed to having anesthesia sensitivity. A vet who knows such things will take appropriate precautions.)

_____

_____

The staff at the clinic should be courteous and willing to answer your questions. Even if you love your vet, two-hour waits and cranky office staff can contribute to bad vet experiences.

Once you've narrowed down the vets to a few choices, call each of the vets and schedule an appointment to visit the facility. Don't drop by unannounced—you may show up during a busy time when the staff may not have a chance to talk with you. When you visit, ask for a tour. The clinic should be clean, and the staff should be friendly and helpful. If you have a chance to talk with the vet, do so. Find out what the vet's training is and whether he or she is familiar with conditions common to your particular dog breed. If you're interested in holistic medicine, find out if the veterinarian uses holistic therapies or is strictly a conventional vet.

You should have a good feeling about the veterinarian and the clinic before bringing your dog there. Usually the final test is when you bring your dog for his first appointment. While some dogs won't get along with any vet, the vet should have a gentle and caring manner toward your dog when you bring him in.

The AAHA

You can find the American Animal Hospital Association (AAHA) online at www.aahanet.org or contact the AAHA at P.O. Box 150899, Denver, Colorado, 80215-0899, 303/986-2800.

Protecting Your Dog's Health: Pet Health Insurance

Veterinary expenses can be high, especially in the first year of your dog's life. However, you must care for your dog with routine medical exams, vaccinations, and dewormings or risk having a sick dog—or worse. Remember, the purchase price of a dog doesn't include health care, training, or food.

Even on the low end, you'll spend a fair amount of money on vet care. Luckily, pet health insurance is available for dogs. It can help with some of the expenses involved in veterinary care. Some insurance plans cover only major medical expenses, while others take care of routine health care.

The following pet health insurance companies are listed here for information only—this is not an endorsement:

AKC Pet Healthcare Plan
P.O. Box 37940
Raleigh, NC 27627
919/859-8222
www.petpartnersinc.com/akcphp.htm

Pet Assure
10 South Morris St.
Dover, NJ 07801
888/789-PETS
www.petassure.com

PetCare Insurance Programs
P.O. Box 8575
Rolling Meadows, IL 60008-8575
866/275-PETS
www.petcareinsurance.com

Pet Plan Insurance (Canada)
777 Portage Ave.
Winnipeg, MB R3G 0N3 CANADA
905/279-7190
www.petplan.com

Petshealth Insurance Agency
P.O. Box 2847
Canton, OH 44720
888/592-7387
www.petshealthplan.com

Veterinary Pet Insurance
P.O. Box 2344
Brea, CA 92822-2344
800/USA-PETS
www.petinsurance.com

While price in pet health insurance is important, it's also important to know that the insurance comes from a reputable source, has been around for a long time, and won't disappear tomorrow. Read the policy information carefully; some policies handle only catastrophic injuries or diseases (like a human major medical policy) and some are like a human's HMO or PPO. Obviously, the more routine services a policy covers, the more expensive it's likely to be.

When checking out pet insurance, be sure to get the AM Best rating—that is, an insurance rating that tells you how good the insurance is and how reliable the underwriter of the policy is. Typically, most experts recommend an A+ or A++ rating. (The higher the rating, the more confidence you should have in the insurance.)

Most pet health insurance won't cover preexisting conditions, elective surgery, or hereditary diseases. Many have a cap on diseases such as cancer. Most insurance is more expensive if you purchase it for an older dog, so it's best to buy it when your dog is a puppy.

Is pet insurance a good value? It depends largely on whether you need to use it and whether you could afford to pay for an emergency or a serious illness on your own. With pet insurance, many pet owners who would normally have to put their pets down because of an expensive illness have the option of treating the disease instead. Usually the owner must pay for the procedure and then get reimbursed by the health insurance.

What You Now Know . . .

- You need to provide a safe place for your dog to spend his time.
- Your dog needs a variety of supplies, from bowls and brushes to food, toys, and treats. If you can, take your time in purchasing dog supplies and buy online or through catalogs so you can save money.
- You should choose a veterinarian whom you'll respect and who has services you and your dog require. Pet health insurance can help with large veterinary bills.

Chapter 5

Dog-Proofing

What's Inside...

- Learn what dangerous things dogs are likely to get into.
- Learn how to dog-proof your house.
- Learn how to make your yard and garage safe for your dog.

Before you bring your dog or puppy home, you'll need to make your home safe for her. It's a lot like child-proofing for a toddler. But in this case, you have a kid with teeth who will taste and chew just about anything and everything.

Puppies are destructive little critters. As with children, it's the very nature of a puppy to explore. Unfortunately, like infants, puppies use their mouths to explore, and they pick up everything. And of course, anything that is picked up gets chewed and swallowed. Consequently, if you have a cluttered home or lots of knickknacks, you're going to have to do some cleaning and rearranging.

Begin by taking a look around your home at a puppy's- or dog's-eye level. Get on your hands and knees and look for anything that might be tempting. Things with strings or tassels, glittery knickknacks, and objects your dog can easily reach are all prime targets. Electrical and curtain cords are also very enticing—and dangerous. Hide them or put them out of reach of inquisitive mouths.

Even if you adopt an adult dog, you don't know the dog's habits. Many dogs are turned in to animal shelters and rescue groups because of behavior problems. Those problems include destructive chewing. For whatever reason, the owners couldn't be bothered with retraining the dog.

After you have determined where your dog is going to stay, be sure you've dog-proofed all areas of your home that your dog will be allowed in. Some owners like to start with a few rooms and gradually allow the dog in other rooms in the house. It gives them time to see what the dog will actually get into before allowing her into other rooms in the house.

Will you have to do all this dog-proofing? Probably not. However, overkill is best when you don't know what your dog will get into. Some things people think are safe from the dogs end up not being so. So, err on the side of caution when you first get your dog until you learn what she can or can't get into.

Dog-Proofing Inside the House

When you begin to dog-proof your house, look in areas that may present the most hazards, such as the kitchen and bathroom. Anything that has enticing items that can be pulled to the floor and chewed may be a danger. The following checklists will help you spot and fix dangers in your house in general and in specific parts of your house. Extra blanks are provided so you can add to these lists as needed.

House Checklist

Here is a general list of items to look for throughout your house:

- ☐ Alcohol of all sorts—very poisonous to dogs
- ☐ Bathroom cleaners and shower cleaners
- ☐ Batteries
- ☐ Candles
- ☐ Cell phones
- ☐ Children's toys, especially those with small pieces that can be chewed off or swallowed
- ☐ Chocolate—extremely toxic to dogs (dark chocolate is more poisonous than milk chocolate)
- ☐ Dental floss—can become lodged in throat or intestines
- ☐ Electrical cords
- ☐ Garbage pails
- ☐ Glass knickknacks
- ☐ Grapes and raisins (toxic to some dogs)
- ☐ Houseplants
- ☐ Irons and ironing boards
- ☐ Kitchen knives
- ☐ Medications—including ibuprofen, acetaminophen, and aspirin—and vitamins
- ☐ Onions—can cause anemia
- ☐ Pennies—can cause "penny poisoning" due to the zinc content
- ☐ Pens, paper, paper clips, and other small items that may be chewed or swallowed
- ☐ Plates and glasses—can be knocked over
- ☐ Scented soaps, potpourri, scented plug-in air fresheners, and other air fresheners
- ☐ Sewing needles, spools of thread, and craft kits
- ☐ Shampoo, conditioner, and mouthwash
- ☐ Socks and other clothing items—can be chewed or swallowed whole and cause obstruction
- ☐ Suntan lotion and insect repellents
- ☐ Toothpaste—extremely toxic to dogs

Kitchen Checklist

Be sure to do the following to dog-proof your kitchen:

- ☐ Fit cabinets with childproof latches.
- ☐ Fit the refrigerator with a childproof Velcro strap (some dogs figure out how to open it).
- ☑ Stow cleaners in cabinets with latches.
- ☑ Remove food from counters and put either in a pantry with a shutting door or in the refrigerator.
- ☐ Stow knives out of the dog's reach or, preferably, in a drawer.
- ☐ Stow trash and garbage behind a locked door.
- ☑ Stow plates, glasses, and cutlery in cabinets or drawer.
- ☑ Make sure air fresheners are out of reach.
- ☑ Cap electrical outlets with childproof covers.
- ☑ Make sure electrical cords are out of reach.
- ☑ Make sure window blind cords are out of reach.
- ☐ Move potpourri out of reach.
- ☑ Move soaps and detergents out of reach.
- ☑ Move kitchen plants out of reach.
- ☑ Remove anything that can fall down or be pulled down onto the dog.
- ☑ Remove dirty dishes from the sink and drying rack. Clean and put away.
- ☑ Put all cutlery and kitchen utensils away in drawers.
- ☑ Stow sponges and cleaning brushes in cabinets.

- ☐ _____
- ☐ _____
- ☐ _____
- ☐ _____
- ☐ _____
- ☐ _____
- ☐ _____

Bathroom Checklist

Be sure to do the following to dog-proof your bathroom:

- ☐ Fit cabinets with childproof latches.
- ☐ Put toothpaste and all medicine into a medicine cabinet, out of reach of your dog.
- ☐ Remove "automatic" toilet cleaners such as those that cause the water to turn blue.
- ☐ Keep the toilet lid closed.
- ☐ Stow cleaners in cabinets with latches.

- ☐ Stow trash under a cabinet.
- ☐ Make sure air fresheners are out of reach.
- ☐ Cap electrical outlets with childproof covers.
- ☐ Make sure electrical cords are out of reach.
- ☐ Make sure window blind cords are out of reach.
- ☐ Stow sponges and cleaning brushes in cabinets.
- ☐ Stow nail clippers, tweezers, and other sharp objects in cabinets.
- ☐ Stow all paper products, including toilet paper and feminine products, out of reach.
- ☐ Remove anything that can fall down or be pulled down onto the dog.
- ☐ Move potpourri out of reach.
- ☐ Move soaps out of reach.
- ☐ Move dental floss out of reach.
- ☐ Move bathroom plants out of reach.
- ☐ Store suntan lotion, skin lotion, scented creams, makeup, perfume, aftershave, and so on in a latched cabinet.

☐ _____

☐ _____

☐ _____

☐ _____

☐ _____

☐ _____

☐ _____

Living Room Checklist

Be sure to do the following to dog-proof your living room:

- ☐ Fit cabinets with childproof latches.
- ☐ Get all items such as books, papers, baskets, toys, and house-plants off the floor and out of reach.
- ☑ Move knickknacks from coffee table and tables to a higher place and make sure a curious dog can't reach them on her hind legs.
- ☐ Keep all shoes and other clothing items in closets.
- ☐ Stow cleaners in cabinets with latches.

- [ ] Stow trash in a cabinet or behind a locked door.
- [x] Make sure air fresheners are out of reach.
- [ ] Cap electrical outlets with childproof covers.
- [ ] Make sure electrical cords—including those to computers, stereos, game systems, and other equipment—are out of reach.
- [ ] Make sure window blind cords are out of reach.
- [ ] Remove anything that can fall down or be pulled down onto the dog.
- [ ] Move potpourri out of reach.
- [ ] Move candles out of reach.
- [ ] Add extra screens around a fireplace or woodstove.
- [x] Remove the ash bucket for a stove or fireplace.
- [x] Keep crafts and games in cabinets.
- [x] Move books, CDs, DVDs, VCR tapes, and other items out of reach.

- [ ] _____
- [ ] _____
- [ ] _____
- [ ] _____
- [ ] _____
- [ ] _____
- [ ] _____

Phone Numbers to Tape to Your Phone

You should always have the following phone numbers taped to your phone or programmed into the speed dial:

- Veterinarian
- Emergency veterinary clinic (for off hours)
- Local poison control center
- ASPCA poison control hotline (see "Poison Control Centers" sidebar on page 75)

Bedroom Checklist

Be sure to do the following to dog-proof your bedroom:

- ☐ Fit cabinets with childproof latches.
- ☐ Get all items such as books, papers, baskets, toys, and houseplants off the floor and out of reach.
- ☐ Move knickknacks from tables where a curious dog can reach on her hind legs.
- ☐ Keep all shoes, socks, and other clothing items in closets and drawers.
- ☐ Move jewelry to drawers.
- ☐ Keep ties, belts, and other pieces of clothing behind a closed closet door or in a drawer.
- ☐ Stow trash in a cabinet or behind a closed door.
- ☐ Make sure air fresheners are out of reach.
- ☐ Cap electrical outlets with childproof covers.
- ☐ Make sure electrical cords—including those to computers, stereos, game systems, and other equipment—are out of reach.
- ☐ Make sure window blind cords are out of reach.
- ☐ Remove anything that can fall down or be pulled down onto the dog.
- ☐ Move potpourri out of reach.
- ☐ Move candles out of reach.
- ☐ Move books, CDs, DVDs, VCR tapes, and other items out of reach.

- ☐ _____
- ☐ _____
- ☐ _____
- ☐ _____
- ☐ _____
- ☐ _____
- ☐ _____

Dining Room Checklist

Be sure to do the following to dog-proof your dining room:

- ☐ Fit cabinets with childproof latches.
- ☐ Get all items such as books, papers, baskets, toys, and houseplants off the floor and out of reach.
- ☐ Move knickknacks from tables where a curious dog can reach on her hind legs to a higher place.
- ☐ Stow cleaners in cabinets with latches.
- ☐ Stow trash in a cabinet or behind a locked door.

- [ ] Make sure air fresheners are out of reach.
- [ ] Cap electrical outlets with childproof covers.
- [ ] Make sure electrical cords are out of reach.
- [ ] Make sure window blind cords are out of reach.
- [ ] Remove anything that can fall down or be pulled down onto the dog.
- [ ] Move potpourri out of reach.
- [ ] Move candles out of reach.
- [ ] Store plates and cutlery in a china closet or other cabinet and drawers.
- [ ] Remove centerpiece from table.

- [ ] _____
- [ ] _____
- [ ] _____
- [ ] _____
- [ ] _____
- [ ] _____
- [ ] _____

Office Checklist

Be sure to do the following to dog-proof your office:

- [ ] Fit cabinets with childproof latches.
- [ ] Get all items such as books, papers, baskets, toys, and houseplants off the floor and out of reach.
- [ ] Move knickknacks from desk and tables where a curious dog can reach on her hind legs to a higher place.
- [ ] Keep all shoes and other clothing items in closets.
- [ ] Stow cleaners in cabinets with latches.
- [ ] Stow trash in a cabinet or behind a closed door.
- [ ] Make sure air fresheners are out of reach.
- [ ] Cap electrical outlets with childproof covers.
- [ ] Make sure electrical cords—including those to computers, stereos, game systems, printer cables, and other equipment—are out of reach.
- [ ] Make sure window blind cords are out of reach.
- [ ] Remove anything that can fall down or be pulled down onto the dog.
- [ ] Move potpourri out of reach.
- [ ] Move candles out of reach.
- [ ] Put away paper shredder and keep unplugged.
- [ ] Put away small items such as coins, paper clips, thumbtacks, and staples.

- [ ] Remove crafts and games from reach and put in cabinets.
- [ ] Move books, CDs, floppy disks, DVDs, VCR tapes, and other items out of reach.

- [ ] _____
- [ ] _____
- [ ] _____
- [ ] _____
- [ ] _____
- [ ] _____
- [ ] _____

Kid's Bedroom Checklist

Be sure to do the following to dog-proof your child's bedroom:

- [ ] Fit cabinets with childproof latches.
- [ ] Get all items such as books, papers, baskets, toys, and houseplants off the floor and out of reach.
- [ ] Move knick-knacks from dressers and tables where a curious dog can reach on her hind legs.
- [ ] Keep all shoes and other clothing items in closets and drawers.
- [ ] Put toys up out of reach and in closets.
- [ ] Stow trash in a cabinet or behind a closed door.
- [ ] Make sure air fresheners are out of reach.
- [ ] Cap electrical outlets with childproof covers.
- [ ] Make sure electrical cords—including those to computers, stereos, game systems, and other equipment—are out of reach.
- [ ] Make sure window blind cords are out of reach.
- [ ] Remove anything that can fall down or be pulled down onto the dog.
- [ ] Store jewelry in a dresser drawer.
- [ ] Put away small toys such as action figures, matchbox cars, and so on that could be chewed up and swallowed.
- [ ] Remove crafts and games from reach and put in cabinets.
- [ ] Move books, CDs, DVDs, VCR tapes, and other items out of reach.

- [ ] _____
- [ ] _____

☐ _____

☐ _____

☐ _____

☐ _____

☐ _____

Laundry Room Checklist

Be sure to do the following to dog-proof your laundry room:

☐ Fit cabinets with childproof latches.
☐ Get all items such as books, papers, baskets, toys, and houseplants off the floor and out of reach.
☐ Move all dirty clothing items to an enclosed hamper with a latch a dog can't open.
☐ Stow cleaners and laundry detergent in cabinets with latches.
☐ Stow trash in a cabinet or behind a locked door.
☐ Make sure air fresheners are out of reach.
☐ Cap electrical outlets with childproof covers.
☐ Make sure electrical cords are out of reach.
☐ Make sure window blind cords are out of reach.
☐ Remove anything that can fall down or be pulled down onto the dog.
☐ Move potpourri out of reach.
☐ Unplug and put away the iron.
☐ Store the ironing board where it can't be knocked over.
☐ Hang hangers out of the dog's reach.

☐ _____

☐ _____

☐ _____

☐ _____

☐ _____

☐ _____

☐ _____

Attic and Basement Checklist

Be sure to do the following to dog-proof your attic and basement:

- ☐ Fit cabinets with childproof latches.
- ☐ Store nails, nuts, screws, and similar items out of the dog's reach.
- ☐ Get all items such as books, papers, baskets, toys, and houseplants off the floor and out of reach.
- ☐ Make sure insulation is covered up completely by drywall.
- ☐ Put all tools in locked cabinets.
- ☐ Remove rat and mouse poison.
- ☐ Remove rat and mouse traps.
- ☐ Store old craft kits and other items in storage containers.
- ☐ Move all shoes and other clothing items to closets.
- ☐ Stow cleaners in cabinets with latches.
- ☐ Stow trash in a cabinet or behind a closed door.
- ☐ Make sure air fresheners are out of reach.
- ☐ Cap electrical outlets with childproof covers.
- ☐ Make sure electrical cords are out of reach.
- ☐ Make sure all furnace, water heater, and other pipes and ducts are blocked off.
- ☐ Remove anything that can fall down or be pulled down onto the dog.
- ☐ Move potpourri out of reach.
- ☐ Block off fans and crawl spaces.
- ☐ Remove paint, turpentine, and other poisons.

- ☐ _____
- ☐ _____
- ☐ _____
- ☐ _____
- ☐ _____
- ☐ _____
- ☐ _____

Poison Control Centers

The ASPCA has a staffed poison control center that is available 24 hours a day, 365 days a year. Its toll-free number is 888/426-4435. The cost is $50 per case, with as many follow-up calls as necessary at no extra charge.

Some local and regional poison control centers will handle cases involving pets for no charge.

Dog-Proofing the Garage

Garages are full of toxic chemicals such as antifreeze and pesticides and may also contain dangerous items such as tools and nails.

Garage Checklist

The garage should be off-limits to your dog, but just in case she gets into it, you should keep a number of items out of reach:

- ☐ Antifreeze and windshield washer fluid (and any on the garage floor)
- ☐ Batteries
- ☐ Lawn and garden chemicals
- ☐ Mouse and rat poisons (These poisons are still dangerous if your dog eats a mouse or rat that has eaten the poison.)
- ☐ Nails, screws, and other hardware that can be ingested
- ☐ Paint and paint remover
- ☐ Saws and other tools that may be sharp

☐ _____

☐ _____

☐ _____

☐ _____

☐ _____

☐ _____

☐ _____

A Partial List of Poisonous Plants

Aloe plant
Azalea
Begonia (wax and tuberous)
Black locust
Buckeye
Chinese lantern
Daffodil
Foxglove
Gladiola
Holly
Hyacinth
Hydrangea
Iris
Ivy
Japanese yew

Laurel
Lily
Lily-of-the-valley
Milkweed
Mistletoe
Nightshades
Oleander
Philodendron
Rhododendron
Star leaf
Tomato plant (green parts only)
Tulip
Water plant
Yew

Dog-Proofing the Backyard

The backyard can be a source of danger for dogs. Both exotic and indigenous plants can be poisonous. You should periodically check your backyard for possible hazards and loose areas in your fencing.

Backyard Checklist

Check your backyard for the following hazards and correct them if possible:

- [ ] High decks—dog can accidentally jump from them.
- [ ] Lawn and garden chemicals—can be absorbed through paw pads or licked off fur.
- [ ] Mushrooms and other fungi—many are toxic or even deadly.
- [ ] Sharp edging—can cut paws.
- [ ] Stones—many dogs love to eat small rocks and gravel that can lodge in intestines.
- [ ] Swimming pools—should be fenced in or otherwise made off-limits to the dog.
- [ ] Toxic plants—these are too numerous to list them all but include evergreen plants such as holly and pods from the black locust tree. The list above names more plants that are toxic to dogs. Contact your local poison control center or state agricultural office for a list of poisonous plants in your area.

- [ ] _____
- [ ] _____

☐ _____

☐ _____

☐ _____

☐ _____

☐ _____

A Shopping List

What do you really need to make your dog safe? Now that you've gone through the checklists in this chapter, you probably have an idea of what's involved. Some areas will be too difficult to dog-proof properly (such as the basement or garage). In such cases, you'll have to declare them off-limits to your dog and make sure she can't get to them.

Most of the items mentioned in the following list are things you can get at a hardware store. If you have a truly cluttered house, you may want to consider using storage containers and perhaps enough shelves and cabinets to keep things off the floor. You should cordon off rooms that you don't want your dog in by using pet gates or keeping the doors shut.

```
         Safety Supplies: A Shopping List

How many childproof latches do you need for:

_____ Bedrooms

_____ Bathrooms

_____ Kitchen

_____ Living room

_____ Dining room

_____ Office

_____ Attic

_____ Basement

                                        continues
```

How many childproof outlet covers do you need for:

_____ Bedrooms

_____ Bathrooms

_____ Kitchen

_____ Living room

_____ Dining room

_____ Office

_____ Attic

_____ Basement

How many pet gates do you need for:

_____ Bedrooms

_____ Bathrooms

_____ Kitchen

_____ Living room

_____ Dining room

_____ Office

_____ Attic

_____ Basement

How many storage containers do you need for:

_____ Bedrooms

_____ Bathrooms

_____ Kitchen

_____ Living room

_____ Dining room

_____ Office

_____ Attic

_____ Basement

What You Now Know . . .

- Dogs can be hurt by a number of household items, so it's important to dog-proof your house and yard before you bring your new dog home.
- Look for and pick up anything that your dog or puppy might be able to chew.
- Keep all dangerous substances away from your dog.
- Keep the ASPCA poison hotline number and other emergency numbers near your phone.

Chapter 6

Bringing Your Dog Home

When to Bring Your Dog Home

Your life is probably pretty hectic. So when it comes time to bring your dog home, don't complicate matters. Choose a time when you have days off to spend with your new pup. You and your dog need time to get acquainted. You'll also be using this time to bond. This usually means vacation days or time off. If you can't take time off, at least wait until a Friday afternoon to bring your new dog home so you have the weekend with him.

If you can, don't plan anything else during this time. If your new dog is a puppy, you'll need this time to get him settled into a routine and catch up on lost sleep. (You will lose sleep the first few nights, until your dog gets used to the new home.)

Other good times might be during summer vacation, when the kids are out of school. That way, you'll know that there'll usually be someone home to play and socialize with your dog, even when you aren't. Slow times during work or school are also good times to bring a puppy home because you'll be able to take a little time off here and there to spend some extra time with your dog.

When Not to Bring a Dog Home

There are times when you shouldn't bring home a dog. One time is the holidays. Yes, you have a lot of time off, but if you're spending the holidays with family and friends, you won't have enough time for a new pup or dog. The other problem is that there are many fun and interesting things to get into around this time. Christmas tree lights, tinsel, and ornaments

Can I Pick Him Up?

Most children want to pick up a puppy or small dog. While this looks cute, it can actually be dangerous to the dog because the child can inadvertently hurt him. Children can be clumsy, and all it takes is one trip and fall to seriously injure or even kill your pet.

The safest thing to teach a child is to only hold the dog when she is sitting on the floor or in a sturdy chair or couch. When the child is ready to get up, she must put the dog on the floor before getting up.

look yummy but could seriously harm or even kill your new dog if he chews on an electrical cord or swallows tinsel or an ornament. Bones and scraps from the holiday dinner or garbage can cause upset stomachs and can present choking, blockage, or perforation problems. Most reputable breeders and many shelters discourage people from getting pets around the holidays for these reasons.

Many puppies are given as Christmas pets only to be given up to shelters by the springtime. If you're planning on giving a puppy or dog to a family member as a Christmas present, consider buying doggy presents such as a new collar and leash, bowls, bedding, and so on, and then plan on getting your dog *after* the holidays.

Other times you shouldn't consider bringing a dog home are when you're going to take a trip, when you have a big deadline at work, and when you have visiting guests.

The Car Ride Home

When you bring your dog home, be certain to have a crate in your car to transport your dog. Many dogs become carsick, fearful, or worse when riding in the car. A crate keeps your dog safe and secure in one place, so you can focus on driving home. Even if you bring a second person along with you, you should still transport the puppy in the crate. Don't trust your passenger to hold your dog—dogs and puppies have the ability to squirm out of people's arms at inopportune moments. A loose puppy can cause a car accident.

Having a passenger with you in the car can be helpful to keep an eye on the puppy or dog and alert you if there's a problem (such as carsickness or if the dog has to relieve himself). Bring paper towels, a few plastic grocery store bags, enzymatic cleaner, unscented baby wipes (moist towelettes), and poop bags so that if there is an accident, you can clean it right up. You'll need a collar and leash so that if your dog or puppy has to eliminate, you can walk him outside the car. Be sure that the collar you put on the puppy or dog is tight enough so he won't slip out, or use a slip collar.

Once you get home, put a leash on your dog and walk him around outside until he relieves himself. He may be too excited to urinate or defecate at first, so be patient. Let him sniff around and allow him to explore the new area. Once some of the excitement has worn off, he'll relieve himself.

Next Up: The Veterinarian

Before you bring your dog or puppy home, make an appointment for him with the veterinarian. This way you can ensure that your dog or puppy is healthy before you bring him home. If you can't visit the vet first thing, plan on it within the next few days. Many breeders and shelters require that you have your dog or puppy checked by a veterinarian within a week after you buy or adopt him.

Some shelters offer coupons for a free or low-cost checkup that many veterinarians will accept. You can get a list of veterinarians in your area from the shelter (and the vet you've already chosen may honor it).

When you bring your puppy or dog to the veterinarian, you may be tempted to have him greet other animals and people. This isn't a good idea for two reasons. First, your puppy or dog is unlikely to have a strong immune system and can pick up diseases other dogs may have, including the fatal diseases parvovirus and distemper (which can even be carried on clothing). Second, while your dog may be friendly, not everyone's dog is, and you need to act as though every dog encountered can be aggressive until the owner assures you otherwise (and even then, some owners are in denial).

Before you bring your puppy or dog in to the vet, be sure to write down any questions you have. Don't be embarrassed to ask questions—vets have heard them all before, and the only dumb question is the one that's not asked. In fact, your vet should be delighted that you're asking questions because it's a sign of a conscientious pet owner.

Your vet should talk to you about basic dog and puppy care. It's important for you to listen to him and ask questions if he says something you don't entirely understand. He may talk with you about basic health care, about spaying and neutering (and their benefits), vaccinations needed, and other procedures your dog may need.

Can I Ride Him?

Children often want to ride large dogs like they are horses. However, dogs have flexible spines and were not bred to carry a child's weight on the back. (When dogs carry packs, the weight is distributed over the shoulder area, not the back.) Riding a dog can cause serious spinal injuries that may lead to lameness or paralysis.

Vaccinations

During their first few weeks of life, puppies have a natural immunity against diseases from their mother. This immunity comes from maternal antibodies in the colostrum—the milk the puppy's mother produces during the first twenty-four hours after whelping. However, this immunity is only temporary. The maternal antibodies begin to fade sometime between the puppy's fifth and sixteenth weeks, leaving the puppy exposed.

Veterinarians try to vaccinate the puppy after the maternal antibodies fade but before the puppy can become exposed to deadly diseases. When the maternal antibodies will fade is uncertain—it varies with each puppy. If a vaccination is given too soon, the vaccine will not override the antibodies. If a vaccination is given too late or if none are given after the antibodies fade, the puppy is still at risk. This is why it is very important to follow your veterinarian's recommendations regarding vaccinations.

If your dog is an adult, vaccinations are still important. Certain diseases, such as rabies and distemper, can affect any dog at any age.

In recent years, veterinarians have discovered that we overvaccinate our pets and have caused a variety of autoimmune types of diseases. However, not vaccinating your dog or puppy can put him at risk of many fatal diseases. It is important that you discuss vaccinations with your veterinarian. In most cases, your vet can recommend a sensible vaccination schedule for your dog to protect him against diseases that are likely in your area and that your dog is likely to become exposed to. Not all dogs should receive all vaccines, but your dog needs to be protected, depending on his level of exposure.

The following pages list vaccines that are currently available. Unless your dog is at high risk for certain diseases, he may not need all these vaccinations. Many veterinarians vaccinate once a year, but the current trend in veterinary medicine is to vaccinate less frequently and check titer levels (that is, the amount of antibodies within a dog) for particular diseases.

A Good Gift?

You may be tempted to get someone a puppy as a gift. I highly discourage you from doing this. Unless you know for certain that the person wants a dog, you should never give a puppy as a gift (and even then, I don't think this is a good idea). Most people want to pick out their own dog.

If you really want to surprise someone with a puppy, try buying some dog supplies like a new collar, a chew bone, and so on and write a note saying that you'll go with the person to pick out her special pet.

Offering a Cookie

Most children hold out a cookie or biscuit like it is an extension of their fingers. This can accidentally cause a dog to nip them and cause the child to be fearful. Show your children the right way to give a treat—they should hold the treat cupped in the palm of their hand and offer it to the dog.

Teach your kids to never tease a dog with treats by holding a treat up high and waving their hands. This can make the dog snappy or make him food possessive. Instead, teach them to offer treats correctly, and they'll have a lot more fun with their dog.

Rabies

Rabies has been feared throughout the ages—for good reason! Rabies is caused by a virus and is nearly 100 percent fatal. Rabies is contagious to humans and is transmitted through the dog's saliva—either through a bite or through wounds in the skin. The incubation period varies considerably: anywhere from three weeks to three months or more.

Rabies takes two forms, which both affect the central nervous system: dumb (paralytic) and furious. In dumb rabies, the dog's throat becomes paralyzed, causing excessive salivation (drooling) and inability to swallow. Furious rabies is the classic "mad dog" form, where the dog becomes vicious and attacks anything. Furious rabies eventually progresses to the paralytic stage, and death follows within a few days.

Most municipalities require dogs to have rabies vaccinations. Rabies vaccines are generally given every three years, after the dog is 18 months or older.

Canine Distemper (CDV)

Distemper is highly contagious among dogs and may be transmitted through the air, on shoes, or on clothing. It is nearly always fatal. Distemper starts with a yellow-gray discharge from nose and eyes, high temperature, dry cough, and lethargy. It may progress to appetite loss, diarrhea, and vomiting. Distemper may affect the intestinal tract or may attack the nervous system, causing seizures and convulsions. Some dogs may have the hardening of the pads, hence the name "hardpad disease."

Canine Adenovirus 2 (CA2)

CA2 is a form of highly contagious kennel cough. Dogs who contract kennel cough have a harsh, dry cough and may sound like they are gagging. Unless the dog is very old or young, kennel cough is more of a nuisance than a danger.

Infectious Canine Hepatitis (CA1)

Infectious canine hepatitis is a form of adenovirus that causes fever, lethargy, jaundice (due to liver involvement), excessive thirst, vomiting, eye and nasal discharge, bloody diarrhea, hunched back, hemorrhage, and conjunctivitis. Infectious canine hepatitis may attack the kidneys, liver, eyes, and lining of blood vessels. CA1 and distemper may occur simultaneously. CA1 is contagious to other dogs only through an infected dog's urine, feces, and saliva.

Canine Parainfluenza

Canine parainfluenza is another form of kennel cough. Dogs who contract kennel cough have a harsh, dry cough and may sound like they are gagging. Unless the dog is very old or young, kennel cough is more of a nuisance than a danger.

Leptospirosis

Leptospirosis is a bacterial infection that causes high fever, frequent urination, brown substance on the tongue, lack of appetite, renal failure, hunched back, bloody vomit and diarrhea, mild conjunctivitis, and depression. It can be fatal to dogs, and deadly forms have caused death in people. Dogs (and humans) may contract leptospirosis from rats, infected water supplies, and other infected dogs.

Canine Coronavirus

Coronavirus, whose symptoms are similar to (but milder than) those of parvovirus, is transmitted through fecal material. Parvovirus and coronavirus may infect a dog simultaneously.

Canine Parvovirus

Canine parvovirus is a dangerous virus that causes severe, bloody diarrhea, vomiting, dehydration, high fever, and depression. Half of all puppies who contract it die. Canine parvovirus is highly infectious in dogs and is transmitted through fecal matter. The virus can live up to one year in the soil and can be carried on shoes or paws.

Bordetella Bronchiseptica

Bordetella bronchiseptica is a form of kennel cough. Dogs who contract kennel cough have a harsh, dry cough and may sound like they are gagging. Unless the dog is very old or young, kennel cough is more of a nuisance than a danger. However, before you can board your dog at a kennel, you usually have to have him vaccinated against *Bordetella bronchiseptica*.

Lyme (Borellosis)

Lyme disease is a tick-borne disease that causes fever, lameness, loss of appetite, and fatigue. Lyme disease is fairly common along the East Coast and Upper Midwest in the United States, and it continues to spread.

Giardia

Giardia is a microscopic organism that lives in streams. Carried by beavers and other wildlife, as well as domesticated animals, *Giardia* was confined to the Rocky Mountains but may now be found in any untreated water. *Giardia* causes severe diarrhea, vomiting, and weight loss.

Medical Records

You should bring any vaccination and health records with you when you visit the veterinarian. These records will help your veterinarian decide whether deworming or vaccinations are required. They will also give a medical history on your dog, which your vet will find helpful.

Deworming

A variety of internal parasites can infest dogs. Many worms and other internal parasites can be detrimental to your dog's health, and some can even be transferred to you. It's very important to eliminate these pests to keep your dog healthy.

Your veterinarian will most likely ask you to bring a fecal sample when you bring your dog or puppy in. Be sure to put it in a plastic zipper-type bag and write your name and your dog's name on it before bringing your dog to the vet.

You might be tempted to treat your dog with over-the-counter dewormers. Unless you have experience with recognizing worms, treating your dog with a dewormer might not be a good idea because different worms require different treatments. Not all dewormers work on all worms, and some touted for certain kinds of worms may not work well or may have adverse side effects. All dewormers are poisons, and even those with a relatively high margin of safety can make your dog sick.

Your dog can basically get two types of worms: those that inhabit the gastrointestinal tract and heartworms.

Worms

When we say that a dog has "worms," we're usually talking about the worms that inhabit the gastrointestinal tract. These include roundworms (*Toxocara canis*), hookworms (*Ancylostoma caninum*), tapeworms (*Dipylidium caninum*), and whipworms (*Trichuris vulpis*).

Can My Kids Get Pinworms from the Dog?

No. Pinworms are contracted through physical contact with another human who has pinworms. Dogs do not get pinworms and cannot pass them along to humans.

With the exception of hookworms, most worm infestations come through an oral-fecal transmission route (meaning that the dog eats something contaminated with fecal material that has worm eggs in it). Roundworms may be transferred from mother to puppies before they're born or through the mother's milk. Tapeworms may be picked up through swallowing fleas or eating roadkill, rodents, or raw game. Hookworm infestation occurs through skin penetration or to a puppy from its mother's milk.

Of all the worms, roundworms are the most common. Roundworm, hookworm, and whipworm infestations can kill puppies and dogs, so it is important to have your vet perform a fecal analysis on your dog. Both roundworms and tapeworms can be transmitted to humans, so it is important to keep your dog worm free.

Heartworms

Heartworms are internal parasites that are transmitted through mosquito bites. Heartworm can kill your dog. Most states in the continental United States have heartworm, although it is less prevalent in the western states than elsewhere. When a mosquito feeds on an infected dog, the *microfilariae,* or heartworm larvae, from the infected dog incubate within the mosquito for several days. When the infected mosquito feeds off another dog, it injects the infectious *microfilariae* into the dog, and the dog becomes infected with heartworm.

Your veterinarian should administer a heartworm test before putting your dog on heartworm preventive medication. It is a simple blood test that screens for the presence of microfilariae. You should have your dog tested for heartworm once a year and put him on a heartworm preventive. In many areas, heartworm is seasonal, and you only have to administer the preventive during the spring and summer months. Heartworm season is year-round in the southern states and in other areas where the temperatures seldom reach freezing.

Can My Kids Get Worms from the Dog?

Maybe. Roundworms and tapeworms aren't contracted directly through a dog but through the oral-fecal route. That is, if your child eats dirt or if he touches dirt contaminated with worm eggs or if he touches fecal material and then puts his hands in his mouth, then there is a possibility for roundworm or tapeworm infection. Because humans aren't the right hosts for these worms, they often travel through the body, finding a place where they can reside. Children have lost vision due to roundworm infestations.

Roundworm eggs live a long time (over a year) in the soil and are not destroyed by heat or cold. Roundworms can be carried by a variety of wildlife as well—not just dogs. Thus, roundworm eggs may have been in the soil even before you got a dog.

This is why teaching your children sanitary methods such as washing their hands with soap and warm water before eating or touching their mouths is vital for their health. Keeping your dog worm free is important as well.

What's Ringworm?

Ringworm, which seems to plague some young children, isn't a worm at all, but a fungus. Some dogs (and puppies), can contract ringworm from the soil or from people. It's characterized by the loss of hair in a circular pattern.

Usually using a betadine and water wash several times a day will cure ringworm, although stubborn cases must be treated with medication from the veterinarian.

Children and adults (although less likely) can contract ringworm from a pet, so it is important to always wear gloves when touching an infected area.

Several different heartworm preventives are available, including some that help control other worms. Most veterinarians now prescribe monthly heartworm preventives, although there are still a few daily preventives available. The daily preventives are less effective if administered incorrectly. The available monthly heartworm preventives include:

* **Heartgard (ivermectin):** Heartgard Plus also contains pyrantel pamoate for control of roundworms and hookworms. Some dogs are sensitive to ivermectin, but this sensitivity is rare.
* **Interceptor (milbemycin) and Sentinel (milbemycin and lufenuron):** Interceptor controls heartworm as well as hookworms, roundworms, and whipworms in a monthly preventive. Sentinel also controls fleas.
* **Revolution (selamectin):** A topical application, Revolution works as a monthly heartworm and flea preventive.

Introducing Your New Dog to Your Family

You may think that having all your friends and relatives show up for a giant puppy party might be a good idea. Avoid this at all costs! Your new companion will need some quiet time to adjust to his new surroundings, and too many people will be overwhelming. He'll be overwhelmed as it is with new owners and a new home—so give him time to adjust.

When you bring your new dog home (after he has relieved himself outside), bring him inside and let him explore a bit. If he hasn't yet met your family, have family members sit quietly in chairs or on the couch and let your dog meet them on his own terms. Be sure to have your children be quiet or, if they're too young to understand, wait until your new dog is a bit more comfortable with his surroundings before introducing him to the children.

If your dog is an adult, be sure that the introductions are done carefully. Your children need to understand that until your dog is used to your family, they shouldn't stare directly into his eyes because that is a threatening gesture. Keep everything calm and low-key.

At What Age Can I Bring My Puppy Home?

Everyone wants to bring their puppy home early, but the earliest you should bring home a puppy is at 8 weeks old. A puppy needs time with his siblings and his mom so he learns how to be a dog. If you bring a puppy home younger than 8 weeks, you run the risk of having a dog with emotional problems.

Now is not the time to introduce your new dog to the rest of the pets if you have them. Keep other animals in another room (dogs crated) while your dog becomes accustomed to you and his new surroundings. When you introduce a new dog to the rest of the house pets, it's better to introduce dogs on neutral ground. (More on this in the next section.)

Introducing Your Dog to Other Dogs

Other dogs may look on your new dog as an interloper. They may behave in unexpected ways, including snarling and biting. Never bring a new dog home and leave him alone with another dog, or they may have a serious dogfight.

Introduce your new dog and your current dog on leashes in a neutral place, preferably a park. Have a family member hold the leash of your current dog as you approach with your new dog. Watch for signs of aggression: walking stiff-legged, hackles raised (hair on the back of the neck and shoulders standing up), hard stares, lifting or curling of the lip, growling or snarling. Correct either dog for aggression (see chapter 7, "Educating Your Whole Family"). One thing to be careful of is not to hold the leashes tightly the first time you introduce the two. You will telegraph your nervous feelings to your dogs, and they will pick up on it and become nervous as well.

Some dogs and breeds are naturally inclined toward aggression and fighting. That tendency will always be there, regardless of training or correction. Don't leave your dogs unsupervised. Either dog may be severely injured or killed. A much larger dog will outmatch the smaller one if a dogfight ensues. But many large dogs are gentle and nonaggressive. Regardless of whether you think your current dog will be friendly with your new dog, never leave them unsupervised until you are certain that they have become good friends.

Introducing Your New Dog to Cats and Other Pets

Some dogs do great with cats; others think cats are dinner. It depends on the individual dog. Some dogs that have sighthound, terrier, or northern breeds in them may have a strong prey drive and may want to chase your cat. If your dog is an adult, you may already know whether he is good with cats and other pets.

If your dog is a young puppy, you may be able to introduce the family cat to him. After the cat has swatted him on the nose once, the puppy will learn to leave the cat alone.

If your dog is an adult but considered good with cats, you can keep your cat in other rooms so your dog can become used to the cat's smell. Take your time with this—most owners tend to rush introductions. After a couple weeks, you can allow your dog into the area where your cat has been to investigate her smell. (Be sure to move the cat to another part of the house while you have your dog investigate where the cat was.)

After your dog gets used to the cat's scent, it's time for introductions. Start slowly and crack the door open and let them see each other. Interest in the cat is okay; wanting to eat the cat is not. Correct any attempts to chase the cat.

After you've had some introductions, you can put your dog in a crate and let the cat out into the dog's area when your dog is crated. The dog should become used to the cat and not react when she's walking around.

Now it's time to have your dog meet your cat face-to-face. Put the dog on a leash and wait. Your cat may want to visit; on the other hand, she may find this boring and go elsewhere. Working on the "Watch me!" command with your dog, as described in chapter 7, can help with this. Sometimes teaching your dog to focus on you while the cat is in the room works well. Give him praise and treats for watching you instead of the cat.

After a while, you can allow the dog and cat to meet while your dog is not on a leash, but be certain your cat has a way out of the dog's reach in case he gets excited and starts to chase her. A dog can outrun a cat in the long run, but your cat should be quick enough to get away if you give her an exit route in each room. Think vertically: Your cat should be able to climb to safety in every room.

If you have other pets, such as birds, rodents, snakes, lizards, and so on, keep them away from your dog. Some dogs may look on them as prey animals. To avoid unfortunate incidents, keeping them away is the best solution.

Will He Bond to Me?

Most people think that they can only bond with a puppy. The truth is that adult dogs who were adequately socialized as puppies will bond with people very quickly. Dogs who do not bond well are ones who were never handled by humans as puppies. Even so, many of those dogs are quite capable of bonding to their new owners in a startlingly short amount of time.

What You Now Know . . .

- ➤ Don't bring your dog or puppy home before he is 8 weeks old.
- ➤ Don't get a Christmas puppy.
- ➤ Plan to take time off to get acquainted with your new dog.
- ➤ Take your dog to the vet as soon as possible, to make sure he's healthy and keep him that way.
- ➤ Keep introductions with family members and other pets low key.
- ➤ Introduce your new dog to other pets in the household slowly. Correct any aggression.

Chapter 7

Educating Your Whole Family

What's Inside...

- Learn what the first few days and nights with your new dog will be like.
- Learn how to get a good night's sleep with a new puppy or dog.
- Learn why establishing a routine is a really good idea.
- Determine what ground rules you need to set with your children before they interact with your dog.
- Learn how to teach house manners to your dog.

I f this is the first time you've gotten a dog, or if this is the first time in a long time since you've had a dog, you're probably wondering what it's like to own a dog on a day-to-day basis. Your success at integrating your dog into your family depends on what you and your family know about dogs before you bring your dog into your home. The first several days are going to be hectic, with lack of sleep (even with an adult dog!), and it's going to take a bit to establish a routine. Once you do, though, you'll enjoy your dog's company that much more.

The First Few Days and Nights

The first few days and nights with your new dog or puppy are likely to be the toughest. You've been going along in an established routine, and now you've added a new family member. However, this family member doesn't understand the rules, nor can you bring her up on the couch and explain it to her. Thus, her presence is going to make your life topsy-turvy for several days.

Plan on spending all your time with the puppy or dog the first few days. All of it? Yes, all of it. You will have breaks during naptime and when your puppy or dog sleeps, but like a baby, she'll need constant attention while she's trying to learn how things work in your household.

So, don't expect a lot of sleep. And don't expect to be able to do many other things while you and your family are getting used to the new addition. You may find your dog or puppy glued to you or getting into trouble. It seems that there's just no middle ground with them.

It's important to enforce all rules now. This can be tough to do, especially with those soulful eyes looking into yours, but you must. Your puppy or dog will remember what you let her get away with and will continue to press the issue long after you think is appropriate.

How to Get a Good Night's Sleep with Your New Dog

A new dog or puppy will most likely whimper or cry the first few nights. After three nights of no sleep, you may be questioning why you fell in love with that oh-so-adorable puppy who is screaming at the top of her lungs now.

Your dog should sleep in your bedroom, in a crate, next to your bed. Not in the basement. Not in the kitchen. Not in the empty bedroom. Your bedroom. Your dog needs to feel secure and to bond with you. Even though you may be asleep, your presence will be comforting to your new dog. It's practical, too—if your dog has to go out, she can tell you and you can let her out or, if she's just fussing, you can lean over and tap the crate and tell her, "No!"

If your dog is a puppy who has recently left her mother, she may be lonely for her mother and siblings. You can fill a hot water bottle with warm water and wrap it in a towel so your puppy can lie against it. Experts claim that the ticking of an old fashion alarm clock imitates the heartbeat of a dog's mom and siblings, but whether this works is an individual thing. (Turn off the clock's alarm, or you're both in for a rude wake-up!)

The most sensible way to ensure that a puppy or dog sleeps through the night is to take her on a long walk, play with her, or exercise her before going to bed. A tired dog is a sleepy dog and one less likely to whine during the night. Be certain she relieves herself before putting her in her crate at night. For the first few days, an hour or two before you go to sleep, you should play with your puppy. Get her to expend her energy playing so that when bedtime comes around, you will both sleep soundly.

Tools to Aid in Getting Your Puppy to Fall Asleep

A few high-tech gizmos may help your puppy fall asleep faster. One is the SnugglePuppy (see www.snuggleme.com), which has an electronic "heartbeat" and a heating pack that helps simulate mom's warmth.

Another interesting product is the Canine Lullabies CD. When played, the music has a heartbeat that helps soothe dogs to sleep. You can order it at www.caninelullabies.com.

Establishing a Routine

Dogs love routine. It makes them feel safe and secure. Getting fed, walking, and going to bed at a specific time each day are important for the well-being of your dog. (Routine also helps with housetraining.) Once your dog learns the routine, it won't take long for her to know what to expect and when to expect it.

Once you establish a routine, consider assigning tasks to each family member. (See the appendix for a handy chart to help with this.) If you have a white board or a computer with a calendar program, you might want to consider entering each of those tasks and assigning a person to each one. Be aware that you will have to check to be sure that those tasks were done, or your dog might go hungry or not be taken out.

Try drawing up a checklist similar to this one to make sure the dog is cared for properly:

- ☐ Take dog out (and in) in the morning
- ☐ Feed dog breakfast and check water
- ☐ Morning walk
- ☐ Take dog out (and in) at noon
- ☐ Feed dog lunch and check water
- ☐ Take dog out (and in) midafternoon
- ☐ Exercise/play with dog one-half hour
- ☐ Training—fifteen minutes
- ☐ Afternoon walk
- ☐ Feed dog dinner and check water
- ☐ Exercise/play with dog one-half hour
- ☐ Take dog out (and in) before bedtime
- ☐ Tuck dog in her crate

Basic Rules for Dealing with a Dog or Puppy

Before you or your children interact with your new dog or puppy, you need to know some basic ground rules about dealing with a dog. Most people don't know or understand that dogs have read a rule book and, unfortunately, it's not the same rule book humans have read. So, let's go over some basic rules your family should follow:

- Never look an adult dog in the eye. This is extremely threatening to a dog who hasn't been trained to look into her owner's eyes. Until you train your dog with the "Watch me!" command, you should never force a dog to look you in the eyes.
- Never tease a dog with food or toys.
- Don't play tug-of-war games with the dog.
- Don't startle a dog.

- If the dog is a puppy or an adult, have your children move slowly and deliberately when anywhere near her. Adult dogs and pups may become agitated with children who are screaming or running around.
- Don't bother a dog while she's sleeping.
- Don't bother a dog while she's eating.
- Don't allow your children to play with your dog's toys, and don't allow her to play with your children's toys.
- Be consistent: Don't allow the dog to do something (like climb on the couch) and then disallow it later.
- Don't feed your dog from the table.
- Don't hit your dog.
- Don't allow your dog to chew on clothing.
- Don't allow your dog to mouth your hands.
- Don't give any command you can't enforce.
- (For children) Don't pick up the dog.
- (For adults) Don't pick up the dog and carry her everywhere.
- Don't punish your dog for something she doesn't understand.
- Don't allow your dog to loom over you or walk on you.
- Don't allow the dog to climb on you or grab you with her forelegs.
- Don't let your dog roam loose.
- Don't leave your dog outside while you're gone.
- Enforce all commands.
- (For children) Don't contradict the rules set forth by the adults.

These rules might seem a little strict, but they're to make sure that you don't cause unwanted behavior later. The basic rule for a puppy is that *what is cute for a puppy may not be cute as an adult*. If you're not sure if something you or your kids are doing isn't a good thing to do, use this rule as your guide. Look at the puppy and then imagine what this behavior will be like in an adult dog. If it's obnoxious or dangerous with an adult dog, don't allow it in your puppy.

How to Pick Up a Dog or Puppy (For Adults Only!)

There are times when an adult needs to pick up a dog or puppy. However, most people don't know how to do it properly. When picking up a puppy or small dog, cradle the puppy in a sitting position, with one hand under her rear end to support her bottom and another hand around her chest and shoulders. Keep her back toward you and support her fully by pressing her gently against your chest.

You'll have to pick up a large dog differently. First of all, be sure to lift with your knees, or you will hurt your back. When the dog is standing up, put one arm around the front of the dog's chest and one arm behind the dog's rear, so that you cradle her body between both arms and carefully lift. The legs will dangle, but this is the safest way to pick up a larger dog.

Teaching House Manners

You may be wondering how to start teaching your dog commands. Commands are great, but often they don't help in the day-to-day living with a dog. Commands don't address things such as table manners or whether it's okay for your dog to lie on the couch. Yet the day-to-day behavior is as important as obedience training. After all, if your dog is raiding your cabinets and destroying your things, you may think "Sit" is the least of your worries.

Preventing bad behavior from the start is almost always easier than trying to correct the behavior after it has started. Before you allow your dog the entire run of the house, start thinking about what should be on and off limits. Maybe you don't care about the ratty old couch and don't mind if your dog sleeps on it, but maybe you will if you buy a new couch. Maybe it's okay that she chews on your son's stinky sweatshirt and sneakers, but will she know the difference between those things and your evening dress and $200 shoes?

What is cute or funny in a puppy may annoy or irritate you when she becomes an adult. Look at the behaviors now and decide which are acceptable and which aren't. Once you figure out which ones are acceptable, you can establish some basic house rules.

Your dog's behavior is largely up to you and how permissive you wish to be. Some people like having brats who "rule the roost" and think it's cute if their dog growls or chews up their furniture. Others want a nicely behaved dog but don't mind it if their dog hops on the couch or the bed. Others want a very well-behaved dog who stays in certain rooms and doesn't ever climb on the furniture.

While you and I might not think the growling dog is ideal, I'm sure someone out there does, and if that makes this person happy and their dog never bites anyone, I guess that's okay. But most of us fall somewhere in between extremely permissive and strict. Just be sure to have rules and make sure your dog knows them.

In addition to establishing what you and your family should and shouldn't do, you need to think about basic rules for your puppy or dog. The following rules are a bit strict, with good reason—they'll help avoid problems later:

- Don't allow your dog to do the following:
    - Jump on people
    - Growl
    - Bark incessantly
    - Mouth people
    - Put her paws on your legs
    - Beg at the table
    - Sleep in your bed or your children's beds
    - Get away with things "just this once"

- But be sure to do the following:
  - Feed your dog or puppy meals—don't leave the food out for her to eat all day.
  - Allow your dog up on the furniture only when you invite her.
  - Have her earn her treats with a "Sit" or "Down."
  - Have her work on her commands for five minutes each day.
  - Have her wait to enter and exit all rooms until after you do.
  - Give her plenty of appropriate things to chew and offer them to her.

Useful Commands

Your dog should learn several commands that are not within obedience training. She probably knows some of them, but they are worth teaching to ensure a well-behaved dog.

The "Off" Command

The "Off" command means "four paws on the floor." Use this command when you want your dog to climb off the furniture or not jump on you. When your dog jumps up on you,

Keeping Your Little Angel from Turning Devilish

Out of sight, out of mind—that's a good philosophy to have with a dog. If she can't see it or get at it, she can't get into trouble with it. There are plenty of things your dog can get into without really trying, so be sure to work on dog-proofing (see chapter 5, "Dog-Proofing"). Kitchen counters, tables, and stuff that is just outside nose reach can easily become within nose reach without a lot of effort. Even a slow and docile pup can be motivated to grasp a roast off the counter. And once your dog has her reward, she'll remember it. Guaranteed.

So, look at what you're doing from a dog's perspective. Is the hot apple pie or Sunday's meat loaf going to tempt her? Do your shoes sit right next to the rawhide on the floor? What about those chocolate chip cookies? That trash smells interesting since you left the chicken bones from last night's dinner in it. Leaving stuff on the counter or out in the open guarantees a temptation that most dogs can't ignore.

Many dog owners have discovered the uses of ovens and microwaves as dog-proof safes for their dinner or food. Cabinets with childproof latches can keep most inquisitive noses out of food areas, and you can always store trash in a cupboard, pantry, or closed bathroom.

If you can't hide the interesting stuff—you have a party at your house, for example, and you have trays of food out—consider putting your pup in her crate until the temptation goes away. It's easy, and she won't snitch the deviled eggs—or angel food cake.

Static mats and gates are available for teaching boundaries. The static mats give an unpleasant sensation just like a static electricity shock you receive when you shuffle your feet on carpet and touch a doorknob (yes, I've felt them!). Gates are useful—up to a point. Some dogs can climb them, and others barrel right through and knock them down.

 push her down and tell her "Off!" Then have her sit and give her a treat for obeying. Because "Off" means all paws on the floor, you can use it when your dog has sneaked up onto the bed or another piece of restricted furniture.

A word of caution: Don't use the word "Down" for "Off." If your dog is lying on the couch, you'll confuse her, even if you're sure she knows what you really meant.

The "Drop It" or "Trade" Command

"Drop it" is a useful command that you will want to teach your dog should she ever pick up something really disgusting or bad for her. Most dogs seem to know that these forbidden items are icky, and the quicker they wolf them down, the better, in their opinion.

You can teach "Drop it" unless your dog's jaws are too strong or you're afraid of getting bit. Start by squeezing open your dog's jaws by applying gentle but consistent pressure with your fingers where the upper and lower jaws meet. Once your dog opens her mouth, say "Drop it" and allow the item to fall from her mouth. Give her a treat for being a good dog and take the items away.

Instead of using "Drop it," you can use the command "Trade." With "Trade" you offer a treat that is better than what your dog has in her mouth. Your dog will usually drop the item for something more tasty.

You can practice "Trade" easily. When your dog is chewing on a rawhide or playing with a toy, offer to trade with something yummy. When your dog drops the toy for your treat, take the toy and give your dog the treat at the same time.

The "Leave It!" Command

"Leave it!" is a command that tells your dog to leave whatever interests her alone—whether it be a dead animal on the ground or a cookie your toddler dropped. Usually you give this command while giving a short snap of the collar.

The "Out" Command

You can tell your dog when to go to the door to go outside by associating the command "Out" with it. When you walk your dog or take her out in the backyard, simply say "Out." It won't take long before she learns what "Out" means.

The "Bed" Command

"Bed" is another command that most dogs learn by association. When you tell your dog to go to her "Bed" or "Crate," she learns quickly what her bed is. You can teach your dog to go into her crate easily by tossing a treat into her crate and telling her, "Bed."

The "Watch Me!" Command

"Watch me!" is a great command for teaching your dog to pay attention to you. It's good for teaching your dog to focus during chaotic situations when you must have your dog's attention.

Practicing "Watch me!" is easy and teaches your dog to not be afraid to make eye contact with you. Hold up a treat and bring it to the tip of your nose. Your dog's gaze should meet your eyes. Say "Watch me!" and give her a treat when you make eye contact. As you continue to practice "Watch me!" you may continue to use treats or vary the times you use treats and when you don't.

Being a Good Neighbor

Part of your family's education includes being a good neighbor when it comes to your dog. Your dog can be a good neighbor or a nuisance, depending on what you and your family allow her to do. Yes, dogs will be dogs, but as the dog owner, you need to set limits.

Does your dog tear up the yard when you're gone? Does she bark and whine until your neighbors call the police or animal control? Does she explore the neighbor's trash?

Good fences make good neighbors. Your dog needs to be behind a fence and not running loose at any time. Surprisingly, some people still believe that their dog should be allowed off leash to do whatever she wants to.

Loose dogs are a nuisance and illegal in many areas. Most municipalities have leash laws that require dogs to be behind a fence, in your house, or on a leash. A loose dog is more apt to be hit by a car, poisoned by unscrupulous people, get into trouble, or get totally lost. Look around at your neighborhood—would you turn loose a 5-year-old child into the street to play? That's what you're doing when you turn loose a dog.

"Oh, she just hangs around home while I'm gone," you say? Want to bet? Dogs are remarkable observers and know when their owners leave and come home from work. You leave the house with Rover sitting on the front porch. You work for eight hours. You come home and Rover is sitting on the front porch. Do you really think Rover hangs out on the porch for eight hours? Ask your neighbors what Rover's really doing.

Okay, so the best place for your dog is behind a fence—but only when you're home. Your dog may bark incessantly while you're gone. What do you expect if you've left your dog alone and bored in the backyard? She'll sleep for a while, sure. But then the meter reader comes by or the postal carrier—and guess what? She barks! Or perhaps she's bored and it's hot. So she digs a nice cooling hole to lie down in. Or maybe she's a canine version of the Army Corp of Engineers and decides that a nice series of tunnels or holes might be a good landscaping project.

Keep your dog inside. It'll thwart dognappers—and yes, mixed breeds and purebreds both get stolen—and people who may try to poison your dog in your own backyard. Your neighbors won't complain about the random barking, and you'll actually have a garden instead of a bomb shelter this summer.

Finally, "share the joy" doesn't mean let your neighbors step in it. When you take your dog for a walk, bring poop bags and clean up after her. Many municipalities have laws that say you must clean up after your dog. Even if yours doesn't, be a good neighbor. No one likes stepping in doggy doo.

What You Now Know...

- Your first few days and nights with your new dog are likely to be rough, so you need to be prepared.
- You *can* get a good night's sleep with a new dog if you help her feel secure and comfortable—and tire her out at bedtime.
- Establishing a routine is a really good idea, for both your dog's sake and yours.
- Your children need to know basic ground rules for dealing with your dog.
- If you teach your dog good manners up front, there will be fewer potential problems later.

Chapter 8

Keeping Your Dog Healthy

What's Inside...

- Learn what's best to feed your dog.
- Learn how to examine your dog for health problems.
- Learn why spaying or neutering is a good idea.
- Learn about external parasites and other canine health problems.
- Learn why exercise is good for your dog.
- Learn the right way to groom your dog.
- Learn how to properly socialize your dog.

Your dog's health is very important. Proper nutrition, health care, grooming, and exercise will help ensure a long and healthy life. This chapter covers the basics of good health.

Feeding Your Dog

Now that you have a dog, you may be wondering what's best to feed him. Dog owners get a lot of mixed signals when it comes to feeding their dogs. On one end, you'll hear that the best thing to feed your dog is commercial dog food, and it really doesn't matter which kind, as long as the food meets or exceeds requirements set forth by the Association of Animal Feed Control Officials (AAFCO). On the other side of the argument are people who swear you are killing your dog if you feed him anything commercial, and you should make your own food. No matter who you talk to, someone will have an opinion about what you should feed your dog.

What are you supposed to do?

Like everyone, I have an opinion, but it's backed with some pretty good data, and it's probably the best bet when it comes to feeding your dog. No matter who you talk to, there are going to be people who will swear that their dogs do great on this or that diet. In truth, they're not lying (at least not intentionally!), and their dogs are probably doing okay on the diets they espouse. However, whether their diet is best for your dog is another matter.

No Bones about It

Lately there's been a lot of talk about raw diets, bones and raw food diets, meat diets, and other homemade diets. There are a lot of people out there preaching that these diets are the only ones to feed your dog.

Before you rush out and start buying chicken wings and celery, step back and think a moment. Many of these diets aren't formulated for a dog's nutritional needs and can actually cause harmful imbalances in your dog's diet. (Balanced dog food is tougher to formulate than you think.) Bones (even raw ones) can cause obstructions. At the very least, these diets can have harmful bacteria such as *Campylobacter, E. coli,* or *Salmonella,* which may or may not make your dog sick but *can* be passed to you or your children and make you sick.

I recommend that you feed a good premium brand of dog food that meets or exceeds the requirements set forth by AAFCO. You want premium because of the quality of ingredients. Generic and bargain-brand dog foods are chock-full of fillers that your dog doesn't need. The protein sources in premium dog foods are highly digestible, meaning that your dog can use more of the protein. As a result, you feed less and have less dog waste to pick up in your backyard.

But what about cost? Premium dog foods are more expensive than other dog foods because of the quality of the ingredients. Because they have more nutrition, you feed less than a generic brand, thus they save you money. With some nonpremium foods, you must feed twice as much or more to obtain the same nutrition and still not receive the same results as you would with a premium dog food.

There are plenty of good premium dog foods on the market, many made by recognizable companies. You should choose a dog food that is readily available so that you don't have to drive all over town looking for your dog's food because the pet boutique where you normally buy it is closed.

You can recognize a premium dog food by its ingredients and its digestibility. The first ingredients should be the protein source of the dog food and should be an animal protein, such as chicken, beef by-products, or poultry meal, rather than soy, corn gluten meal, or bone meal. Dogs use animal protein more efficiently than plant proteins, and overall the quality of animal protein is better.

The digestibility of a dog food is usually not stated on the package; however, you can contact the manufacturer of the food and ask about the digestibility of its dog foods. Dog food that is over 80 percent digestible is considered premium dog food.

Whichever dog food you buy, be certain to purchase one that is complete and balanced. This means that the dog food has all the necessary nutrients and that they are balanced so as not to cause a deficiency. Complete and balanced dog foods will have a label stating that the dog food meets or exceeds the requirements as set forth by the AAFCO. The AAFCO has established guidelines for dog foods, and most major dog food companies comply with AAFCO's guidelines, but you should still check the packaging to be certain.

Finally, it's important to choose a dog food that your dog likes. While this may seem trivial, it certainly isn't. The best nutrition in the world isn't worth anything if your dog won't eat it.

Dry, Canned, Semisoft, Compressed Meat Rolls, or Frozen?

When you look at commercial dog food, you have a dizzying array of choices. The following are the main options:

- **Dry food:** Pound for pound, dry food is the most economical choice. It's easy to handle and relatively easy to store. The shelf life is not as great as that of canned food because most dog foods now use natural preservatives such as tocopherols (vitamin E) to prevent rancidity. Dry food tends to come in the most varieties, too. On the negative side, dry food is not as palatable as other forms, and some dogs may turn up their noses at it.
- **Canned food:** The next most popular dog food, canned food is expensive compared to dry. Much of what you pay for is water and processing. You must usually feed more canned food than you would dry food. Canned food is very palatable, and many pet owners mix canned and dry food to make the dry food more palatable. It has an excellent storage life.
- **Semisoft food:** Semisoft food usually comes in the shape of hamburger patties. Most semisoft food includes sugar or corn syrup and lots of preservatives to make the food soft. It usually has some sort of artificial color added to it as well. For the amount of food you must feed, semisoft food can be expensive. Semisoft food is extremely palatable, but I don't recommend it as a daily food.

Switching Dog Foods

To avoid stomach upsets, it's a good idea to keep your dog on the same dog food that the breeder fed him and then slowly switch over to whatever brand you prefer. When you do switch over, follow the 10 percent rule. Start with 90 percent of the old dog food mixed with 10 percent of the new dog food the first day. Then increase the new dog food by 10 percent and decrease the old dog food by 10 percent each day until you're feeding the new dog food 100 percent.

- **Compressed meat rolls:** Compressed meat rolls are a type of semisoft food that's made from quality ingredients (usually lamb and rice, beef and rice, or some other meat and grain) and looks a bit like a salami. Highly palatable and expensive, it needs to be refrigerated once opened.
- **Frozen food:** This food is relatively new. It's made from meat and is highly palatable, but it can be expensive. As with canned food, you're paying for the water, but you're also paying for storage. You'll need freezer space, and it's highly perishable because it has no preservatives. It must be kept frozen until used.

Life-Stage and Breed-Type Foods

If you look at the various premium dog food brands, you may notice that there are brands for different life stages of your dog (puppy, adult, senior, lite, and so on) and even brands for the size of breed (toy breed, medium breed, large breed) or even a breed itself (Labrador Retriever, German Shepherd Dog, Poodle). How do you decide among those?

First, consider your dog's age. If he's a puppy, you should probably be feeding puppy food. An adult naturally gets adult food. A senior should get senior food. However, if your dog is active or thin, he may need more energy and may require a performance food to maintain his weight. A heavy dog will need a lite or a maintenance food.

Finally, if the dog food you buy is split into breed sizes, consider those formulations. However, *you should feed your dog according to his weight and activity level*. If you have a skinny senior dog who is active, a higher-calorie and higher-protein food may be in order. Likewise, a fat puppy might do better on an adult food that is good for all life stages but may have fewer calories. Consult your veterinarian about the proper choice for your dog.

Minimum AAFCO Requirements

AAFCO requires the following minimums on a dry-matter basis (that is, the nutritional values are measured according to the weight of the dog food minus the weight of any added water):

	Puppy	Adult
Protein	22%	18%
Fat	8%	5%

How to Read Dog Food Labels

Dog food labels can be a bit confusing. When you pick up a package of dog food, you'll see information as required by the U.S. Food and Drug Administration (FDA). This includes:

- The product name
- The manufacturer's name and address
- The net quantity, in weight
- The guaranteed analysis
- Ingredients
- A nutritional adequacy statement
- Feeding directions

The manufacturer may put other information on the label, including calories and digestibility, but this is voluntary and at the sole discretion of the company.

The guaranteed analysis on the label states the following:

- The minimum percentage of crude protein
- The minimum percentage of crude fat
- The maximum percentage of crude fiber
- The maximum moisture or water

These percentages are listed as "as is" or "as fed" percentages, sometimes called "by-weight." Some dog foods list ash as well. These percentages guarantee a certain amount of protein and fat. However, they don't guarantee the quality of the ingredients. Through this type of analysis, protein can be from indigestible or digestible ingredients.

When you look at the ingredients list on dog food, you'll see that the ingredients are listed according to weight. So, the first ingredient is the most common ingredient, followed by the second most common, and so forth. With most dog foods, you'll want the protein source first, followed by other ingredients.

If the first ingredient is chicken, does that mean the food is mostly chicken? Not necessarily. For example, if a dog food contained chicken, corn gluten meal, wheat middlings, corn, and poultry fat (preserved with BHA) as the first five ingredients, the corn gluten meal, wheat middlings, and corn might outweigh the chicken. Also, "chicken" includes the water that is in the chicken, whereas chicken meal and chicken by-product meal have water and fat extracted. Technically, chicken meal could have a higher percentage of available protein than chicken on a pound-for-pound basis.

Dog Food Worksheet

To use this worksheet, you need to make several copies. When you're considering a certain dog food, write in the name of the dog food and the availability and then fill out the rest to comparison shop.

Name of dog food:

_____

_____

Is it readily available? Where can you buy it?

_____

_____

What size is your dog? Is there a size-specific formula for dogs that size?

_____

_____

Is your dog a puppy, an active adult, an overweight adult, or a senior? Is there a formula for that?

_____

_____

What form of food does your dog prefer (dry, canned, etc.)? What form does the dog food come in?

_____

_____

What is the minimum protein of the dog food?

_____

_____

What is the minimum fat of the dog food?

_____

_____

Is this food AAFCO compliant?

_____

_____

What is the main protein ingredient in this food?

_____

_____

Does the dog food come in varieties for different life stages or breeds?

_____

_____

Feeding Your Dog

You should follow the dog food manufacturer's feeding recommendations for your dog's weight and age and split them up into two or three meals a day. Usually the amounts are larger portions than what your dog needs, but it is a good start. If your dog doesn't eat it all or if he is gaining weight (rather than maintaining a healthy weight), cut back the portions until your dog is maintaining a healthy weight.

Canine Health Care

Nobody likes going to the doctor—not even a dog! But it is as important for a dog to visit the vet as it is for you to visit the doctor occasionally—at least for a checkup every year or so. After the initial series of vaccinations and a spay or neuter, most dogs don't need to go to the vet's office more than once a year, unless a problem arises, until he starts creeping into middle age. After that time, you may notice some health problems like arthritis, bad teeth, or other middle-age to old-age ailments.

Is Your Dog Too Fat?

Most people's dogs are too fat. It's hard to resist those soulful eyes at dinnertime, and that one scoop of dog food looks woefully inadequate. But being fat isn't healthy for your dog any more than it is for you.

The easiest way to determine if your dog is fat is to look at his shape. (Don't rely on the scale—the dog's health is dependent on fitness, not weight!) There should be a tuck where your dog's abdomen (waist) is, both in profile and looking from above. Place your thumbs on your dog's spine and feel his ribs. If you have an "amazing ribless dog" or if you can barely feel your dog's ribs through the heavy padding, your dog is obese and needs to shed some pounds. You should also be able to feel your dog's hip bones and spine.

If your dog is too fat, talk with your veterinarian. He can recommend a diet and exercise program that's right for your dog.

You can prevent a lot of health problems simply by taking good care of your dog. That includes:

- A home health exam every week
- Spaying or neutering your pet
- Preventing heartworm (discussed in chapter 6, "Bringing Your Dog Home")
- Brushing your dog's teeth (discussed later in this chapter, in the section "Grooming Your Dog")
- Controlling fleas and ticks
- Grooming your dog (discussed later in this chapter, in the section "Grooming Your Dog")
- Knowing how to recognize a health problem
- Knowing how to recognize an emergency

The Home Health Exam

A weekly health exam is very important for your dog's health. Take the time to check your dog over for any abnormalities. Sometimes pet owners are so used to seeing something on their pet that they don't think it's abnormal until they really examine the dog or until someone points it out to them. So take time to do this. A good time is usually while grooming your dog (which you should do once a week).

To conduct a home health exam, first run your hands along your dog's body to feel whether he's gaining or losing weight or muscle mass. If your dog is getting bony, it may be a sign that you're not feeding him enough or he may have a disease that is causing him to lose weight. Conversely, a sudden weight gain or puffiness without a drop in activity may also be a sign of disease. Look for abnormalities such as bumps and lumps. If you feel a lump, check the other side of the body to see if it is normal. For example, if you feel something lumpy on the right elbow, check the left one in the same place. If there is a similar lump on the left elbow, you can safely discount the lumps as normal. Check the following body parts as you do this exam; if a dog has some anomalies, it's time for a trip to the vet:

- **Eyes:** Your dog's eyes should be clear and bright, without excessive or puslike discharge. There should be no redness or tearing.
- **Nose:** Your dog's nose should be cool and moist to the touch. Hot and dry may indicate a fever. There should be no discharge or blood.
- **Ears:** Your dog's ears should be clean and sweet smelling. Any foul odor or excessive buildup of wax indicates a potential ear problem.
- **Mouth:** Your dog's teeth should be white and clean, without tartar buildup. Your dog's breath should not be foul smelling; foul breath may suggest tooth or gum problems. The gums should be a healthy pink rather than red.
- **Legs:** Feel down your dog's legs to check for any lumps or bumps. Inspect the footpads for cuts and foreign objects such as foxtails. Look at the toenails—they shouldn't be red or broken. If you find an unusual bump, check the other side of the body to see if it is normal or if it is only on one side. If the bump is unilateral, then it might be a tumor or some other problem. Check the legs for full range of motion, moving them slowly and gently in full range. There should be no clicks or pops.
- **Skin and fur:** Look for sores, bald patches, or redness to the skin and check whether the skin is dry or flaky. Also look for dark grains through the fur that turn red when wet.
- **Tail:** The tail should be healthy looking rather than hanging limp. Note whether your dog has been chewing it.
- **Sex organs:** Is there discharge from the vagina or penis? In intact female dogs, discharge is normal during estrus.

Spaying and Neutering

Spaying and neutering—that is, removing a dog's sex organs—causes concern for some pet owners. There are many reasons, mostly misinformed, why pet owners keep their dogs intact. Many owners of purebred pets erroneously think that keeping a dog intact makes the dog somehow more valuable. Because so many pets are not neutered, about five million pets are euthanized each year. By spaying and neutering, you're doing your part in ending this problem.

But there are health and behavior reasons for spaying and neutering dogs. Let's look at them:

- It reduces aggression in both male and female dogs.
- It reduces the urge to roam to look for mates.
- It makes your pet a better pet because his focus is on you.
- You don't have to worry about your female dog accidentally becoming pregnant.
- It eliminates ovarian and uterine cancer in females.
- It eliminates testicular cancer in males.
- It greatly reduces breast cancer in females.

- It greatly reduces anal tumors in males.
- It eliminates full pyometra (uterine infection) in female dogs.
- It eliminates the heat cycle in females, so there is no need to lock up a female dog during heat.
- It may reduce prostate cancer in male dogs.

Those are quite a few benefits for a single operation. But what about all the things you've heard about spaying and neutering? You may have heard the following statements:

- *Your dog will get fat and lazy*. Dogs get fat and lazy from eating too much food and not getting enough exercise. You may have to cut back a bit on dog food after you spay or neuter your dog (dogs seem to show more interest in food after being spayed or neutered).
- *Your dog will miss sex*. Dogs don't enjoy sex the way people do. It's an instinct, and they get very little pleasure from it.
- *Your dog won't be a tough, protective dog anymore*. If your dog has protective instincts, he won't be any less protective after he is neutered. Neutering will help reduce aggression—an aggressive dog is a liability—but will not change his work ethic or his protectiveness.
- *Your purebred will be more valuable intact*. Actually, this is untrue unless you show your dog in conformation shows, he is a champion, and you are planning on breeding him. Otherwise, the puppies your dog produces will be mediocre.
- *A female dog needs to have a litter of puppies to improve her temperament*. A female dog's temperament changes when she has puppies but may or may not change for the better afterward. Most female dogs keep the same temperament they had before they had puppies.
- *It's healthy for a female dog to have a litter of puppies*. Actually, it's healthier for a female dog to *not* have a litter of puppies. Dogs have had complications and even died in the birth process, and if she's spayed early, a female dog actually has a reduced chance of mammary cancer.
- *You want to show your kids the miracle of birth*. Buy a DVD or videotape. What will you show them when there are complications such as a dead puppy or stuck puppies or massive blood loss? What will you do with all the puppies? It's better to show your kids responsible pet ownership and spay or neuter your dog.
- *Your male dog won't act male*. Actually, he will. It's a little-known fact that neutered males will try to mate with females in season—and will succeed, except that they won't reproduce. Neutered males may take a little extra time to lift their legs, but they eventually do. Neutering will actually make a young dog bigger because the growth plates close later.

Spaying and neutering can be done any time after 8 weeks. It used to be that you had to wait until the dog was at least six months old because of anesthesia risks, but the latest anesthetic is safe enough to use on very young puppies.

Any competent vet can perform a spay or neuter. In some cases, there may be minor complications, such as undescended testicles (cryptorchid) that require the veterinarian to perform a slightly more complex surgery.

Also, many shelters and rescues offer low-cost (or even free) neutering or spaying for dogs adopted from their establishments.

External Parasites

Fleas, ticks, and mites can cause misery for a happy, healthy dog. But more than just making your dog miserable, external parasites can cause severe health problems and, in certain instances, carry dangerous diseases to you and your family.

Fleas

Fleas are nasty little bloodsuckers that carry wondrous diseases such as bubonic plague and parasites such as tapeworm. They carry other diseases, too, and they cause allergic reactions in some dogs. While canines tend to have a high resistance to plague, you don't, so treat these critters like the dangers they are.

```
          Flea Systemics
```

The following are some of the systemic flea treatments currently on the market:

- **Frontline (fipronil) and Frontline Plus (fipronil and methoprene):** These work by killing fleas within twenty-four to forty-eight hours. Frontline Plus contains an insect growth regulator that keeps immature fleas from reproducing. It is a topical, spot-on systemic that works for up to three months on adult fleas and one month on ticks.
- **Advantage (imidacloprid):** Advantage works by killing both adult fleas and larvae within forty-eight hours. It is a topical, spot-on systemic that works for six weeks on adult fleas.
- **Program (lufenuron):** Program works by preventing flea eggs from hatching or maturing into adults. It is a pill you give once a month.
- **Biospot (pyrethrins and fenoxycarb):** Biospot is a topical spot-on systemic that kills fleas and ticks for one month. It has an insect growth regulator that keeps immature fleas from reproducing. I've also seen it repel flies.

Different treatments may be recommended for different areas of the country. For example, in areas where both ticks and fleas are a problem, vets may recommend Frontline over some of the other types of treatments. When you apply one of these treatments, put it directly on the dog's skin, in a place the dog can't get to, such as on the back of his neck. Be sure to wash your hands after applying any spot-on systemics.

Fleas flourish everywhere except places that are very cold, very dry, or at high altitudes. I live in such a place (in the Rocky Mountains) and have very few problems with fleas, but those fleas that we see tend to carry plague. So fleas are a no-win situation wherever you go.

If you suspect a flea infestation, search for fleas on your dog around his belly and groin area, at the base of his tail, and around his ears. A common sign of fleas is deposits of black flea feces that turn red when wet. Of course, seeing the little suckers jump is a sure sign of flea infestation.

If you find fleas on your dog, you can guarantee that you have a flea infestation in your home. How do you declare war on fleas? Talk to your veterinarian about ways to combat the problem. Often, your veterinarian can recommend a system that will combat fleas in the yard, in your house, and on your dog. Your vet will recommend products based on your climate and your dog's age and health. He will also recommend products that are safe to use together. Be very careful about mixing products and always read the label.

You'll have to vacuum all carpets and furniture—anywhere fleas hide. I've heard of putting a piece of flea collar in the vacuum cleaner bag to kill the fleas. Systemic flea treatments have made most drastic measures (flea bombs and the like) obsolete except in the worst infestations.

Ticks

Ticks are blood-feeding relatives of spiders and carry a host of dangerous diseases, including the following—all of which can be fatal:

- **Babesiosis:** Common signs of babesiosis are fever, lethargy, and lack of appetite.
- **Canine ehrlichiosis:** Common signs of canine ehrlichiosis are fever, discharge from the eyes and nose, and swollen limbs (edema). A dog with canine ehrlichiosis may lack appetite, be unusually tired, and have swelling of the lymph nodes.
- **Lyme disease:** Common signs of Lyme disease are lameness and fever. A dog with Lyme disease may lack appetite, be unusually tired, and have swelling of the lymph nodes. The dog may have bouts of unexplained lameness that may become chronic.
- **Rocky Mountain Spotted Fever (RMSF):** Common signs of RMSF are high fever, abdominal pain, coughing, lack of appetite, lethargy, swelling of face or limbs, depression, vomiting, diarrhea, and muscle or joint pain.

These diseases can greatly affect your dog's health or may even be fatal in extreme cases. Your vet can test for tick-borne diseases through a blood test and can treat them with medications. If your dog tests positive for one of these tick-borne diseases, you may wish to consider having your own doctor test you and your family for the same disease. Ticks can transmit these diseases to humans, and in rare instances, contact with your dog's bodily fluids may transmit these diseases to you and your children. However, if a person and a dog both contract a disease from ticks, they were probably bitten by similar ticks.

In some places, ticks are so prevalent that you must check your dog (and kids!) after every time he has been outside. In other places, you may need to check your dog only when he goes through deep grasses or brush.

If you find a tick on your dog, avoid handling it, or you may risk exposing yourself to any disease it carries. Instead, treat the area with a good tick insecticide approved for use on dogs, wait a few minutes, and then try to remove the tick. Wear latex gloves and use tweezers. Firmly grasp the tick with the tweezers and gently pull. Don't try to pull the tick out if it resists. You may leave portions of the tick embedded in your dog, which may become infected. Instead, wait for the tick to drop off and dispose of it.

Mites

Mites are small arachnids, relatives to spiders and ticks. There are several types of mites, including those that cause sarcoptic and demodectic mange and those that enter the ears and cause infection. Your vet can determine what type of infestation a dog has, based on skin scrapings. There are three major mites:

- **Ear mites (*Otodectes cynotis*):** These mites often appear as reddish-brown earwax in your dog's ears. Your dog may scratch or shake his head frequently. Don't try to treat ear mites with over-the-counter solutions because there may already be a secondary infection. Your vet will need to clean out the reddish-brown gunk and then give you ear drops to kill the mites and handle any infections.
- **Demodectic mites (*Demodex canis*):** These mites, which feed primarily on the cells of hair follicles, cause demodectic mange. An infestation of demodectic mites appears as dry, scaly, red skin, with hair loss, mostly around the face. Demodectic mange exists on all dogs but is thought to be triggered by a depressed immune system. Most of the time, localized demodectic mange clears itself up on its own. If it is generalized or doesn't clear up, it is hard to treat.
- **Sarcoptic mites (*Sarcoptes scabei*):** These mites are highly contagious. The mange they cause may spread quickly in kennels. Affected skin is itchy, with hair loss and a red rash. The dog may have ugly sores from scratching. Your vet can prescribe a topical product to treat sarcoptic mange. You may have to treat your dog with medicated baths and body dips. If the sores are infected, your vet may prescribe antibiotics.

Common Canine Health Problems

Dogs get plenty of different conditions and health problems, and it's impossible to cover all of them here. A good book about canine health care is the *Dog Owner's Home Veterinary Handbook* by James M. Giffin, M.D., and Liisa F. Carlson, D.V.M. (Howell Book House). This chapter covers some of the basic problems, but you need to be aware that many more do exist.

Allergies

Allergies and intolerances seem to be occurring more frequently in dogs today than they have in the past. Perhaps it's the pollutants in today's environment or perhaps it's because of the plethora of puppy mill dogs whose breeders don't care if they breed dogs with allergies. When we think of allergies, we might think of the sit-com version of a person sneezing all the time—and certainly, there is that component to allergies! But allergies include food allergies, contact allergies, and allergies to fleas, and they can cause rashes, coat problems, and other trouble:

- **Dietary allergies:** Dietary allergies are becoming common among dogs. They're a bit tricky to diagnose. Your vet will recommend a hypoallergenic diet for several weeks. This diet usually has a novel protein source—that is, a protein source that dogs generally don't eat, such as fish or venison. (Contrary to popular belief, lamb is not a hypoallergenic meat.) The diet may have an unusual carbohydrate source too, such as potatoes or barley. After your dog is on this diet several weeks, you add the potential problem ingredients to determine what the allergy is. Some dog owners are so relieved to have their dogs free from the allergy that they keep them on the hypoallergenic diet.

- **Contact allergies:** Contact allergies occur when a dog comes in contact with an allergen external to his body. Some contact allergies are apparent; some aren't as easy to diagnose. For example, if your dog's skin looks irritated and is itchy after using a particular shampoo, you might guess that the dog is allergic to a chemical in that shampoo. However, you might not know why your dog's nose and face are swollen and irritated. Many dogs are allergic to plastic or rubber and may react to the plastic bowls you feed them out of. Most contact allergy diagnoses are based on the owner's observations.

- **Flea bite dermatitis (flea allergy dermatitis):** Flea bite dermatitis can cause itchy skin. With flea bite dermatitis, the dog becomes allergic to the flea saliva. Eliminating fleas from your dog and your home will solve the problem and provide welcome relief. Your veterinarian can prescribe medications to alleviate the itching.

Allergy or Intolerance?

Dogs who are allergic to certain foods will show their allergies in the form of rashes, poor coat, and other conditions. Dogs who are intolerant of certain foods will not be able to digest the food. For example, dogs are typically lactose intolerant, meaning that they can't break down the milk sugars in milk; ingesting milk often results in diarrhea and gastric upsets. Dogs who are allergic to certain foods (beef, for example) may be able to digest the food just fine, but the problems manifest themselves in skin and other problems.

Be Careful with Over-the-Counter Medicines

Some over-the-counter human medicines—for example, aspirin, Pepto Bismol—are safe for dogs. However, other over-the-counter medicines, such as acetaminophen (Tylenol) and ibuprofen (Motrin, Advil), are poisonous to dogs and should never be given to dogs except under direction of a veterinarian. Do not give these medications to your dog, or you may have a very sick dog!

Broken Toenails

Your dog may experience cracked or broken toenails, especially if you allow them to grow too long. Trim each toenail and file off any rough edges if the toenail has broken below the quick, or blood supply to the nail. If the nail is bleeding, you can stop the bleeding with styptic powder, silver nitrate, or an electric nail cauterizer, available through pet mail order catalogs. You can then paint the nail with a skin bond agent, available from your veterinarian or through veterinary supply houses.

Diarrhea and Vomiting

Changes in diet, overeating, strange water, and nervousness can cause diarrhea, but so can parvovirus, internal parasites, rancid food, allergies, and other serious ailments. If your dog is dehydrated, has a fever (over 102 degrees Fahrenheit), or has extreme or bloody diarrhea, bring him to your veterinarian as soon as possible.

If your dog has mild diarrhea (soft stools—not liquid and without mucus) and does not have dehydration and is not vomiting, you can give one to two teaspoons per ten pounds of body weight of a kaolin product (such as Kaopectate) or .5 milliliters to 1.5 milliliters per pound of body weight every twelve hours of a bismuth subsalicylate product (such as Pepto Bismol). Withhold your dog's next meal to see if the diarrhea improves. Encourage your dog to drink water or an unflavored pediatric electrolyte solution. If there is no diarrhea or vomiting, you can feed a mixture of boiled hamburger and rice. If your dog's condition does not improve or becomes worse, contact your veterinarian.

Dogs vomit for a variety of reasons. Dogs will sometimes eat grass and vomit. Dogs also vomit due to obstructions, enlarged esophagus, parvovirus and other serious illnesses, allergies, and rancid food. If your dog vomits more than once or twice, projectile vomits, starts becoming dehydrated, has severe diarrhea along with vomiting, has a fever (over 102 degrees Fahrenheit), or retches without vomiting, bring your dog to the veterinarian immediately.

How to Take a Dog's Temperature

Occasionally, you may have to take your dog's temperature. Buy an ordinary digital rectal thermometer (don't get it mixed up with your human one!) and wash it well with soapy water. Sterilize it with isopropyl alcohol. Then lubricate it with petroleum jelly and insert it into your dog's rectum. Hold your dog quiet for about two minutes to get a reading. Don't allow your dog to sit down while taking the temperature, or you could break the thermometer or cause damage to the rectum. Remove and read. Normal temperatures for dogs are 100.5 degrees Fahrenheit to 101.5 degrees Fahrenheit.

Foxtails

Foxtails, or grass awns, are seeds from grasslike plants. They have a sharp, burrowing head with a tail that looks like a fox's tail (hence the name). These seeds have a nasty habit of getting into a dog's fur and ears. With each movement, they burrow further into the dog's skin.

After your dog has been outside, check him thoroughly for burrs and foxtails. Check his ears, too. I've seen foxtails bury themselves deep into a dog's skin. They can cause abscesses and can even enter organs.

Hot Spots and Other Skin Problems

Your dog could have itchy skin for a number of reasons—anything from poor diet to allergies to hypothyroidism to hot spots. If your dog's coat is dull and dry, try adding a teaspoon or two of canola oil to your dog's meal once a day and feeding him a hard-boiled egg three times a week. If your dog's coat remains dry and brittle or thin, consider having him tested for hypothyroidism. Some dogs are allergic to certain ingredients in their foods. Your veterinarian can prescribe a special hypoallergenic diet.

"Hot spots"—another name for moist eczema—are areas of moist dermatitis (skin inflammation) that may become infected. The symptoms are reddening skin, missing hair, and oozing, woundlike lesions. Allergies, matted fur, or some other form of irritation frequently causes them. Shave or clip all hair surrounding the hot spot and clean twice daily with a 10 percent betadine/90 percent water solution. If the hot spots are too painful, infected, or extensive, your veterinarian may have to anesthetize your dog to shave him and prescribe corticosteroids and antibiotics.

Lumps and Bumps on the Skin

Most lumps are usually benign. You can usually determine whether a lump is normal by checking the same place on the opposite side of the dog's body. Typically lumps that appear on both sides of the dog in the same place are normal.

Show any suspicious lump or bump to your veterinarian. Lumps that are oozing, red, dark-colored, irregular in size and shape, or swift-growing may be serious. If your female dog has lumps on her mammary glands, they may be cancerous mammary tumors requiring surgery. A large doughy lump on the stomach might be a hernia that your veterinarian may have to fix.

Rapidly growing lumps may be a form of abscess or infection. Abscesses occur when foreign bodies (such as foxtails) enter the skin or when an injury closes, with bacteria inside. Abscesses are serious. Your veterinarian must drain an abscess and prescribe antibiotics. Do not attempt to drain the abscess yourself, or the wound may become more infected.

Incontinence

Incontinence is generally a sign of a more serious problem, such as a bladder or urinary tract infection or bladder stones. Have your vet examine your dog to determine the cause of incontinence. Occasionally, spayed female dogs "dribble" and may require medication to correct the problem.

If your dog crouches down and urinates when you yell at him or touch him, it may be a form of submissive urination. It's important to know that this is a behavioral problem, not a medical one. It's a sign that he respects your authority and is submissive. Some dogs are more submissive than others. Scolding or yelling at your dog will only aggravate the problem. You can stop this behavior by remaining calm and speaking quietly. Pet your dog under the chin gently and don't act angry. Most dogs who are overly submissive may require some gentle confidence builders, such as training and other positive-reinforcement techniques.

Exercising Your Dog

One thing you can do to keep your dog healthy is to exercise him regularly. Like people, dogs can become couch potatoes and can be afflicted with diseases due to obesity. I have sled dogs, and most people are amazed to hear that my big dogs (fifty to eighty pounds) usually live past 14 years (I've had a few who have even lived to 17). However, my dogs get a lot of exercise. You should consider a variety of exercises, including the ones I've listed here, and check out the various activity books to get some ideas about what to do with your dog.

Naturally, you'll need to get your dog checked out by your vet before starting an exercise program, but once you do, long walks are a good way to get your dog in shape without over-stressing him. If you're both athletic types, you may want to consider some fun activities such as playing fetch or Frisbee. There are plenty of dog sports available, including agility, flyball, flying disc, and freestyle dancing. Oftentimes, a dog likes activities that are similar to the activities for which he was bred: water dogs such as Irish Water Spaniels love to swim, retrievers such as Labs love to play fetch, and herding dogs such as Corgis love to play soccer. The best way to determine whether a sport is right for you is to try it out a bit and see if your dog likes it. If he doesn't, try another one.

Dog Activity Books

You can learn more about activities in these books:

The Simple Guide to Getting Active with Your Dog by Margaret H. Bonham (TFH Publications) gives you ideas for various organized dog sports.

Beyond Fetch: Fun and Interactive Activities for You and Your Dog by D. Caroline Coile, Ph.D. (Howell Book House), describes fun games and activities to do with your dog.

Dog Parties: How to Party with Your Pup by Arden Moore (BowTie Press), gives you ideas about fun ways to interact with your dog.

Walking Your Dog

Always walk your dog on a leash. You'll need some sort of collar for control (usually a flat collar isn't enough for bigger dogs) and a good leash. Most collars I recommend are the slip-type collar. These are usually made of cloth or nylon, but some are made of chain (use the nylon ones if you can). Teach your dog to walk nicely on a leash, as described in chapter 12, "The Basics of Training," and you won't need anything other than a standard slip collar.

You'll need a six-foot leash to walk your dog. If your dog is a young puppy, you can use a nylon leash, which is slightly harder to chew through if your puppy whirls around and chomps the lead. Otherwise, choose a leather leash. This will help save your hands (nylon cuts into your hands when the dog pulls) and gives you more control. Unless you have a small dog, avoid retractable leashes. They give little or no control over the dog and can tangle in an instant. Unless you make it a habit to carry a pocketknife while walking, your dog can accidentally tangle with something—or worse, another dog—and get into a dog fight.

The correct side for walking your dog is your left side, but unless you're planning on competing in obedience, it doesn't really matter what side your dog walks or heels on, as long as you have control.

Bring bags to pick up poop when you walk your dog. Many municipalities have laws requiring you to pick up after your dog. Even if yours doesn't, it's the right thing to do.

Never allow your dog off leash while walking or in an unenclosed area. In most places—including national parks and some portions of national forests—having a dog off leash is illegal. In other places it might be legal, but unless you have a good recall with your dog, you're more likely to have to chase your dog to get him back and he may make himself a nuisance to other people. In any case, find out what the rules are before you let your dog off leash.

Going to Dog Parks

One fairly recent phenomenon that has cropped up is dog parks. These are normal parks that have been set aside for off-leash work with dogs. Some are fairly spacious, and some are tiny. Some have activities such as agility courses and are outfitted for pampering pooches with grooming stations. Before you head over to a dog park, be aware that other dogs are likely to be loose there, and your dog must be friendly with other dogs. Even so, there are owners whose dogs aren't friendly who may let their dogs loose there—so always be careful.

When you go to a dog park, be sure to have bags to pick up your dog's poop and bring his own ball or other toys to play with. While that doesn't guarantee that he won't try to steal another dog's ball, it can at least provide a distraction.

Playing Games in the Backyard

If you have a backyard, you can play with your dog there. You can play fetch with a Frisbee or ball, play soccer, and play other types of games. Have fun with your dog while you're both getting exercise!

Agility

You may have seen agility on TV. Dogs jump over hurdles and go over, under, and through various obstacles and compete against time and each other. It's as fun to do as it is to watch and makes for a great sport for the entire family. (Lots of adults do this, as well as kids.) Your dog can earn titles from various organizations and in most cases, your dog doesn't have to be a purebred to compete.

There are plenty of good resources for agility. You can learn more about them in my two books, *Having Fun with Agility* (Howell Book House), for those who aren't interested in competition, and *Introduction to Dog Agility* (Barrons), for those looking at seriously entering the sport.

Grooming Your Dog

One way to ensure a beautiful and healthy dog is to keep him groomed. Your dog will have healthier skin and hair, not to mention look beautiful and be sweet smelling. A clean dog is enjoyable to have around. A dirty dog is, well, a dirty dog.

But should you groom your dog yourself or should you hire a professional? And grooming doesn't just stop at brushing and combing or bathing! Cleaning ears, clipping toenails, and brushing your dog's teeth are all part of grooming.

Should You Hire a Professional Groomer?

If you don't have the time or if your dog has a high-maintenance coat, grooming can be a daunting task. If you're a busy person or your family is busy, paying a groomer to bathe and clip your dog once every two weeks or once a month isn't extravagant—it's a necessity! Be honest with yourself; if you just don't have time to groom your dog, have an expert do it. But don't wait until your dog is filthy and his fur is matted. The groomer will charge you more for that, and detangling the mess may test your dog's patience. Keep in mind that if your dog has a long coat or requires more clipping, it will cost more than one with a shorter coat or one whose coat has been maintained.

How do you find a good professional groomer? Ask other dog owners which groomers they use and if they would recommend them. Ask your vet who he or she would recommend. Some vets have a groomer on staff. Many large pet stores also have adjacent grooming facilities.

Once you find a groomer you're interested in, contact the groomer and ask what certifications he or she has. Although there are many good groomers without certifications, you may wish to only have a groomer who is certified. Ask what services he or she performs (for example, some groomers will trim toenails, clean ears, and express anal sacs). Find out if they are familiar with grooming your dog's breed. Ask the groomer how many regular clients he or she has.

Be aware that some groomers tranquilize dogs, especially if the dog is aggressive or difficult to work on. If your dog is prone to seizures, certain tranquilizers can cause seizures. In most cases, it's better to use a groomer who doesn't tranquilize.

Once you've prescreened a groomer, visit the grooming shop. If the groomer is especially busy, you'll see hair and water on the floor, but otherwise the grooming shop should be neat and orderly. Watch how the groomer and staff (if there are any) handle the dogs. Are they gentle or rough? If there are dogs in cage dryers, does the groomer check on them frequently to be sure they are not becoming overheated? Finally, does the groomer have enough room to put all the dogs in adequate crates?

Grooming Your Dog's Coat

Different breeds have different coats and different grooming needs. If you have a mixed breed, you may indeed be getting a mixed bag when it comes to his coat. Does your dog have a single coat (one without an undercoat) or a double coat? Is hair terrierlike or poodle-like, requiring trimming, or is it huskylike, with a thick undercoat? Is it short and sleek like a Labrador's or long and fluffy like a Samoyed's? Maybe he's a mixed breed and it's all of the above!

How often you groom your dog depends on the type of coat, whether he is shedding, and whether he is dirty. Naturally, a dirty dog requires grooming. Dogs with single coats may need extra clipping, and dogs with double coats may need extra grooming, especially when they shed. Regardless of the coat, you'll need to brush and comb your dog at least weekly. Dogs with long hair that tangles easily will require more frequent brushings. Dogs with short coats can probably get by with a quick brushing. Dogs with double coats shed once or twice a year, depending on the breed and your climate.

Grooming Implements

You'll need some standard supplies for grooming your dog. These include the basic brushes and combs described in chapter 4, "Preparing for Your Dog," but also include what might seem extravagant, such as a dog blow dryer and grooming table. These items, however, will make your job much easier. Grooming tables will help save your back, and dog blow dryers won't burn your dog's skin. Here's what you'll need to groom your dog:

- Electric clipper (for single-coated dogs)
- Flea comb
- Grooming table with noose (never leave your dog on it unattended)
- Appropriate dog comb
- Blow dryer for dogs (not human blow dryers—they are too hot)
- Shampoo and conditioner formulated for dogs
- Mat splitter, mat rake, or detangler solution (for dogs who get mats—usually long-coated and double-coated breeds)
- Nail clippers or nail grinder
- Shears (for single-coated dogs)
- Slicker brush
- Styptic powder
- Thinning shears (for single-coated dogs)
- Toothpaste and toothbrush for dogs
- Undercoat rake (for double-coated dogs)
- Zoom Groom or curry brush (for short-coated dogs)

Brushing and Combing

How you brush your dog depends on the coat, but you should start by brushing the hair and untangling any mats. (Use a mat splitter or a detangler solution if your dog has mats.) Never use scissors to cut out a mat! You can severely cut your dog's skin even if you are careful. If your dog has too many mats, take him to a groomer, who may have to use clippers to cut away the matted fur.

Next, brush your dog's hair against the lay of the hair. This helps stimulate oils in the coat. Then, brush the dog's hair back.

Baths

Although it's tempting, you should never bathe a dog without first brushing him out. Some breeds are prone to tangles, and the mats will be worse if you bathe the dog first. Instead, brush your dog out and then bathe him with a good pH-balanced shampoo for dogs. Do not use human shampoo, as it can dry out a dog's skin. Follow it with a conditioner made for dogs and rinse thoroughly.

Some dogs hate baths. If your dog is one of those, you might want to procure a restraining noose that attaches via a suction cup so you can keep your dog in the tub while you wash him. (Never leave a dog unattended in one, or he might strangle.) You may want to consider putting a small piece of cotton in each ear so that water doesn't get in them. Be certain that the bathwater is tepid to touch. Rinse your dog really well because soap and conditioner residue will attract dirt.

Pat down your dog with thick towels and keep your dog away from drafts while he's drying. Use a dog hair blow dryer to dry your dog. Don't use a human hair dryer, as these get too hot and will burn your dog's skin and scorch his fur. Use towels to get rid of the excess water and then blow his fur dry.

Clipping

Unless you're a pro at clipping, you might want to leave the clipping to a professional, who can shape your dog's coat into a nice style. The groomer can show you how to maintain the cut in between grooming sessions. If you plan to learn how to clip your dog's coat, ask an expert. Some trainers and groomers will be happy to help you. Other people to ask would be breeders and show people with dogs that are clipped. The wire-coated terrier breeds are hand-stripped for the show ring but that's a time-consuming process, so pets are usually clipped. Even if your dog isn't a purebred, any of these people can show you a nice pet cut that would work with your dog's coat.

Doggy Dental Care

Your dog has two sets of teeth while growing up. The first set, called puppy teeth or milk teeth, drop out when your puppy is three or four months old so the adult teeth can come in. Dogs suffer dental problems such as tartar and gum disease like humans, but cavities in a dog's mouth are rare. Still, infected teeth can cause severe health problems, including heart problems, in your dog. Teeth cleaning requires anesthesia and its associated risks—not to mention expense!

Many vets recommend brushing your dog's teeth every day with toothpaste specially for-mulated for dogs. Many dog owners don't have the time or patience to do that, so I recommend brushing your dog's teeth twice a week to reduce plaque, which leads to tartar. If your dog has good teeth (healthy teeth and gums largely depend on genetics and diet), you might be able to get away with brushing his teeth less, but that's inadvisable.

If your dog isn't used to having his mouth handled, you won't be successful in brushing his teeth. Start by holding your dog's head gently and flipping up his lip and touching his teeth and gums. Do this gently and praise him. Practice this often, so he becomes used to you touching his mouth.

After he becomes used to you handling his mouth, get a soft washcloth and wet a corner of it. Now, with your finger, gently massage your dog's gums with the tip of the washcloth.

Recognizing a Tooth or Gum Problem

The following are potential warning signs of tooth or gum problems that suggest that it's time to visit the vet:

- Bad breath
- Loss of appetite
- Lump above or below a particular tooth
- Nasal discharge
- Red, swollen gums
- Sudden, unexpected chewing on inappropriate items

Purchase a toothbrush and toothpaste for dogs. These are available at pet supply stores. You must use toothpaste formulated for pets, as human toothpaste is poisonous to dogs. Most pet toothpastes are chicken or malt flavored, so the taste is appealing. Brush your dog's teeth, making sure you get all the teeth, at least once a week. No, he doesn't have to rinse and spit.

Cleaning Your Dog's Ears

Some dogs develop ear problems frequently, and others never seem to have a problem. Breeds that seem to have a predilection for ear infections and injuries tend to be sporting dogs and hounds, due to their dropped ears, which make an ideal place for bacteria to grow and mites to hide.

Regardless of whether your dog has up or dropped ears, you should keep his ears clean. Your dog's ears should be clean and sweet smelling. If there is an odor, your dog may have an infection.

Clean your dog's ears once a week. Use a mild over-the-counter otic solution for dogs. Squeeze some into your dog's ears and then gently massage the outside of the ear canal. Using sterile gauze or sponges, gently wipe out the excess. Don't leave any behind, or it could lead to an ear infection. Don't use insecticides or mite treatments, as they can cause irritation. If you suspect ear mites, see your vet for the appropriate treatment.

Clipping Your Dog's Toenails

Most dogs hate having their toenails clipped. You can minimize the stress by getting your dog used to you handling his feet. Start by touching and picking up each foot gently. For the first few times, it may be no longer than a few seconds. Gradually increase the time you hold your dog's feet.

Recognizing an Ear Problem

These are the signs of potential ear problems, which suggest that it's time to visit the vet:

- Blisters or abrasions on ears
- Dog yelping when you touch his ears
- Crusty or red ears
- Excessive waxy buildup
- Foul smelling odor coming from the ears
- Red or black waxy buildup
- Dog's scratching at, pawing, or shaking his head

Clip your dog's nails once a week to keep them short and healthy. Long nails may break and cause pain. Dogs have a pink part where nerves and blood supply to the nail are, called the "quick." Because many dogs' nails are dark, you have to make an educated guess where the quick is. If you cut into the quick, your dog will let you know in no uncertain terms—and won't want you near his paws again! He'll also bleed profusely. Have styptic powder or sodium nitrate on hand, in case you do cut the quick. Packing the nail with styptic powder will stop the bleeding. You can buy styptic powder at pet supply stores.

When you start clipping your dog's nails, use a dog nail clipper (either a guillotine or scissors action) and snip off a small portion of the nail at a time to trim back the nails. If the nail feels spongy or hard to cut, stop immediately. You can use a nail grinder, which will help file the nail instead. Some dogs handle the nail grinder better than clippers.

Emptying Your Dog's Anal Sacs

A dog has two glands at the four and eight o'clock positions around his anus. These usually empty themselves when the dog defecates, but occasionally they become overfull or impacted.

If your dog starts scooting around on his rear or chewing the fur on his rear or tail, he may have full or impacted anal sacs. The best time to empty these is when you are bathing him. The liquid matter expelled is smellier than a skunk, and you'll want to clean him off thoroughly after you've expressed them.

Fold up a wad of paper towels and place them over your dog's anus. Now press gently on the four and eight o'clock positions. The glands should express themselves. If the problem still persists, take your dog to the vet. He could have impacted anal glands, which your vet may have to express.

Socializing Your Dog

Socializing your dog is very important for his mental health and well-being. Like exercising, socializing your dog isn't done once and then it's over with. For a dog to be well socialized, he must interact with people and experience new things every day. Otherwise, he will become used to not seeing and doing new things and will slip into fearful reactions toward new things.

I had an Alaskan Malamute named Kiana who was very experienced with people and unusual situations. Kiana could go everywhere and do anything, even though she wasn't socialized in all situations. At book signings, people's little children would hang off her, and she would patiently tolerate them—even though this dog had never grown up with or been around many children. Her socialization combined with training made her very trustworthy. (Consider the bite statistics in chapter 2, "A Good Match—What Dog Is Right for You?")

A properly bred, properly trained, and properly socialized dog can perform some pretty amazing tasks. Although I can't guarantee that you'll have the level of trustworthiness I had with Kiana with your own dog, socializing your dog is a start.

If your dog is a puppy, start socializing him right after his last series of vaccinations. You need to socialize him in the following situations:

- On car rides (make it fun for him—go someplace fun)
- At dog parks
- Outside shopping centers
- At dog supply stores
- On walks
- At outside seating by coffee shops
- On trips to the groomer or vet
- Visiting friends and friends' pets
- Any other place where there are people

Puppy KPT or puppy kindergarten classes (offered through professional trainers) are aimed at helping you socialize your puppy right. (See chapter 12 for info on choosing a trainer.)

If you have an adult dog or a fearful puppy, you should take socialization very slowly. Don't force your dog into situations where he is frightened or fearful, or you will just increase his fear and you may create a worse problem. If your dog is fearful of strangers, start by walking him in a park far enough away from people so he is not afraid of them but can still see them. As he becomes more comfortable, decrease the distance so that it is just on his edge of comfort and let him instigate interaction. Usually this takes time and patience in desensitizing. A professional trainer can help you with this problem.

One problem dogs seem to have is with car rides—and little wonder! If all you did was go to the vet or leave home for the boarding kennel or the groomer, you might think cars were no fun. Start taking your dog to fun places like the dog park, the pet supply store, a friend's house, or even for a quick snack at a local fast-food drive-through (order a hamburger plain for him). I guarantee that car rides will quickly turn into fun things to do.

If your dog gets carsick, your vet can recommend an appropriate motion sickness medication and the dosage.

What You Now Know...

- Your dog needs proper nutrition from a dog food that is complete and balanced to AAFCO nutritional standards.
- You are the first line of defense in your dog's health. You need to examine him weekly to make sure he is healthy.
- Spaying and neutering will make your dog a healthier and happier pet.
- Consult with your veterinarian about external parasites and other canine health problems.
- Exercise will help your dog live a long and healthy life.
- Grooming will help keep your dog healthy and looking good.
- Socialization is important for your dog's mental health and well-being.

Chapter 9

Emergencies

What's Inside . . .
- ➤ Learn what constitutes an emergency for a dog.
- ➤ Learn what to do in case of common canine emergencies.
- ➤ Stock a canine first aid kit.
- ➤ Prepare your family for a disaster.

E mergencies are scary. But you can be ready for them if you plan ahead. The main thing is, don't panic. Your dog is relying on you to remain levelheaded and calm during this time. You need to take charge for the sake of your dog's health and well-being.

In most emergencies, time is of the essence, and you'll need to get your dog to a veterinarian as soon as possible. You'll need to know where the nearest emergency veterinarian is as well as your vet's after-hours emergency numbers (if he or she has them). Keep these numbers taped to the phone or on your speed dial in case of an emergency.

How to Recognize an Emergency

How do you know when to take your dog to the vet? And how can you recognize an emergency?

When to Go to the Vet Immediately

If any of the following is true, take your dog to a vet immediately (your regular vet or an emergency vet, if necessary):

- ☐ Dog isn't breathing or is having difficulty breathing.
- ☐ Dog is shaky or weak.
- ☐ Dog has collapsed.
- ☐ Dog's face is swollen or there's extreme and rapid swelling on the body or legs.
- ☐ Dog's gums are gray or sticky.
- ☐ Dog has been burned.
- ☐ Dog has suffered broken bones or severely injured legs.
- ☐ Dog is bleeding profusely.

- [ ] Dog has been electrocuted.
- [ ] Dog has been hit by a car.
- [ ] Dog has a seizure.
- [ ] Dog's temperature is 103 degrees Fahrenheit or higher.
- [ ] Dog's stomach swells rapidly.
- [ ] Dog is in obvious pain or distress.
- [ ] Dog is shocky (see "Shock," later in this chapter).
- [ ] Dog projectile vomits.
- [ ] Dog has forceful or bloody diarrhea.
- [ ] Dog is dehydrated.
- [ ] Dog has heatstroke.
- [ ] Dog's temperature is below 99.5 degrees Fahrenheit.
- [ ] Dog has suffered frostbite.
- [ ] Dog has eaten something poisonous.
- [ ] Dog has suffered an injury severe enough that underlying tissues or bones can be seen.
- [ ] Dog has been bitten by a poisonous snake or insect.

A general rule for emergencies is that if you think it is an emergency, it probably is. If there is still some question in your mind, try calling your vet or an emergency veterinarian and *asking*.

When to Go to the Vet as Soon as Practical

What conditions aren't quite emergencies but still call for you to take your dog to a vet as soon as practical? Some of these conditions are easy to figure out; others aren't so easy. If any of the following is true of your dog and doesn't clear up in a few days, you should consider taking her to a vet:

- [ ] Dog hasn't eaten any meals all day.
- [ ] Dog has mild diarrhea or vomiting.
- [ ] Dog has a cough.
- [ ] Dog has a limp.
- [ ] You feel a strange lump or bump on the dog.
- [ ] Dog is itchy or has a rash developing.
- [ ] Dog is starting to lose hair.
- [ ] Dog is drinking excessive water.
- [ ] Dog's temperature is above 101.5 degrees Fahrenheit but less than 103 degrees Fahrenheit.
- [ ] Dog shakes her head or paws her ears.
- [ ] There is unusual discharge coming from the dog's nose, eyes, or other mucus membranes.
- [ ] Dog is sensitive to light.
- [ ] You see cloudiness in your dog's eye.
- [ ] Dog is acting reluctant to do things she normally likes doing.

In these situations, anything that appears unusual is probably a reason to take your dog to the veterinarian as soon as practical. If you notice something out of the ordinary that doesn't appear to be an emergency,

Emergency Veterinarian Numbers

Contact	Name	Telephone Number
Primary veterinarian	_____	_____
Primary veterinarian's on-call number	_____	_____
Secondary veterinarian	_____	_____
Emergency clinic	_____	_____
Alternate emergency clinic	_____	_____
Local poison control hotline	_____	_____
24-hour poison control hotline ($50/case)	ASPCA Animal Poison Control Center	888/426-4435

make an appointment as soon as you can to get your dog checked out. If you aren't sure if the problem is an emergency, contact your vet (or an emergency vet) and ask.

How to Muzzle Your Dog

Even the gentlest dog may bite if frightened or injured. It's therefore important to know how to muzzle your dog. Have a quick muzzle (sold by pet supply stores) handy. If you don't have one, you can fashion a makeshift muzzle from a bandage, a rope, a belt, or a tie. Here's what you do:

1. Check your dog's breathing and temperature. Never muzzle a dog who is having problems breathing, is overheated, or has a sucking chest wound.
2. Find a piece of bandage, rope, or whatever will work to make a muzzle.
3. Start in the middle of the bandage, rope, or other muzzle material and place it beneath the dog's muzzle.
4. Wrap both ends of the bandage upward.
5. Cross the ends and tie.
6. Bring the loose ends back downward under the chin and tie.
7. Tie the two loose ends behind the dog's head securely. Make sure the muzzle is tight enough so the dog is unable to bite you. Be sure to not leave it on for very long—only to treat the dog.

Once the dog is muzzled, you can examine or treat her as needed.

Assembling a Canine First Aid Kit

First aid kits aren't just for people. Dogs need them, too, with their own supplies. When you put together a first aid kit for your dog, be sure it is someplace where you'll use it. Have one at home and one in the car for when you travel. Be sure to include the following items:

- ☐ Aspirin
- ☐ Bandage scissors
- ☐ Bandage tape
- ☐ Betadine solution
- ☐ Cortisone cream
- ☐ Disposable latex gloves
- ☐ Hydrogen peroxide
- ☐ Kaolin product (such as Kaopectate)
- ☐ Large and small nonstick bandage pads
- ☐ Mineral oil
- ☐ Petroleum jelly
- ☐ Pressure bandages
- ☐ Quick muzzle
- ☐ Rectal thermometer
- ☐ Self-adhesive wrap (such as VetWrap or Elastaplast)
- ☐ Sterile gauze wrappings
- ☐ Sterile sponges
- ☐ Styptic powder
- ☐ Surgical glue or VetBond (available through veterinary supply stores)
- ☐ Syrup of ipecac
- ☐ Triple antibiotic ointment (the same as what's used for humans) or nitrofurizone (available through veterinary supply catalogs)
- ☐ Tweezers
- ☐ Unflavored pediatric electrolyte fluid (such as Pedialyte)
- ☐ Your veterinarian's phone number, pager, or after-hours number
- ☐ Local poison control center phone number
- ☐ An emergency veterinary hospital's phone number

Handling Common Emergencies

Broken Bones or Dog Hit by Car

Fractures to the head, chest, or back may be life threatening. Use a stiff board to transport the dog (slide the board under the dog) and seek immediate veterinary attention. If your dog has broken her leg, you can fashion a splint from a stick, a rolled-up piece of stiff cardboard, or even a rolled-up newspaper. Put the splint alongside the broken leg and wrap either VetWrap or tape around it. Transport your dog to the veterinarian as soon as possible.

Burns

A severe burn, where the skin is charred or where underlying tissue is exposed, requires immediate veterinary attention. You can treat minor burns over a small area with ice packs or cold water. Do not use water on extensive burns, or you may risk shock. Aloe vera is a good burn treatment after the burn has blistered.

Choking or Difficulty Breathing

Signs of choking and breathing difficulty include gagging, coughing, gums and tongue turning pale or blue, and wheezing. Do not muzzle your dog, but do loosen your dog's collar and anything else that might restrict breathing. Seek immediate veterinary attention. Check your dog's throat for any object caught in the throat. If you see something that you can remove with tweezers, do so. Do not use your fingers; you can accidentally push the item farther down. If the item is lodged in the throat, try pushing on the dog's abdomen to expel the object.

If your dog has stopped breathing, perhaps the only way to save her life is to give mouth-to-mouth resuscitation. Make certain your dog's airway is clear. Close her mouth, hold her jaws together, and blow gently into her nose. Don't blow hard or overinflate her lungs, or you may rupture a lung. Her side should move only as if she were breathing. Release and let the air leave the lungs. Blow in again and release. Continue to do this until your dog is breathing on her own. Ask your veterinarian for information on how to perform CPR on a dog.

Cuts, Injuries, and Animal Bites

You can clean minor cuts and scrapes yourself with a solution of 10 percent betadine/ 90 percent water. Then apply a triple antibiotic ointment, but watch for signs of infection. Seek veterinary attention if you see signs of reddening, inflammation, or infection (such as oozing pus).

Severe cuts and lacerations will most likely require suturing. Use pressure bandages to slow or stop the bleeding, except in severe crushing injuries. If injuries are severe, such as in a car accident, there may be internal bleeding. Use a stiff board to transport the dog and seek veterinary attention.

In the case of arterial bleeding, the blood is bright red and sprays out with each heartbeat. In such a case, use pressure bandages and apply pressure directly to the artery. Seek immediate veterinary attention.

 For deep puncture wounds, determine how deep the puncture is. If the object is still embedded, do not remove it, if practical, and seek immediate veterinary treatment. If the puncture is a dog bite that is not serious, you can clean the wound with a betadine/water solution. Your veterinarian might want to prescribe antibiotics to prevent infection. Be certain that both your dog and the biting dog have had their rabies vaccinations.

Cut pads tend to bleed badly. Staunch the bleeding with styptic powder and then apply an antibiotic to it. You can wrap the foot with gauze and put a bootie on, similar to those you can buy at a pet supply store or from a sled dog outfitter. (www.dogbooties.com is one possible source.) If the cut or split is minor, you can affix a piece of leather a little larger than the cut to the pad by using surgical glue or superglue. This will help the pad heal.

Dehydration and Heatstroke

Signs of dehydration and heatstroke include elevated temperature, weakness, extreme thirst, watery diarrhea, vomiting, lethargy, high temperature (over 103 degrees Fahrenheit), skin around muzzle or neck that does not snap back when pinched, difficulty breathing, weakness, and pale gums. Note that dehydration can occur during any season.

The onset of heatstroke is very sudden, and sometimes it takes only a few minutes to reach an emergency situation. Blood pressure falls, mucous membranes turn icy blue, and the dog becomes confused, staggers, is comatose, and then dies.

If you suspect heatstroke, get the dog to someplace cool and shady. Pour cool water over her body and head or, if possible, submerge her body in a tub or tank. Fan her and lift her coat with your fingers so that her skin will directly benefit from the cooling breeze and water. Don't apply ice or ice water because that will tend to close skin pores, shrink her skin's surface vessels, and exacerbate the heatstroke.

When she comes around, give your dog small quantities of water to drink or pediatric electrolyte solution and repeat as often as she wants. If possible, measure her body temperature with a thermometer and stop the physical cooling process when her body reaches about 103 degrees Fahrenheit because the cooling will continue after you take her from the water, and your target temperature is about 100 degrees Fahrenheit.

The most common cause of heatstroke is leaving a dog in a car. Even with the windows cracked, the glass of the car magnifies the sun's temperature, and the inside can easily reach 150 degrees Fahrenheit, even when the day is overcast and the outdoor temperature is moderate.

Electrocution

If your dog is still touching the source of electricity, do not touch your dog, or you might be shocked also. Use a wooden broom handle or other nonconductive item to unplug the cord. Treat as you would for traumatic shock (see "Shock," later in this chapter) by maintaining proper body temperature and seek veterinary treatment. Administer mouth-to-mouth resuscitation, as described previously in the section "Choking or Difficulty Breathing."

Make sure to give puppies lots of supervised outdoor playtime. These two Golden Retriever siblings
obviously enjoy their time outside.

There's always something interesting to see
outside. Eager to go on a walk and explore,
this English Setter checks out the scenery.

Puppies tend to stick close to their mothers. This West Highland White Terrier pup enjoys some quiet time outdoors with his mother.

These Border Terriers join their family on a trip to the local park.

Some dogs, like these Alaskan Malamutes, were born to work. It's essential that working breeds get lots of exercise.

After a long day, this Bullmastiff puppy is ready for a nap.

Dogs, especially puppies, love
to explore their surroundings.
This Bulldog puppy must have
found something interesting
around that tree.

Dogs need lots of exercise.
This Rottweiler is waiting
for a companion to come out
and play ball.

It's a good idea to research any breed you are interested in adopting. The curious expression on this Jack Russell Terrier's face hints at the breed's intelligent and active nature.

Demonstrating his mastery of fetch, this chocolate Labrador Retriever brings in the morning paper.

Self-confident Bearded Collies are devoted members of the family, but they have no qualms about exploring on their own.

A nap in the sun is the order of the day for this Chinese Shar-Pei.

Many dogs and their families find competing in dog sports, for fun or for ribbons, to be reward- ing. This Pug completes an agility trial.

Your dog's ancestry can tell you a lot about how he may behave. True to his nature, this Bloodhound picks up a scent in the air.

Even in play, these Rhodesian Ridgeback puppies are establishing a pecking order.

Virtually everything looks like a toy to a dog. This French Bulldog runs off with a garden hose left out in the yard.

Fishhooks

If your dog has stepped on a fishhook or had one pierce her lips, take her to a vet. If no vet is available, you may have to muzzle your dog and look for the hook's barb. Push the barb through the skin if necessary to expose it and then snip it off with a pair of wire cutters. Then remove the hook. Contact your vet; he or she may wish to prescribe antibiotics. Only your veterinarian should remove swallowed fishhooks.

Frostbite and Hypothermia

Signs of hypothermia include lowered body temperature, shivering, and lethargy, followed by stupor, shock, unconsciousness, and finally, death. Lack of food for energy and dehydration can greatly affect your dog's ability to keep warm. Dogs expend energy and heat while working, but if the heat loss is too great, your dog may experience hypothermia.

Treatment for hypothermia is mostly common sense. Warm your dog slowly by wrapping her in blankets or lying next to her in blankets to help warm her. If she is conscious, you should offer her warm broth to drink. Seek immediate veterinary attention.

Frostbite is skin damage as a result of cold. The skin will turn white if frostbitten. With severe frostbite, the skin will actually turn black. Sometimes the affected skin will slough, leaving a raw sore. If the skin is white and intact, warm it slowly in tepid water (not hot, which can damage the skin further). It will be painful to warm the skin. In frostbite with sores, wrap with an antibiotic ointment and gauze. In all cases of frostbite, seek veterinary attention.

Insects Bites and Stings

You can treat most insect bites and stings with Benadryl (diphenhydramine), 2 milligrams per pound of body weight every eight hours. If your dog shows any allergic reactions to bites or stings (severe swelling or difficulty breathing), seek immediate veterinary attention. This can be a life-threatening condition known as an anaphylactic reaction.

Spider bites can be very serious. The two most dangerous spiders are the black widow and the brown recluse. Bites from both of these spiders can be fatal if left untreated. If you suspect that a spider has bitten your dog, seek veterinary attention.

Poisoning

Contact your veterinarian or local poison control center and have available the substance or chemical that your dog has ingested so that you can properly describe the poison. Follow the veterinarian or poison control center's instructions. Do not induce vomiting unless told to do so. Some acids, alkalis, and other substances can harm your dog more if they come back up.

Shock

Signs of shock include pale mucous membranes, slow respiratory rate, weak pulse, and unconsciousness. Keep the dog quiet and maintain body temperature. That means if the dog is cold, keep her warm. If she's hot, keep her cool. Get the dog immediate veterinary attention.

Skunks

There aren't many things worse than getting skunked. But don't buy out the local supermarket's stock of tomato juice, or you'll just get a stinky pink dog.

Purchase a good commercial skunk-odor remover or use the following do-it-yourself baking soda/hydrogen peroxide remedy:

$\frac{1}{2}$ quart hydrogen peroxide
$\frac{1}{8}$ cup baking soda
1 teaspoon of shampoo or liquid soap

I've never used a commercial skunk-odor remover, so I can't vouch for their effectiveness. However, I had the most unfortunate luck of having one of my dogs get skunked while he was playing in our backyard. The skunk decided to spray him from the other side of the fence. I decided to try the baking soda/hydrogen peroxide remedy for getting rid of skunk odor. Suffice it to say, it works extremely well. My dog came out smelling better than he had before he got skunked. You can double the recipe with ease, if your dog is big or if he is particularly stinky. Wash the dog with this and rinse thoroughly. Don't get any in your dog's eyes. Don't save any of it in a container—it might explode.

Family Disaster Planning

Pet owners must prepare not only for injuries and severe illnesses, but also for disasters due to wildfires, floods, tornadoes, hurricanes, and even terrorist attacks. Your dog is relying on you to keep her healthy and safe. How do you prepare for a potential disaster? By being prepared and planning your strategy now, before trouble hits.

For most of us with pets, the thought of leaving our best friends behind is intolerable at best. But many shelters set up by the American Red Cross and other organizations won't take pets (although they do accept service dogs). Where will you stay if you have to leave your home and take your pets with you?

Locate friends or family members out of the potential disaster area who will take you and your pets. (Don't assume that they will take you and your pets and then find out later that they won't! Ask now, before you're forced into a bad situation.) If you don't have family or friends to stay with, have a listing of hotels and motels within a certain radius of your house (five miles, ten miles, twenty-five miles, fifty miles) that will allow pets. Locate kennels that are outside the potential disaster area in case you must stay in a place that doesn't allow pets.

Disaster Preparedness Checklist

The following is a checklist for disaster preparedness. Have this on hand to make sure you have everything you need.

- ☐ Pet first aid kit
- ☐ Enough pet food and potable water for three days
- ☐ Copies of your pet's health records and vaccination records
- ☐ Pet's medication
- ☐ Photos of your pet in case she gets lost
- ☐ Bowls, leashes, and can opener
- ☐ Travel crates
- ☐ Hotel contact #1: _____
- ☐ Hotel contact #2: _____
- ☐ Hotel contact #3: _____
- ☐ Hotel contact #4: _____
- ☐ Hotel contact #5: _____
- ☐ Emergency vet #1: _____
- ☐ Emergency vet #2: _____
- ☐ Emergency vet #3: _____
- ☐ Emergency vet #4: _____
- ☐ Boarding kennel #1: _____
- ☐ Boarding kennel #2: _____
- ☐ Boarding kennel #3: _____
- ☐ Boarding kennel #4: _____
- ☐ _____
- ☐ _____
- ☐ _____
- ☐ _____

A last resort can be to contact animal shelters and find out if they can care for your pets in an emergency. Shelters are frequently crowded and usually have pets that have already been displaced.

There is advanced warning before many disasters—such as hurricanes, wildfires, and tornadoes—hit. If you have warning, make plans to get both your family and your pets out of the area. Once the disaster hits, it's going to be very difficult to find places for your family and your pets to stay. It's better to leave early rather than at the last minute. Have a disaster preparedness list for your family and your pet and make sure you take all important items with you when you leave.

What You Now Know...

- Seek veterinary advice if you're unsure whether a situation is an emergency.
- Know how to handle common canine emergencies.
- Have a pet first-aid kit available in your home and car in case of an emergency.
- Plan ahead for disasters so that you are not caught unaware.

Chapter 10

Hereditary and Congenital Diseases

What's Inside . . .
- ➤ Learn what hereditary and congenital diseases are.
- ➤ Learn how hereditary and congenital diseases can affect your dog.
- ➤ Learn whether and how hereditary and congenital diseases can be treated.

What Are Hereditary and Congenital Diseases?

Hereditary diseases—which may appear in a dog at different stages of his life, depending on the disease and the dog—are diseases that dogs can inherit genetically. There are many hidden diseases and conditions in a dog's genes that carry undesirable traits and potential health problems. No animal is 100 percent disease-free in his genes. However, there are diseases we know are hereditary that we can screen for.

Some diseases are dominant, meaning that the disease will show up if the puppy inherits the dominant gene from his mom or dad. (A dog with such a dominant gene will always have the disease but will not always pass that gene along to the puppy.) Many diseases, however, are recessive, meaning that the gene must be paired with another recessive in order for the disease to show up. Oddly, some dogs may have a gene that leads to a disease only in the presence of certain environmental conditions.

Let's look at some of the hereditary and congenital diseases that can affect dogs.

Elbow Dysplasia and Osteochondritis Dissecans

Elbow dysplasia (ED) is a hereditary disease in which the elbow joints are malformed. Surgery, anti-inflammatories, and nutriceuticals (nutritional supplements intended to help mitigate disease) are recommended treatments for elbow dysplasia. Arthritis often sets into the joints, further complicating matters. Surgery can be very expensive.

Osteochondrosis dissecans (OCD) is a condition where the cartilage thickens in joint areas. This thickened cartilage is more prone to damage and may tear and form a flap or rejoin to the bone. OCD may appear in several joints or only one. If your dog has this condition, he may limp after exercising, and this limp may be mistaken for an injury. However, OCD causes persistent lameness. You may feel the joint pop or crackle as you examine it. Its onset is usually between 4 and 8 months of age.

If your dog is diagnosed with OCD, your veterinarian may recommend that you rest your dog for several weeks. Your veterinarian may treat it with analgesics and nutriceuticals. OCD can be very painful, causing a cartilage flap to form over a joint. That flap may tear or reattach, and surgery is needed to remove the flap. Although OCD can be due to trauma, when it is paired with elbow dysplasia, it is most likely due to hereditary conditions.

Both ED and OCD can be diagnosed. When looking for a puppy, look for one whose parents were certified as being free of these diseases either with the Orthopedic Foundation for Animals (OFA) or the University of Pennsylvania Hip Improvement Programs (PennHIP).

Epilepsy

Epilepsy exists in all breeds and mixed breeds. It can be hereditary in dogs, and it is quite prevalent in some lines. Studies show that some breeds have a genetic predisposition to epilepsy. Idiopathic epilepsy (that is, epilepsy where the specific cause is not known) in dogs is very similar to epilepsy in humans. However, other causes of epilepsy—including head trauma, poisoning, tick paralysis, parasites, vitamin deficiencies, overheating, intestinal obstructions, liver problems, and calcium imbalances—must be ruled out before a condition can be declared idiopathic.

There are two types of epileptic seizures: petit mal and grand mal. Petit mal seizures are usually of short duration, where the dog has a sudden twitch or blank-out. Grand mal seizures are usually spastic seizures that last for several seconds to minutes. The dog may shake, urinate and defecate uncontrollably, and whimper and groan involuntarily. It is very distressing to see a dog undergo either type of seizure.

If your dog has seizures, your vet must test to rule out other causes to determine if he has epilepsy. If the seizures are frequent or become worse, your vet usually will prescribe a medication to help control them, such as phenobarbital. If the seizures are still uncontrolled, adding other drugs, such as clorazepate, potassium bromide, clonazepam, or valproric acid, may help.

There's really no test to determine whether a dog will get epilepsy. This is why it is important to get a dog from a responsible breeder who knows his or her lines and knows whether the disease exists in those lines.

Eye Diseases

Purebreds and mixed breeds are susceptible to hereditary and congenital eye diseases. A veterinary ophthalmologist can determine whether your dog has an eye condition. To ensure that you get a dog who doesn't have these eye diseases, be sure the breeder whom you get your dog from has his or her dogs tested and registered through OptiGen and Canine Eye Registry Foundation (CERF). The following are the most common genetic eye diseases, but there are many others.

Cataracts

A common eye disease in dogs, cataracts are cloudiness of the eye's lens. The lens may have a small dot or may become opaque, causing complete blindness. Cataracts can be due to either hereditary or environmental reasons.

Many dogs get cataracts as they grow old; however, there is a form of juvenile cataracts that can lead to blindness. Juvenile cataracts are usually hereditary.

Entropion and Ectropion

Entropion is a hereditary condition where the eyelid turns into the eye, causing the eyelashes and fur to rub against the eyeball. It is obviously irritating to the dog and usually requires minor surgery to correct.

In ectropion, the lower eyelid droops, exposing its interior. In mild cases, your veterinarian may prescribe eye drops and antibiotic and corticosteroid ophthalmic ointment. In severe cases, surgery may be required.

Progressive Retinal Atrophy and Central Progressive Retinal Atrophy

Both progressive retinal atrophy (PRA) and central progressive retinal atrophy (CPRA) affect a dog's vision and may cause blindness or near blindness (with CPRA, the rate of vision loss is slower). There are no treatments or cures for these diseases. These diseases may start as early as 4 to 6 months of age or may appear several years later. They are generally tied to recessive genes, but in certain breeds, CPRA can be a dominant gene. PRA appears in more than eighty-five breeds and in many cases has specific genes associated with it. In both PRA and CPRA, the retina degenerates. The dog may show night blindness before his eyesight deteriorates entirely.

Glaucoma

Glaucoma is a painful condition that leads to blindness in dogs. It can be hereditary or occur as a result of disease or trauma to the eye. The eye overproduces fluid inside the eyeball and builds up intense pressure. Some forms of glaucoma are due to injury and other conditions, but some forms are inherited. If it's diagnosed early, you may be able to control glaucoma with medication. Glaucoma may require surgery to reduce pressure, or even require the removal of the entire eye.

Heart Problems

Dogs suffer from a variety of heart conditions, both congenital and hereditary. They can be extreme, such as a severe heart defect that will lead to death, to minor, such as a slight heart murmur. Your veterinarian may be able to diagnose certain heart conditions by listening with a stethoscope, but some heart diseases may be diagnosable only by a cardiologist and complex machinery.

Congenital Heart Diseases

Congenital heart disease is usually present at birth. It occurs when there are malformations of the heart or the great vessels surrounding the heart. This condition may develop more fully as the puppy gets older. No one knows if congenital heart defects are hereditary, but many believe that they are. They can be mild or serious—anything from a heart murmur to life threatening.

Aortic Stenosis and Subaortic Stenosis

Aortic stenosis (AS) and subaortic stenosis (SAS) are insidious hereditary conditions that may show no outward signs in an apparently healthy dog. Then, the dog may suddenly simply drop over dead. AS and SAS are caused by a narrowing of the outflow tract of the left ventricle. In the case of SAS, the narrowing occurs below the aortic valve. The heart must work harder to push more blood through the narrow opening, causing more problems.

SAS can be difficult to diagnose. The heart murmur, a common symptom of SAS, may be difficult to detect. The dog may also have arrhythmias. A veterinary cardiologist can diagnose SAS through either Doppler echocardiography or cardiac catheterization. The prognosis for a long, healthy life is poor, and unfortunately, there is no treatment or cure.

Hip Dysplasia

Hip dysplasia is a crippling hereditary disease. No amount of good nutrition and care will stop it. Nor can you cause it if you feed an Association of Animal Feed Control Officials (AAFCO)–formulated diet. It is caused by the malformation of the hip socket.

In mild cases of dysplasia, your vet may be able to help mitigate the effects with nutriceuticals such as glucosamine, chondroitin, and creatine and anti-inflammatories such as aspirin, Metacam, Rimadyl, Zubrin, or Deramaxx. Some cases are so bad that the dog must have surgery. In some extreme cases, the dog must be euthanized. Surgery is extremely expensive, costing thousands of dollars in most cases. If you buy a puppy, you should only buy one from a breeder who registers their dogs either through the OFA, PennHIP, or a similar registry.

Hypothyroidism

Hypothyroidism occurs when a dog's thyroid produces insufficient thyroid hormone. Symptoms can include lethargy, dull and dry coat, obesity or weight gain, and a thinning haircoat. The dog may seek warmer areas. Your vet can diagnose hypothyroidism through a blood test. If your dog has hypothyroidism, your veterinarian may prescribe a form of thyroid hormone.

The OFA provides a database for breeders to register their dogs as being free of thyroid problems. It appears that hypothyroidism can be hereditary (many breeds are predisposed to it), so it is a good idea if the parents of the puppy you intend to buy are screened for this disease.

Von Willebrand's Disease

Von Willebrand's Disease (VWD) is a type of hemophilia in dogs. There are various levels of VWD—it is more severe in some dogs than in others. There are two types of VWD: inherited and acquired. The acquired form of Von Willebrand's is associated with familial autoimmune thyroid disease. Your veterinarian can diagnose VWD through a blood test.

More than fifty breeds are affected by some form of VWD. Parents of puppies in breeds that are affected by VWD should be registered with Veterinary Genetic Services (VetGen). (Genetic testing is available for certain breeds.)

Other Hereditary Diseases

There are certainly more hereditary diseases than the ones listed here. If you are interested in learning what diseases your dog breed may have, contact the breed club or consult a breed book about your particular breed. One series worth looking at is the Your Happy Healthy Pet series published by Howell Book House.

What You Now Know...

- ➤ Hereditary diseases exist in all dog breeds and mixed breeds.
- ➤ Some of the most prevalent diseases include hip dysplasia, elbow dysplasia, epilepsy, eye diseases, hypothyroidism, heart diseases, and Von Willebrand's Disease.
- ➤ To find out more about the diseases that may affect your breed, you can contact the national breed club or consult a breed book.

Chapter 11

Crate Training and Housetraining Your Dog

What's Inside . . .

- Learn how and why to crate train your dog.
- Learn how to clean up after accidents.
- Learn how to reliably housetrain your dog.
- Learn how to solve housetraining problems.

You probably know that housetraining (or housebreaking, as it is commonly called) is important for dogs. But perhaps you don't know just how important it is. Whether your dog is a champion or just a pet, she has to be housetrained. Think about it. You can probably deal with a dog who doesn't do a perfect sit or down. But you aren't going to tolerate a dog who uses your house as her toilet.

If there is one type of training you *must* get right, it's housetraining. You aren't likely to want to put up with your house smelling like a sewer, and there will be a wedge driven between you and your dog. So commit to housetraining your dog, and your dog will become a member of your family.

Common Housetraining Misconceptions

Before you get started with housetraining, there are some misconceptions you may have heard that can hinder housetraining. Here are some questions you might have:

- *Can I paper train before I housetrain?* In a word, no. When you paper train, you teach your dog to relieve himself indoors—something that can be very confusing to a dog unless you're planning on litter box training only.
- *I heard I should hit my dog with a rolled-up newspaper or rub her nose in it. Is this something I should do?* No! This is very confusing to the dog and very cruel. She will not understand what you are doing by punishing her in this fashion.

- *I heard I could housetrain my dog in a week—can I do this?* Maybe, if you have an adult. But, if you have a puppy, it may take months until your puppy is reliable. Some puppies are unreliable until 6 months to 1 year old. It really depends on the breed as well as the individual dog.
- *I think crate training is cruel (or I've been told it's cruel). I don't want to do it.* Crate training is vital for housetraining (as you soon will see). It is not cruel. It uses a dog's basic instinct for keeping her den clean.

Crate Training 101

You may be thinking, "I can't lock my puppy up in a cage. That would be cruel." But dogs aren't humans; they think in terms of safe places and hidey-holes when they consider a place to sleep. After all, if you look at canines in the wild, you'll find that none of them sleep out in the open—all of them live in dens. A den is usually a hole in the ground that the wolf, coyote, or fox has excavated. These dens are not very big; in fact, we would consider them downright cramped. But to the wolf, coyote, or fox, it's a secure place to raise young and escape the elements without worry.

What does this den talk have to do with a puppy? Believe it or not, your puppy still has those basic instincts when it comes to what makes a suitable den. She's hardwired for it, and she instinctively knows that a cozy crate is what will keep her safe. (Many dogs like sleeping in the crates with the doors open or going to an enclosed place when something scary, like a thunderstorm, happens.) When she's properly trained in the crate, she doesn't mind the door being shut or locked.

A crate is useful for you as a pet owner because it is a place where you can put your dog when you can't watch her (until she's trustworthy and housetrained). It's a safe place for her if you have people coming and going in your house, such as a party, repairmen, or movers.

Most dogs look on their crates as their beds. I've caught a few of my dogs in their crates napping or waiting for me to close the crate when it's their bedtime. However, a few dogs positively despise crates—no doubt due to incorrect usage or never having had a safe, secure place. In this case, you may try to use an X-pen or confine the dog to a small area. Don't give up on crates easily, though. You will have a much harder time housetraining without a crate, even if you have problems crate training.

For a handy crate-training schedule, consult the "Daily Crate-Training Chart" in the appendix.

The Crate

To get started with crate training, first, you need a crate—but not just any crate will do. Get one too big, and your dog will eliminate in part of it and sleep in the other part. Get one too small, and you're likely to have a very uncomfortable pooch.

Choose a crate that is large enough for your dog to stand up, turn around, and lie down in. You'll have the crate in your bedroom, but you may want to move it to an area such as your den or living room when you're home and need to crate your dog near you. The best time to crate a dog is anytime you can't watch her—at least until she's trustworthy enough to be loose in the house. For this reason, having more than one crate—one in the bedroom and one in the kitchen, for example—might be a good idea.

Crates come in two styles: wire and travel style. A third type is made of PVC tubes and cloth mesh, but you should avoid those because they're only for dogs who are crate-trained, and they are intended for crating at obedience, agility, and other such events.

The wire type looks more like a cage than the travel type, but it allows air to circulate more freely. The plastic travel style is usually the type of crate allowed on airplanes (which is useful if you're planning on traveling with your dog). Both have advantages and disadvantages. Whichever you decide on, choose a sturdy one with a secure latch. Some escape artists have chewed or dug through crates or opened latches. A good-quality crate is worth the initial investment.

Training Your Dog to Accept the Crate

So how do you get started with crate training? Optimally, you should start putting your dog in the crate for a very short amount of time (such as five minutes) and work your way up. Unfortunately, life isn't optimal, is it? That won't work for you? What usually does happen is that you'll probably have to go to work or school, or leave the house, or—heaven forbid!—get some sleep, so you may need to slip the puppy in the crate for longer periods. She may cry, annoying your neighbors or keeping you up all night.

That doesn't work either, does it? Instead, you need to teach your dog that going into the crate and staying there is a good thing. Don't force your dog to go into the crate. Instead, toss a treat into the crate to get her to enter. After she enters the crate, give her a toy or favorite chew. If the chew isn't interesting enough, find a treat that is or use something really tempting—a piece of hot dog or cold cuts. Give her treats for going in the crate. Feed her meals in the crate. Soon, she'll be associating good things with being in the crate.

Before you put your dog in the crate for longer periods (at bedtime, when you leave for work or school, and so on), exercise your dog. Take her for a long walk, play ball with her, or go on a ten-mile hike (just kidding!). Also, make sure that she eliminates before you put her in the crate. The idea is to tire out your dog so all she wants to do is sleep. A sleepy puppy is a happy puppy and one who is not likely to fuss.

If you are leaving for a few hours, turn on a classical music or light jazz station on the radio. Dogs are great at associations, and you'll be teaching her that a particular type of music means naptime. A favorite trick of mine is to turn the TV on to the Weather Channel. Its format is repetitious, and it uses classical or light jazz. (My dogs have their own favorite weather forecasters.) Avoid TV or radio stations with news or talk shows—many have arguments, and their voices are stressed or angry. You want a calm puppy, not one who is unhappy and educated in partisan politics! One veterinarian I know recommends that her clients read a boring book into a tape recorder and then play it back while they're gone. Your voice will be soothing and will help calm your pup.

Use the same command to get your dog to go into the crate every time. I use the word "Bed" or "Go to your bed," but I've heard people use "Crate" or "Place." It doesn't really matter what you use; I just think "Bed" just sounds nicer, and it's a one-word command.

Crate Training for Older Dogs

Crate training older dogs is much like crate training puppies. Some older dogs are already crate-trained, and if yours is, you're lucky! However, some older dogs are resistant to crate training because they've never been introduced to crates before. Patience is key here, as are treats and praise. If—for any reason—you can't keep your dog from carrying on in the crate, you may have to resort to using an X-pen instead.

Housetraining 101

Housetraining, as I've said, is a very important part of your dog's training. Old, outdated training methods usually work poorly, if at all (see "Housetraining Don'ts," below) and may result in a neurotic dog who still urinates on the carpet. Instead, you need to take the right approach, using a schedule.

Housetraining a Puppy

If your dog is a puppy, it may take some time to housebreak her. Some puppies catch on fast; others do not. I've heard of some dogs taking as long as a year to be completely house-trained. I've had dogs who have taken nearly that long.

Housetraining Don'ts

- Don't rub her nose in it.
- Don't force your dog to "hold it"—take her out.
- Don't leave your dog for longer than nine hours in a crate; four hours if she is a puppy.
- Don't paper train.
- Don't restrict water, especially in hot weather.
- Don't whack her with a rolled-up newspaper.
- Don't use household cleaners to clean up accidents.
- Don't leave your dog in a large area alone.

Housetraining Do's

- Take plastic bags on walks and clean up after your dog.
- Clean up poop in your yard once a week. You can compost dog feces and use it on nonfood plants (flowers, trees, shrubs) or throw it out.
- Crate your dog when you are unable to watch her.
- Create a schedule for taking her out and stick with it.
- Praise your dog every time she eliminates outside.
- Use vinegar and water or enzymatic cleaner to clean up accidents.

When housetraining a puppy, it's important to create and stick to a good schedule. Your puppy needs to be ushered outside:

- When she first wakes up
- After meals (breakfast, lunch, dinner)
- After drinking water
- After exercising
- Before being put into a crate for longer than a few minutes
- After she comes out of the crate
- Before bedtime

This sounds like quite a bit of work, but you will have fewer accidents than if you don't follow this sort of schedule. You should keep an eye on your puppy when she's loose—and keep in mind that puppies will often sniff or circle when they're getting ready to eliminate. When you take your puppy outside, watch her and praise her for eliminating. You may want to use a command such as "Go potty!" while the dog is urinating or defecating. Then the dog learns that when you say "Go potty!" it's time to eliminate, thus teaching the dog to go on command.

But how does a crate work into all this? You need to keep your puppy in the crate when you can't watch her. Dogs naturally don't want to eliminate in a place where they lie down, so they will wait until they are out of the crate. This is why it is important to establish a routine and why you should never make a puppy younger than 6 months stay in a crate longer than four hours, except at bedtime.

When you can't watch your puppy, put her in the crate. It only takes a single moment of inattentiveness for her to piddle on the carpet behind your back. Many trainers believe that you shouldn't correct a dog for having an accident on the carpet, saying that the dog will not associate the correction with the evidence. It's been my experience that you can correct a dog for relieving herself inside, but without all the old, revolting techniques. If you catch your puppy in the act, you'll probably gasp or exclaim "No! No!" anyway. Whisk her outside and praise her when she finishes outside. Then clean up the mess with either a good enzymatic cleaner or soap, followed with white vinegar and water to eliminate the smell. (See "Cleaning Up Accidents" on page 151 for more information.)

If you find the evidence after the fact—a puddle or a pile—pick up your puppy or lead her to the pile and show it to her. In a low voice, tell her, "No! This is bad!" Don't hit your dog and don't rub her face in it. Don't yell at her. Just show her the evidence and show how displeased you are. Some trainers believe that dogs have poor memories for these things, but I've found quite the contrary. Dogs have exceptional memories for places and things; I've found that my own dogs recognize places from over a year ago.

When you show the pile or puddle, your puppy will probably become submissive when she hears your tone. Take her outside and wait until she urinates or defecates outside. (Bringing the pile outside may help your puppy associate where you want her to go.) Praise her when she goes outside. Then clean up the accident with an enzymatic cleaner or soap, followed by white vinegar and water.

I can't emphasize enough how patient you must be with your puppy. Many dogs pick up housetraining quickly, but some are more difficult. Your training methods must be consistent. Each time your puppy has an accident in your house, you will have to work harder to prevent the next accident.

Eventually, your puppy will learn to ask to go outside. But sometimes you don't pick up her signal, and she may be waiting by the door for a long time. One way to avoid this is to teach her to ring a bell to go out. (See "Teaching Your Dog to Tell You She Needs to Go Out," below.)

Housetraining an Older Dog

Housetraining an older dog is a lot like housetraining a puppy—only easier! Most older dogs are quite capable of controlling themselves and usually have some experience with housetraining already. Stick with a schedule and crate your dog when you can't watch her. Most adults can "hold it" for nine hours, but you may wish to work up from four hours at first. A few times teaching her to eliminate outside is usually all that's needed, and the dog is housetrained.

Teaching Your Dog to Tell You She Needs to Go Out

You can teach your dog to nose a bell to tell you she has to go out. It's easy to teach. Hang the bell from the doorknob, at nose height. When your dog needs to go out, make her physically nose it before you open the door. Smart dogs will learn this quickly, but even the most stubborn ones figure out this trick if you're consistent. I've actually had other dogs learn to nose the bell by watching or even hearing other dogs nose the bell to go out!

Cleaning Up Accidents

Accidents can and do occur. Before you invest in fancy cleaners and expensive carpet cleaning machines, you need to know how to stop accidents from recurring in the same place again and again. Dogs' noses are very sensitive to the smell of urine, which is mostly ammonia. That means that if you use a fancy cleaner with ammonia, you'll enhance the smell of the urine—not eliminate it. Detergents and other cleaners often hide the smell from our noses, but they won't fool a dog's nose. Her nose will tell her that she has used the spot, and she will continue to return to it.

So how do you clean up a mess? You use something that will eliminate the smell entirely. Two things that work extremely well are white vinegar and water and enzymatic cleaners. (Keep both on hand.) Vinegar helps neutralize the odor with its acidic content. Enzymatic cleaners (available at any pet supply store) will break down the urine and feces and will eliminate the odor in that way.

When your dog has an accident, clean it up using liquid soap and water and then follow that up with white vinegar and water or a professional enzymatic cleaner. If you want to use some sort of carpet or air freshener, you can. Just make sure it's not ammonia based.

If you smell an accident or if one slips by your notice, you can still find it and treat it. Several makers of enzymatic cleaners have black lights (an ordinary black light will do, too) that will fluoresce the urine when shined on the patch. You can then treat the area with enzymatic cleaner.

Litter Box Training

If you own a toy-sized or small dog and live in an apartment where it's not practical to bring her outside, you may wish to consider litter box training. You can now purchase dog litter and dog litter boxes at pet supply stores.

Litter box training is very much like housetraining, with some important exceptions. First, you will have to situate the litter box in a place where your dog can get to it and where you are unlikely to move it. Otherwise, you may find puddles beside the closed door or where the litter box used to be. Second, you will need to clean the box frequently to avoid having your home smell. Finally, instead of taking your dog outside, you will bring her to the box and praise her when she eliminates. You may be able to facilitate training by putting her feces in the box and praising her when she goes. Otherwise, you use the same training techniques and the same routine to teach her to eliminate in the box that you'd use in regular housetraining.

Does litter box training teach a dog to go indoors? Yes. So if at all possible, you should avoid litter box training. But if you have no choice, it is an option. Do not teach a dog larger than thirty pounds to use a litter box—the amount of waste makes it impractical.

Being a Good Neighbor

Whenever you walk your dog, you should bring along poop bags for cleanup. Many municipalities require that dog owners clean up after their dogs as they walk them. Some dog-friendly cities and parks actually provide poop bags along trails and sidewalks for people to use to pick up after their pets.

Cleaning up the yard is another issue. Many cities and towns require that dog owners clean up the messes in their backyards within a certain time period. This can be anywhere from one day to one week, but it's best that you clean it up to avoid "doggy land mines" from spoiling your next barbecue. Some enterprising souls have started businesses for cleaning up after pets in yards. Look for them under "Pet Services" in the Yellow Pages.

Solving Housetraining Problems

Unfortunately, dogs can and do have housetraining problems. Some are due to not really being housetrained—the dog only partially learned how to go outside. Other problems might have to do with emotional issues. Other problems are biological and require treatment by a veterinarian.

Be aware that no puppy can be considered completely reliable until she has been housetrained and has had no accidents at all for an entire month. Even then, your puppy may have relapses in her housetraining until she is fully grown—that is, about a year old. If your dog or puppy has never been completely housetrained, put her on the housetraining schedule discussed above. It's really the best way to train your dog to eliminate outside.

Is It a Health or a Behavior Problem?

Your dog has relapsed in housetraining, and you're wondering what to do. Before you start retraining her, you need to determine whether the elimination problems exist because of health reasons or because of a behavior problem. Believe it or not, many problems that appear to be behavioral are actually biological in nature. Your dog may have the following problems, which may cause her to relieve herself in the house:

- Diarrhea
- Kidney or bladder infection
- Incontinence
- Prostate problem (in males)
- Diabetes insipidus
- Cushing's disease
- Diabetes mellitus
- Kidney or bladder problems (including stones)
- Intestinal problems

Before you try retraining, have your veterinarian give your dog a thorough examination, even if you're pretty certain it's a behavioral problem. (Many a dog expert has been proven wrong by a vet's diagnosis.) Even if your veterinarian doesn't find something, keep an eye out for possible health problems, like blood in the urine (overly dark urine) or intestinal problems. Such a problem very well could've been missed in an earlier exam.

Is It Housetraining or Marking?

Once you've ruled out a health problem, the next step is to determine whether the dog is having a relapse in housetraining or whether it is a marking behavior. Marking behavior—that is, putting a dribble of urine on something as a scent mark—can be linked to dominance issues. (See "Types of Problem Behaviors" in chapter 13, "Problem Pups.")

If your dog is leaving fairly big puddles in one or more spots and is defecating indoors, she is most likely having a relapse in housetraining. That means she never really has gotten the idea when it comes to housetraining. Start housetraining her just as you would a puppy and stick with the schedule.

If your dog is urinating only and is leaving piddle on vertical surfaces, on new things, and in various places, she is marking her territory. (Female dogs mark, too, so don't think this is only a male problem!) When your dog goes into marking behavior, there's usually something to trigger it—a new house, a new dog, a new person in the house, or a female in estrus nearby can all be causes of marking behavior. You will have to work on housetraining (just as you would with a dog who has problems with housetraining) and with dominance behavior.

Is It Submissive Urination?

Some dogs may urinate when excited, frightened, or scared, and some dogs may urinate when you touch them or pet them. This behavior, known as submissive urination, is common among dogs who want to please their owners and who are not dominant in nature. By piddling a little, these dogs are trying to tell you that they accept your authority as number one. Problem is, that behavior can soil the carpet.

Dogs who do this are often worried about pleasing their owners. Loud talking, exuberant greetings, or yelling can trigger submissive urination, so it does no good to yell at your dog when she does it because she will just piddle more. As an owner of this type of dog, you should greet your dog quietly and in a nonoffensive manner. Don't pet your dog on her head or back; instead, gently stroke her along the sides or under the chin. Keep all comings and goings low-key and don't talk loudly.

You can build up your dog's confidence by working with her in obedience or agility. A submissive dog needs only positive training; negative training will cause her to piddle more. As her confidence starts building, you'll see less of the submissive urination.

What Do I Do When She Sneaks into Another Room?

One thing that stymies owners of delinquent dogs is when their dog sneaks out of the room to urinate or defecate. They're pretty sure the dog is doing it to spite them. Actually, the dog is sneaking out so that she won't be noticed when she does the deed, and she slinks because she's being submissive.

Whether or not she is spiteful is an argument that isn't very helpful. Your first step as an owner is to stop your dog from slinking away from you. One way is to tether her to you while she is out of her crate.

I first learned about tethering nearly twenty years ago with my first dog, Conan, who had a bit of a housebreaking issue. Some trainers call it "umbilical cording," but whatever the name, the theory is the same. Whenever your dog is out of the crate, she must be attached to you via a long line. Wherever you go, she goes. It forces the dog to focus on you instead of on what she wants to do.

Tethering also helps keep your dog from sneaking out of the room and doing naughty things like marking or defecating or chewing things up.

Surprisingly, most dogs like tethering—it's people who have problems with it. It takes a *long, long* time to break bad habits—usually a month or longer—so be committed to it. It *does* work, and it keeps the dog focused on you.

Housetraining a Paper-Trained Dog

If your dog is paper-trained, you'll need to teach her to go outside. This may be somewhat of a challenge, especially for dogs who expect to go in the house and look for any scrap of paper to relieve themselves on. However, with time and patience, you should be able to move your paper-trained dog to the outside.

Start right away by putting papers outside where you want your dog to go. When she relieves herself on the paper, praise her and then bring her inside. Be sure to keep all papers off the floor inside. Follow the same regimen discussed earlier, in "Housetraining a Puppy," and take her outside to relieve herself on paper.

As your dog gets used to going outside, start decreasing the size of the paper. There should be enough paper for her to go on but less and less as the days go by. As she continues to use the paper, continue to decrease its size gradually until there is no more paper left. If at any time your dog acts confused, increase the size of the paper again so that she still has a cue to use it.

Once you have decreased the size of the paper to less than a postcard size, see if your dog will go without the paper. When she does, praise her and continue to train as though she is still working on housetraining until she is consistently going outside.

Housetraining a Puppy Mill Puppy

Puppy mill puppies tend to have been kept in cages during their lives and subsequently been taught to eliminate in the cage. These dogs do not have the basic instinct to keep their dens clean anymore, so it is very difficult to teach such a puppy by using a crate.

It can be done, however, with time. You'll have to have a very shortened schedule for training a puppy who eliminates in her crate. Start by exercising her and letting her outside to urinate and defecate before putting her in her crate. Do not keep the puppy in this crate longer than two hours in the daytime. If she fusses after she's been in the crate awhile, let her out to do her business; otherwise, she may eliminate in the crate.

When you take the puppy out of the crate, take her outside immediately and praise her when she goes. If she urinates or defecates in the crate, put her outside and clean her crate up. Then clean her up. You will have to catch her before she relieves herself in the crate so she learns that when she has to go, you'll be there. Once she understands this, you can lengthen the time spent in the crate, but never do so to a point where she eliminates in the crate.

You will find this training very frustrating, but it is one of the downsides of purchasing a puppy who has spent most of her life in a cage.

What You Now Know . . .

- Crate training simulates a canine's den in the wild.
- Housetraining (housebreaking) takes time and patience.
- Most dogs will not be fully housetrained until they are 6 months of age; some dogs take as long as a year to housetrain.
- Do not paper train your dog if you can help it.
- To clean up accidents, use soap and water followed by white vinegar and water or a good enzymatic cleaner.
- Dogs can "forget" their housetraining for a number of reasons, including medical (biological) problems and poor training, or because they are marking.

Chapter 12

The Basics of Training

What's Inside...

- Learn why training your dog is best for both the dog and your family.
- Learn how to find a good trainer.
- Learn the basics of clicker training.
- Learn how to teach your dog basic obedience commands.
- Learn what the Canine Good Citizen program is and why you should train for it.

Y ou may be wondering why you should train your dog, especially if time is at a premium. After all, many people don't train their dogs.

If you've ever met an untrained dog, the reason for training should be obvious. Untrained dogs are obnoxious. They're a nuisance. And, what is more important, they're dangerous. An untrained dog is a brat with teeth, and since he has no discipline, you're running the risk of getting a dangerous reaction every time you do something the dog doesn't like. Training your dog is important not only for you and your family but for your dog. A dog who knows good house manners and who respects you as his owner will be safer around your family.

There are other bonuses, too. A well-behaved dog is a joy to own. You can often go places with a well-behaved dog where the average dog won't be allowed, and you're more likely to be invited back—such as hotels, motels, stores, and parks.

Your dog doesn't have to have obedience-title responses to commands to be well-behaved. He doesn't need to know how to fetch or catch a ball in midair (but you can teach him that, if you wish). He doesn't need to be perfect—just good enough. Many owners find that knowing how to walk nicely on leash, come when called, sit and down on command, and stay is all that a house pet needs to know.

Training Your Dog on Your Own vs. Hiring Professional Help

People are funny when it comes to training their own dogs. We expect to be experts in training dogs, but you probably call a plumber when you have a backed-up sewer pipe, buy a ticket on a commercial airline instead of fly your own plane somewhere, and have someone teach your kids in a school. Nobody expects you to be an expert in everything—that's why we pay for experts to do certain jobs. But when it comes to training dogs, people are hesitant to hire a professional.

Dog training isn't rocket science, but trying to teach you the nuances of dog training in a book is a little like teaching brain surgery through correspondence courses. I don't think either you or I would find the results entirely acceptable. If you've trained dogs before, you probably have a good idea what I'm talking about when I describe the "heel position," but you've also gone through some trial and error. You've made mistakes with earlier dogs, and either you were able to fix them before they became a problem or the dog was smart enough to compensate. Then again, maybe you didn't.

If you have the time and experience to train your dog on your own and are willing to work through the mistakes novices make, then go for it. But, if you're realistic about your time and know that you don't have the patience to study and learn the right techniques, then look for a professional trainer to teach you how to train your dog.

Yes, dog training can be expensive. But it isn't college tuition, and I'd bet that it costs less than the leather shoes your dog just chewed up. While cost is an important factor, remember that your time is also expensive. Are you willing to spend hours and hours and maybe not make much headway on training? Or goof something up that takes time to fix? With the help of a professional, in six to ten weeks you could have a dog who is pretty obedient.

Consider choosing a professional trainer if some or all of these statements fit you:

- ☐ I don't have much time to train a dog.
- ☐ I've never trained a dog successfully before.
- ☐ I need to have a dog who is reliable enough to come when I call.
- ☐ I want a pet who is enjoyable to be around.
- ☐ I am willing to spend some money to properly train my dog.
- ☐ I don't want to have to fix my mistakes later.

Finding the Right Trainer

Different dogs need different training. Some dogs are "easy"—they're quick learners and pick up on things without much effort. Other dogs are stubborn and independent—they know what you want but they just don't want to do it. Then there are the clueless ones—you're speaking a whole other language, and they can't fathom what you want. Then there are the clueless and stubborn . . .

You get the idea. A professional dog trainer will have seen all of these dogs and more. But how do you find a good dog trainer? Anyone can hang a sign up and call themselves a professional dog trainer, and you need to figure out which one to trust. Talk to your dog-owning friends, your veterinarian, and the shelter if you adopted your dog from one. (Some veterinarians and shelters offer dog training.) Talk to dog owners who compete in conformation, obedience, and agility. These people will know good trainers.

Some community colleges and pet supply stores offer pet training classes, but be careful! Bargain trainers are often no bargain, and not everyone can train certain dogs. If you need a quick puppy socialization class or basic obedience class, they'll probably be just fine, but if you have real issues with your pet, such as aggression, you should look for a trainer who is skilled in all training methods.

When looking for a professional trainer, look for one who uses primarily positive reinforcement training techniques. This means that the trainer uses food and other motivational items to teach the dog rather than using harsh corrections or punishments. Most trainers use a combination of positive and negative techniques, with an emphasis on the positive side. However, there are still some trainers who use harsh, coercive techniques in all their training. You should avoid those trainers.

Trainers should be happy to give you a tour of their facilities. Ask them what titles they have put on their dogs and what types of training they're proficient in. They should be able to show you ribbons and photos from dogs in conformation, obedience, agility, or other titles.

When you find a trainer you think you might like, ask if you can watch a class. Most trainers will be happy to have you observe their training. If a trainer doesn't want you to watch because you might "steal her secrets," look elsewhere. There are no secrets in dog training. You need to find a trainer who teaches you how to train your dog. It does no good to have a dog who obeys the trainer perfectly but will not respect and obey you.

When you look for training classes, be sure you look for the right ones. There are many different types of training classes available, including the following:

- Puppy kindergarten or KPT—Socialization and training for puppies 3 to 6 months.
- Beginner's obedience or basic obedience—For dogs who have not gone through a training class other than puppy KPT.
- Clicker training—An alternate method of training with dogs. Can be beginner to advanced.
- Attention—A class that teaches dogs to focus on their owners. Can be beginner to advanced.

As a beginning dog owner, you'll want to start your dog in beginner's obedience or puppy KPT, depending on your dog's age. Once your dog has finished beginner's obedience, you should have a dog who knows the basics and should do well enough in a home environment provided that you continue to refresh his training five to ten minutes a day. If you want to continue training your dog, you certainly may. You can go as far as you want to when it comes to training—you'll have a fun companion.

What Should Your Dog Learn in Training?

Now that you're set on training your dog, you may wonder what your dog should learn. Most dogs need to know five basic commands—"Sit," "Down," "Stay," "Come," and "Heel"—and how to walk nicely on a leash without dragging you around. No doubt, you are familiar with some or even all of these commands. You can teach them in a number of ways. As mentioned earlier, positive training methods are best. One method I especially like is a relatively new type of positive training called clicker training. I describe how to use this method and how to use more basic positive reinforcement to train your dog to obey the five basic commands and to walk nicely on a leash.

Clicker Training

Clicker training uses operant conditioning—that is, the dog learns something according to his actions. Operant conditioning is how most animals learn. Using positive operant conditioning, the animal does something you approve of and receives a reward. (Operant conditioning works with negative reinforcement as well: The animal does something and receives a punishment. But this chapter focuses on positive training.)

With clicker training, you use a little device called a clicker that looks like a box with a little metal button that you push down. That little metal button makes a loud and definite click.

Clicker training uses primarily positive reinforcement—i.e., the animal does something and receives a reward. With the clicker, you teach your dog to associate the sound of the click with a treat. When your dog does something right, you click and treat. When he performs a behavior you don't want, you ignore it. Sounds pretty simple, doesn't it?

Clicking works much the same as praise does, although instead of saying, "Good dog!" you click. Click; treat. Click; treat. It's very simple and quite effective. Your dog will associate the correct action (the one you clicked for) with the treat.

Why Clicker Training?

Why bother to use clicker training instead of some other form of positive training? This is a very good question because there are many good training methods out there that do work well with dogs.

There are several reasons you should use clicker training, but the one overriding reason is a question of timing. In training, timing is everything. You can instantly tell your dog he's done a good job with a single click before the words "Good boy!" have a chance to leave your lips. Your dog gets an instant confirmation that what he's done is correct, and there's no guesswork. The treat will come later because that's how the clicker works. The dog figures out that to get the treat, he has to perform a certain behavior. It's both fun and rewarding for the dog and the owner.

If you don't want to use a clicker, that's okay. The following section describes how to use clicker training. Then I describe how to train your dog to follow the five basic commands and walk nicely on a leash—both using clicker training and by using more basic positive reinforcement.

Teaching the Clicker

To get started with clicker training, you must have the proper tools:

- Clicker
- Target stick (a stick that you'll use to direct your dog)
- Flat collar
- Six-foot leather leash
- Training collar
- Retractable lead or tracking lead
- Treat bag
- Treats

The treats should be cut up in small portions so that you can give a lot to your dog without getting him fat, ruining his appetite, or upsetting his digestive system. Lots of people use diced up cold cuts, hot dogs, or cheese, but you can try other favorites as well. Just be sure to cut them into tiny portions because you're going to be feeding a lot of them.

The following sections describe how to get started with clicker training. When your dog has mastered these four lessons, you can move on to using the clicker method to train your dog in other commands, as described later in this chapter.

Lesson 1: Introduction to the Clicker

Here's how to teach your dog to respond to the clicker:

1. Start while your dog isn't doing anything in particular, preferably before his feeding time, when he's a little hungry. Show him the clicker. Now, click and give him a treat. If your dog is startled by the loud noise, try muffling it in your hand when you click it.
2. Again, click and give him a treat. Click; treat. Click; treat. You may have to do this for a bit, but at some point, your dog will start picking up that when he hears a click, he's going to get a treat. You should click, and he should look expectantly at you for the treat.

Sometimes it takes a while for the dog to make the association. This is okay. If, after five minutes or so, you haven't made any progress, put away the clicker and play with your dog. Try again tomorrow.

At some point, your dog is going to make the association between the click and the treat. When he does, you'll be ready for Lesson 2.

Lesson 2: Varying the Response Times

Once your dog has figured out that treats come with clicks, the next step is to vary the time between the click and the treat and where your dog receives the treat. This will teach your dog that he can expect a treat even if it's a little delayed or tossed on the ground rather than fed from your hand. Remember that your dog must first associate the click with the treat before you proceed to this next step.

Here's how to vary the response times:

1. Click the clicker and silently count to five. Your dog may look expectantly to you or even drool a bit before you give him the treat.
2. Give him the treat.
3. Click again and count to three silently and then treat him.
4. Click and silently count to ten and then treat. If your dog gets insistent or pushy, don't do anything. Just wait until he stops before you give him the treat. He must wait patiently before you give him the treat.
5. Once your dog is used to varying times, click and toss the treat in front of your dog. Your dog should eat the treat, but if he has problems, show him the treat and tell him "Good dog!" when he picks it up.
6. Click the clicker and toss the treat somewhere else once your dog has figured out that the treat doesn't have to come from your hand.

Lesson 3: Training with the Target Stick

Once your dog is used to hearing a click and receiving a treat, the fun begins! You can now start with target stick training. Target sticks are great for teaching your dog where to go or to touch certain things with his nose or paw.

Here's how to use a target stick:

1. Get out your clicker, your bags of treats, and your target stick.
2. Hold the target stick out for your dog to sniff.
3. If he touches the stick, click and treat. You may have to wiggle the stick a bit to get him interested in it. Even if he accidentally touches it, you must click and treat.

    If your dog doesn't touch the stick, you can start by shaping the behavior. *Shaping* is a fancy term for teaching the behavior you want in small increments. For example, you will click and treat when your dog looks at the stick. Every time your dog looks at the stick, you should click and treat. Then, after he looks at the stick and waits for you to click, wait and see what he does next. Your dog may stare at the stick longer or perhaps nudge or paw the stick. If he needs encouragement, wave the stick close to him, but don't touch the stick to him—instead, let your dog touch the stick. Click and treat.
4. After your dog touches the stick and subsequently hears a click and gets a treat, he may be puzzled. After all, before now, he's done nothing to get a click and treat, but now he

has to work for it. Offer the stick again and see if your dog will touch the stick (accidentally or on purpose). Click and treat when he does.

Some dogs learn touching the target stick quickly. Others take time, and you may have to have several sessions before your dog starts touching the target stick.

5. Once your dog touches the target stick consistently, start using a cue word, such as "Touch," before your dog touches the target stick.

Lesson 4: Adding Commands or Cue Words

In Lesson 3, you began using cue words when you started saying "Touch." Although we tend to call them *commands*, these words are actually *cues* for the action you want your dog to do. Your dog may already know some cue words, such as "Sit," "Down," or "Come."

Here's how to add cue words:

1. Since your dog already knows "Touch," you can begin to differentiate between touching the target stick with the nose ("Nose it") and touching it with the paw ("Paw it"). Let's start with "Paw it." Make it easy for your dog by putting the target stick close to his paw.
2. Wait for him to touch the stick with his paw. Click and treat.
3. He should start pawing the target stick. Click and treat each time.
4. Now that he's primed for pawing the target stick, say "Paw it" before your dog paws it, and then click and treat.
5. Move the stick around so your dog has to work a bit to touch it with his paw. Give him the command "Paw it" each time, and click and treat when he responds appropriately.
6. Teach your dog "Nose it" the same way you taught "Paw it," but click and treat when he noses the target stick.

Teaching Basic Obedience

When you start training your dog to do commands, remember that sometimes it's very difficult for a dog to understand what you're trying to teach him, so you need to be patient. If at any time the training is going badly, stop and have your dog do something he knows how to do. Praise him and then end your training with a play session.

You'll need your dog to either use a training collar or have his flat collar on snugly enough that he can't pull out of it. You'll also want to clip his leash to his collar so that he's with you and not doing something else, and you'll want to train in an enclosed area with few or no distractions so that your dog will focus on you and not on the neighbor's

Training Checklist

☐ Always end a training session on a positive note.

☐ Always enforce a command.

☐ Always reward good behavior.

☐ Always reward your dog for coming to you. Never punish a dog when he runs away and then comes back, or the dog will think you're punishing him for coming back.

☐ Always set your dog up for success. Think through what you are training your dog to do and what possible responses he can have. Be prepared for them.

☐ Become a person your dog will respect. Don't yell and scream when he does something wrong. Don't wheedle and cajole him to obey a command. Corrections and praise should be swift and meaningful to the dog.

☐ Before you can teach a command, you must first have your dog's attention. Always precede the command with your dog's name, such as "Buddy, come!" Don't say, "Come, Buddy!" Buddy is likely to have not heard the command before you got his attention.

☐ Choose one command and stick with it. Don't say "Buddy, down!" and then "Buddy, lie down!" the next time.

☐ Choose one-word commands that don't sound like each other. "Sit down" and "Lie down" are perfect examples of what will confuse your dog. Use "Sit" for "Sit down" and "Down" for "Lie down."

☐ Don't repeat a command, or you'll teach your dog how many times it will take before he has to do it. A caveat to this rule is that you need to teach the dog to obey a command the first time; a dog needs to hear and associate the cue word with the actual command.

☐ Don't use "Down" for "Off." "Down" should mean lie down. "Off" should mean four paws on the ground.

☐ It is easier to teach good habits than it is to undo bad ones.

☐ Never force a frightened dog to do something. You will most likely get bitten.

☐ Never get angry at your dog. If you feel yourself becoming angry at or frustrated with your dog—stop. Take a time out. Stop training. Play with your dog, take a walk, or read a book. Don't take your frustration out on your canine partner.

☐ Never give a command that you cannot enforce.

☐ Don't yell. Your dog probably isn't deaf. If he is, you'd better be teaching him with hand signals instead.

☐ Take time to play. Your dog needs some playtime with you to relieve stress and release excess energy.

☐ Teach your dog to pay attention to you. You can do so with food and the "Watch" command.

cat or the kids playing softball next door or a thousand other fun things. What you're doing is fun, too, but it needs some attention from your dog.

The following sections describe how to train a dog to walk nicely on a leash and obey the five basic commands: "Sit," "Down," "Stay," "Come," and "Heel." For each training skill, I've included both a section that describes how to teach the skill using clicker training and a section that describes how to teach it using positive reinforcement. Try them both and see which works better for you.

Walking Nicely on a Leash

It is no fun for a dog to drag you around, and in some cases, it can be dangerous. Therefore, every dog needs to learn how to walk on a leash without pulling.

Walking Nicely on a Leash: Clicker Training

To teach your dog to walk nicely on a leash using clicker training, get your clicker and treats, and then follow these steps:

1. If your dog has never been on a leash before, put a training collar on him and clip the leash to the training collar.
2. At first, your dog might whirl around you or start pulling. Ignore the bad behavior and just wait for now. When he no longer pulls, click and treat. You'll have to be patient with him and wait for him to do the right thing—that is, not pull. Continue to click and treat the dog for maintaining a loose leash. You're rewarding your dog for not tugging on the leash.
3. Once your dog is waiting for you without pulling, start walking. If he keeps his leash loose, click and treat. If he starts pulling on the leash, stop immediately and wait for him to give you a loose leash. When he does, click and treat, then start on your way again. Your dog will soon figure out that walking with a loose leash means going forward and getting clicks and treats, and that pulling means nothing fun is happening.
4. Because walking is a reward in itself, once he has learned the loose leash concept, you can fade the clicker (that is, slowly remove the clicker and treats to leave the command and the action).

Walking Nicely on a Leash: Positive Reinforcement

To teach your dog to walk nicely on a leash using positive reinforcement, have a handful of treats in your pocket and then follow these steps:

1. If your dog has never been on a leash before, put a training collar on him and clip the leash to the training collar.
2. At first, your dog may whirl around you or start pulling. Take a treat out of your pocket and use it to lure him into the proper position, so he isn't pulling on the leash.
3. Praise your dog and give him the treat when he focuses on you instead of pulling.
4. If he forges ahead or lags behind, give a gentle tug on the leash to bring him back to where you want him to be.

5. Whenever he walks nicely, tell him, "Good boy!" and give him a treat.
6. As your dog starts walking nicely, you can slowly reduce the number of treats and increase the praise.

"Sit"

"Sit" is an important command for your dog to learn. It provides some control over the dog so he's not bouncing off the walls. It also helps your dog to calm down.

"Sit": Clicker Training

Here is how you teach your dog "Sit" with the clicker:

1. Hold a treat or the target stick over your dog's nose.
2. Tell your dog "Nose it" and bring the treat or target stick backward. As he follows the treat or the target stick, his rump will start to drop.
3. When your dog's rump touches the floor, click and treat.
4. Repeat several times. Some dogs may not naturally sit. If yours won't sit or if he backs up instead of sitting, try teaching him to sit with his back to the wall so that he must sit because he doesn't have anywhere to go.
5. Once you have your dog sitting with the clicker, add the command "Sit." Tell him "Buddy, sit!" before having him sit with either the treat or the target stick.
6. Once your dog is familiar with the command, you'll need to fade the lure treat or target stick and stop telling him to nose it. Instead, substitute the command "Sit."

"Sit": Positive Reinforcement

Here is the positive reinforcement method of teaching "Sit":

1. Hold a treat just above your dog's nose.
2. Bring the treat backward while gently pushing down on his rear end and give him the command "Sit!"
3. When he sits, give him the treat and praise him.
4. Practice this several times, and your dog should sit on command. Vary between giving your dog treats and praise, and eventually fade the treats.

"Down"

"Down," like "Sit," is an important command. It can be used both for control purposes and to help calm down a dog.

"Down": Clicker Training

Here is how you teach "Down" with the clicker:

1. Have your dog sit.
2. Hold a treat or the target stick below your dog's nose.

3. Tell your dog "Nose it" and bring the treat or target stick downward toward his chest.
4. As he follows the treat or the target stick, his front legs should start to drop.
5. When his elbows touch the floor, click and treat.
6. Repeat several times.
7. Once you have your dog lying down when you use the clicker, add the command "Down." Tell him "Buddy, down!" before having him lie down with either the treat or the target stick.
8. Once your dog is familiar with the "Sit" command, you'll need to fade the lure treat or target stick and stop telling him to nose it. Instead, use only the command to "Down."

"Down": Positive Reinforcement

This is how you teach "Down" with positive reinforcement:

1. Put your dog into a sit and clip a leash to his collar.
2. Lower a treat from your dog's nose level to the floor, while gently pulling downward on the collar or leash.
3. Give him the command "Down." You can also help him by gently lowering his front legs into a down.
4. Give him a treat and praise him each time.
5. Some dogs find this command particularly threatening because it puts them in a submissive position. If your dog is one of them, try the following:
   a. Try teaching "Down" with your dog sitting next to the wall. (His rear should be touching or almost touching the wall.)
   b. Use a treat to lure him down by starting at the nose and bringing the treat down and toward his chest.
   c. Give him the command "Down!" He should lie down to get at the treat.
   d. Give him the treat and praise him for doing such a good down.

"Stay"

After "Sit" and "Down," the next command your dog should learn is "Stay." "Stay" is useful because you will sometimes want your dog to hold a sit or down for more than a few seconds.

Most trainers like to use the word "Okay!" to release a dog from a stay. It's an easy word to remember, and your dog will figure it out after only a few times. To release your dog from a stay, say in a happy voice, "Buddy, okay!" If your dog still holds the stay, a quick pat will convince him that he's done. After a couple stays, your dog will be waiting for the release word.

You can practice sit-stay and down-stay when you're watching TV or reading a book. You can slowly lengthen the amount of time *or* the distance of the stay, but not both at the same time. If your dog gets up during a stay, decrease the amount of time or distance until he stays reliably. Only increase the distance or time when he is staying reliably. If you're using the clicker, you will have to click and treat at the end of the time you expect your dog to stay. Remember that you must build up slowly to ensure success.

Note that a puppy younger than 6 months can't be expected to stay longer than a few seconds.

"Stay": Clicker Training

This is how to teach "Stay" with the clicker:

1. Have your dog sit beside you while on a leash. Do not click yet.
2. Tell him "Stay!" and hold up your open hand in front of his face for emphasis.
3. Take a step or two away and then turn to face your dog.
4. If he gets up, put him back in sit and don't click.
5. Once you are facing your dog and he has held the sit for a few seconds, click and treat.
6. Return to your dog, release him with "Okay," and click and treat.

"Stay": Positive Reinforcement

This is how to teach "Stay" using positive reinforcement:

1. Put your dog in a sit beside you while on a leash.
2. Tell him "Stay" and hold up your open hand in front of his face for emphasis.
3. Take a step or two away and then turn to face your dog.
4. If he tries to move, tell him "No! Stay!" and put him back in his position. It usually takes a few tries for the dog to learn that you want him to stay.
5. Keep him in a stay for a few seconds.
6. Return to him, release him with the "Okay" command, and praise him and give him treats.

"Come"

"Come" is a vital command for your dog to learn. Unfortunately, too many dogs don't have a reliable recall. This can be dangerous, if not deadly. A dog who won't come when you call him may be hit by a car or may take off into the wilderness. Don't let this happen!

Start by teaching your dog that good things happen when you call him. Give him a treat every time he comes to you. Always praise your dog for coming, and never call your dog to you when you correct him—always go to him.

You should train your dog to come in an enclosed area. This is very important because if your dog sees something he'd rather chase or if he is not reliable, he'll learn that he only has to come when he feels like it. If you're unable to train in an enclosed area, an alternative is to use a retractable leash or a tracking lead. Keep your dog on the tracking lead or the retractable leash when training in an area that isn't enclosed.

"Come": Clicker Training

This is how to teach your dog "Come" using the clicker:

1. Let your dog loose in an enclosed area (or have him on a retractable leash). Most dogs, when they know you have the clicker, will come right to you. If yours does, click and treat.

2. If your dog doesn't come to you while he's loose, try showing him the treat, then click and treat when he comes.

3. As he comes to you, start using the command "Come." You can pair it with your dog's name, such as "Max, come!" and click and treat when he does.

4. Once your dog comes reliably, put a leash on him and put him in a sit-stay.

5. Walk out to the end of his leash. Be careful that he doesn't break his stay in his enthusiasm to come to you. If he does, put him back in his sit-stay.

6. Give him the "Come" command again. Click and treat when he comes.

7. Practice "Come" at short distances.

8. Gradually lengthen the distance with a long-line or a retractable leash. When you call your dog in, either retract the leash or quickly reel in the long-line. If at any time your dog fails to come directly to you, return to shorter distances.

"Come": Positive Reinforcement

To teach your dog "Come" by using positive reinforcement, do the following:

1. Clip a six-foot leash onto your dog's collar.

2. Put him in a sit-stay and walk out to the length of the leash.

3. Hold a treat in one hand and call your dog: "Buddy, come!"

4. If he does not come, show him the treat and gently reel him in.

5. When he arrives, give him the treat and praise him. Practice this several times each day.

6. Once your dog is reliably coming on a short lead, lengthen the distance. For this you need a long-line or retractable lead. Follow the same procedure as for using the six-foot leash. If your dog doesn't come immediately, reel him in and shorten the distance next time. Always give him a treat, regardless of whether you have to reel him in or he comes directly. But if he doesn't come directly, shorten the distance next time.

"Heel"

The correct position for your dog to heel is beside you, on your left side, with the dog facing forward. This is known as the *heel position*. When you walk your dog, you should be holding the leash loosely in your left hand to control the dog, with any excess length of leash looped in the right hand. This will give you the maximum control over a dog—even a large, strong dog.

"Heel": Clicker Training

To teach your dog to heel by using clicker training, follow these steps:

1. Have your dog on a leash but let him move about freely.

2. As he approaches your left side, click and treat.

3. Your dog may be surprised by your click and treat, but he will try to repeat the performance. As he does, click and treat and shape the behavior until he is standing at your side.

4. When he stands or sits for a few moments in the heel position, click and treat. Use a one-word cue such as "Place" or "Heel" to mean the heel position. Practice putting your dog in the heel position and click and treat when he stands or sits straight in that position.

5. Once your dog knows the heel position, you can teach him to heel while you're both moving. Your dog should be sitting in the heel position with his training collar and leash on. Have a treat in your left hand. Say "Buddy, heel!" and start walking, putting your left foot forward first.

6. If your dog starts to forge ahead or lag behind, get his attention by showing him the treat and luring him into the correct position. Click and treat when he is in the correct position.

7. If he lags because he is unsure of what to do, pat your leg and encourage him to get beside you. If he forges ahead, stop and wait for him to stop pulling and go back to the heel position. When he does, click and treat. When you stop, have him sit in the heel position and click and treat.

8. When you start again, always start by moving the left foot forward first. Your dog will see the left leg movement before the right. Also, it becomes another signal to your dog that he is to move with you.

"Heel": Positive Reinforcement

To teach your dog to heel by using positive reinforcement, follow these steps:

1. Clip a leash on your dog's collar. Move your dog to your left side.

2. When he stands or sits for a few moments in the heel position, give him a treat, and praise him.

3. Use a one-word command such as "Place" or "Heel" to mean the heel position. Practice putting your dog in the heel position and rewarding him when he stands or sits straight in that position. Do not reward sloppily performed commands. Instead, try again and give your dog the treat when he is in the proper position.

4. Once your dog knows the heel position, you can teach him to heel while you're both moving. Your dog should be sitting in heel position with a training collar and leash on. Have a treat in your left hand. Say "Buddy, heel!" and start walking, left foot forward.

5. If your dog starts to forge ahead or lag behind, get his attention by showing him the treat and luring him into the correct position.

6. When he is in the correct position, praise him and give him a treat. If he lags because he is unsure, pat your leg and encourage him to get beside you. If he forges ahead, pull him back using the leash or have him focus on the treat and lure him back.

7. When you stop, have him sit in the heel position and give him a treat. When you start again, always start with the left foot forward. Your dog will see the left leg movement before the right leg moves. Also, it becomes another signal to your dog that he is to move with you.

The Canine Good Citizen Program

In 1989, the AKC recognized the need to show that dogs can have good manners and be well socialized. This was partially due to the increasing number of dog bites and attempts at breed legislation. The AKC developed the Canine Good Citizen program. Unlike other AKC titles, the Canine Good Citizen is available to all dogs, purebred or mixed breed, at any age, spayed, neutered, or intact. (For more information on the Canine Good Citizen test, see the AKC Web site, at www.akc.org.)

What the Canine Good Citizen Program Involves

What exactly is the Canine Good Citizen program, and why is it of interest to pet owners? It is a series of tests where the judge gives a pass or fail to the dog. It shows the world that you have a dog whom you're proud to have as a companion. Because your dog earns a title and certificate, you've proven yourself a conscientious dog owner. It might not get you into the local bistro with your dog, but you'd be surprised where you can go when you have a Canine Good Citizen on your pet. I've taken my Canine Good Citizen dogs to special events inside malls, to book signings, and to people's houses. People have bought expensive bottled water for my dog because she was so well-behaved.

I can't say you'll have the same experience, but most people who have well-behaved dogs leave people with favorable impressions. Your dog must pass the following tests to earn his CGC:

- **Accepting a friendly stranger:** The dog must show no fear when someone strange approaches the dog's owner and talks to him or her.
- **Sitting politely for petting:** The dog must accept petting by a stranger when the dog is with his owner.
- **Appearance and grooming:** The dog must accept being brushed gently by the evaluator and allow the evaluator to examine the dog's ears and to pick up each foot. The dog is also judged on whether he is clean and groomed.
- **Walking on a loose lead:** The dog must walk on a loose lead and walk with the handler including turns and stops.
- **Walking through a crowd:** The dog must walk through a crowd of people without pulling, jumping on people, or acting fearful.
- **Sit and down on command and staying in place:** The dog must sit and lie down on command. The dog must then stay in place while the owner walks twenty feet away and returns to the dog. The dog may change position, but must stay in the same place.
- **Coming when called:** The dog must wait while the owner walks ten feet and then calls the dog. The dog must come to the owner.
- **Reaction to another dog:** The dog must show no more than a casual interest in another dog as that dog and his handler approach the first dog and his owner.
- **Reaction to distraction:** The dog must show no fear when faced with two everyday distractions. The dog may show curiosity, but not aggression or shyness.
- **Supervised separation:** The dog must accept being left with the evaluator for three minutes while the owner is out of sight.

How to Train for the Canine Good Citizen Test

As you can see from the list above, the Canine Good Citizen test is a basic temperament and obedience test. Your dog should learn the basic obedience commands, as described earlier in this chapter. Usually a good obedience class will help your dog prepare for the obedience portion and some of the socialization portion of the test. In obedience, your dog will be able to encounter other dogs and people in a controlled environment.

You can prepare for the temperament test portion by socializing your dog. Socialization starts when your dog is a puppy. Your puppy is ready for meeting the world after he has had his last series of vaccinations—usually after 16 weeks. If you have adopted your dog as an adult, you can still socialize him. You'll need to make an extra effort to catch up for lost time. Bring your dog to different places and allow him to greet strangers. Training classes, fun matches, and dog parks are a great way to socialize your dog.

If your friends are dog people, have them join you for a walk at a park or another public place where your dog is allowed. Make the experience a positive one for your dog. Your friend may bring dog cookies or other treats. If, at any time, your dog becomes fearful or shy, reduce the contact a bit until he becomes comfortable. For example, if your dog is shy when your friends or strangers try to pet him, don't insist on it. Instead, walk your dog on leash with your friends nearby or have just one person pet your dog.

What You Now Know . . .

- ➤ Training is good—and fun—for both you and your dog.
- ➤ It's a good idea to find a trainer in your area to help you train your dog.
- ➤ You can train either using the clicker method or positive reinforcement.
- ➤ It's important for every dog to know at least the five basic commands—"Sit," "Down," "Stay," "Come," and "Heel"—and how to walk nicely on a leash without dragging you around.
- ➤ Passing the Canine Good Citizen test is a way to prove you have a well-socialized dog.

Chapter 13

Problem Pups

What's Inside...

🦴 Learn how to prevent problem behaviors before they start.

🦴 Learn to recognize a problem behavior in its early stages and correct it.

🦴 Learn about typical dog behavior problems and how to correct them.

🦴 Learn what your options are if you can't correct problem behaviors in your dog.

You know the phrase "the wolf at the door"? The truth is that when you bring a dog into the house, you've brought the wolf into your house and made her part of your family. No, the dog isn't a wolf, per se, but the wolf is the dog's ancestor, and the dog has inherited behaviors from the wolf that 20,000 or 125,000 years of domestication (depending on which experts you listen to) can't change.

In our zeal to make dogs domesticated, we sometimes forget that they are dogs. Domestication has caused *neoteny*, which is a fancy word that means retaining juvenile traits. These juvenile traits enable a dog to look to us as part of her pack and to look for someone to lead her, thus forming the bond that dogs are so famous for. But you must always remember that dogs are, in essence, juvenile wolves. That means that while you can train a dog to do things and be a very civilized animal, there are underlying traits in the dog that will surface if they are not managed appropriately. Many of these traits, such as aggression, destructive behavior, and digging, are intrinsic to the dog. Through training, the dog learns to curb these instinctive behaviors and substitute behaviors we find acceptable.

A dog will naturally exhibit behaviors you don't want, and if you're not willing to correct them or provide acceptable ones in their place, the dog will show those unacceptable behaviors over and over, especially if doing so gets the dog the kind of response she's looking for. Your job as a dog owner is to prevent those misbehaviors from occurring or to recognize when they're starting and halt them in their tracks.

How to Recognize a Problem Behavior

Many problems start rather innocently, and most dog owners are unaware that certain behaviors can lead to problem behavior. Maybe your dog growls when your kid walks by her while she is eating. Or maybe she's forgotten her potty manners in the house a time or two. Maybe when you leave some chicken wings out, your dog filches them. Or maybe you've caught her up on the couch. Or maybe someone left the gate open once, and now your dog is digging around the fence.

You might explain this behavior away ("She was protecting her food" or "She loves chicken"), or you might ignore it and hope it was a one-time deal. Maybe it wasn't that big of a problem ("I can clean that up" or "I really don't care if she sleeps there"), but it is a problem that can get out of hand quickly. Soon, the problem becomes big ("She's always having accidents in the house" or "She snapped at me"). Before you know it, you have a problem dog.

The easiest way to correct a bad behavior is to prevent it entirely. That means stopping a bad behavior before it starts. Look at what entices your dog: food on the counter, a weak fence, a trash bin left out, etc. If you take away the things that tempt your dog, you won't give her an opportunity to behave badly. After all, your dog can't raid the garbage if she can't get to it. Nor can she annoy the neighbors with her barking if she's inside at night or during the daytime when you're gone.

Is Problem Behavior a Biological Problem?

Before you enroll your dog in a class for doggy delinquents, make sure that the behavior isn't being caused by a biological problem. Arthritis and joint problems can make anyone crabby; certain diseases, such as Cushing's, can cause a dog to become ravenous and bossy about food. Hypothyroidism (among other conditions) can cause aggression in dogs; urinary tract infections can cause incontinence. Whenever a behavior changes, take your dog to the vet.

If a problem appears out of nowhere—or even if it doesn't—take your dog for a thorough health check. Talk with your veterinarian about the problem and see if he or she can find a root cause for the bad behavior. Your veterinarian may or may not be able to find a cause. Even if your vet rules out a biological component, keep it in mind in case the condition is subtle and your vet may have missed it.

I've had many "problem dogs" whose problem was actually biological in nature. I recommend that if you see a potential problem, you should look for an underlying condition. While there *are* naughty dogs who simply need good training, look first for medical problems.

Don't Take It Personally

If you own a dog who has a problem, you may be tempted to take your dog's actions personally. "Look what she's done!" you might say. "She knows not to do that!" Or you might say, "She's being spiteful." As pet owners, we're tempted to anthropomorphize our pets. But dogs aren't little people in fur suits.

You may be surprised to learn that dogs don't feel guilt, and (contrary to what you may think after she's peed in your shoes), they don't feel spite. Dogs who do the wrong things may know you are displeased with them when they do something, but something is rewarding them for doing it. They don't feel guilt in the way you or I do; when you yell at your dog, you may see her crouching and slinking away, but that's not guilt—it's submissiveness because you're using an angry tone. Your dog will still pee in your shoes, but she will become submissive when you're angry.

So, the first thing to do is to realize that you're not dealing with a human. Your dog is peeing in your shoes not because you haven't taken her for a walk and she's mad at you, but because the shoes smell of her urine and she is marking those shoes as her territory. It's your job to put those shoes someplace she can't get at them and start figuring out why she's marking in your house. (Marking is usually a sign of dominance aggression.)

No Quick Fixes

Many people who have problem dogs look for quick fixes. If you're one of those people, I have bad news for you: There are no quick fixes for bad behavior. Yes, you can do something that will stop the behavior while you retrain your dog, but in reality, your dog has probably had a long time to develop this bad habit, and it isn't going to go away overnight.

If the behavior is truly dangerous or obnoxious, you should consult a dog behaviorist as soon as possible to get recommendations about what you need to do to correct it. In chapter 7, "Educating Your Whole Family," I've given you rules about how you and your family should interact with your dog. If you haven't begun following them, do so now! It will help with problems such as dominance aggression and other issues you may be accidentally causing without knowing it.

A few things help curb problem behavior. One is spaying or neutering. If your dog isn't spayed or neutered, have it done now. Second, getting your dog involved in some sort of dog sport or other activity works well. Walking and playing with your dog isn't enough; you've got to focus your dog's attention on something that is challenging and make her a partner with you. By improving the bond, you improve your dog's focus on you and make her more apt to listen to you. She will also be tired out, and a tired dog is a happy dog and one less prone to mischief.

Finding a Behaviorist

You may be wondering whom to turn to when looking for a dog behaviorist. Ask your trainer or vet for a recommendation. If you still can't find one, try contacting the closest veterinary college, or you can look for a specialized trainer with the Association of Pet Dog Trainers, at www.apdt.com.

Types of Problem Behaviors

Aggression

Aggression is a serious problem that you should not ignore. Aggression has various causes, and once you understand your dog's aggression, you can work to correct it. I'm not talking about an occasional growl or a dog fight between your and someone else's pet where the play turned nasty. I'm talking aggression—where the dog is constantly aggressive toward other dogs or people.

Some types of aggression have biological causes. Pain, hypothyroidism, seizures, and other medical conditions can cause a dog to show aggression. Some deadly diseases, such as rabies, can cause aggression. If your dog shows aggression, you should first take her to a veterinarian to determine if the condition is medical. If it isn't, you should take your dog to an experienced trainer or animal behaviorist who has had success in working with aggressive dogs.

Aggression is serious business, especially if you have kids. As I've said in earlier chapters, kids are often the ones who suffer from dog bites. Even if you don't have kids, aggression is still a serious problem. In this litigious society, an aggressive dog is a liability. If you own a dog who has an aggression problem, you must correct it. Otherwise, your dog may injure or even kill a person or another dog. Aggressions such as pain aggression or fear aggression are understandable, and the behavior clearly occurs when the dog is under duress, but you should do all you can to avoid having your dog bite anyone.

Here are some of the types of aggression you may see in dogs:

- **Prey aggression:** With prey aggression, which is seen in a number of breeds, the dog mistakes another animal as a prey item (dinner on the run) and chases it. The dog will usually not back down, because she sees the object of the aggression as food. This behavior has been modified in herding dogs where the dog exhibits all the behaviors of prey aggression but doesn't attack the animal.
- **Dominance aggression:** In dominance aggression, the dog shows aggression because she thinks that a person or an animal has overstepped his or her authority. The dog may not back down with this aggression.

- **Fear aggression:** With fear aggression (also known as fear biting), the dog is frightened by something and is trying to get away. Usually, after a few quick snaps or a bite, the dog retreats.
- **Pain aggression:** When a dog is in pain, she might bite out of pain aggression. As with fear aggression, usually, after a few quick bites, the dog retreats.
- **Guarding or territorial aggression:** With territorial aggression, the dog is trying to prevent someone from taking away something of hers or entering her territory. The dog usually doesn't pursue the intruder once the intruder leaves.
- **Frustration or redirected aggression:** Sometimes a dog bites because of frustration or because she can't get at something her aggression is focused on. The dog may snap or bite once or twice if it's a case of frustration. Redirected aggression can take the form of any of the other aggressions the dog is trying to display.
- **Sexual aggression:** When a dog suffers from sexual frustration, he or she is competing for mating. Once the suitor is driven off, the dog isn't concerned with that other dog.
- **Idiopathic aggression:** Idiopathic aggression, which is often manifested as a seizure-like aggression, is usually biological and has no apparent triggers. The dog attacks without any provocation or signal. The dog may give a quick growl and snap all the way to a full-on attack, and she appears to be unaware that she is doing it at all.

Some dogs show a mixture of these aggressions. For example, a dog showing dominance aggression may also show guarding and prey aggressions.

The best way to stop aggressive tendencies is to give the dog proper training and socialization. Spaying and neutering will help reduce hormone-caused aggression due to sexual urges and dominance behavior, which can show up as several types of aggression but often are seen in sexual aggression and dominance aggression. Teaching your dog to "Trade" for items and teaching her that she mustn't guard her toys or food will help eliminate guarding aggression. It's important to keep your dog away from other aggressive dogs to prevent her from learning to be aggressive toward other dogs.

If your dog is aggressive, immediately seek a professional trainer who is an expert in canine aggression to evaluate and retrain your dog.

Chewing

All dogs love to chew. It's natural for them. But when they chew the wrong things, there's a problem. If your dog is chewing inappropriate items—shoes, purses, furniture—think about when your dog is chewing them. Did you leave her alone at home loose and able to chew up any item she cares to? Is she sneaking into another room while you're in the kitchen? Once you pinpoint when and why the behavior occurs, you can work on a solution.

If your dog is normally an angel and has turned into a chewing fiend, you may wish to have your vet examine her. Tooth, mouth, and digestive problems can all cause excessive chewing. Puppies who are teething will also chew until their puppy teeth fall out and their permanent teeth come in. Sometimes a puppy tooth will not fall out and will become inflamed, causing pain. (Your vet may have to extract it.)

If you've determined that the chewing behavior is not related to biological problems, your next step is to stop the chewing. That means that any time you can't watch your dog, she needs to be in her crate. That includes when you're out of the house or asleep. You can't expect to give your dog full run of the house unsupervised. It's like inviting a group of teens to your home and having a tapped keg of beer: an invitation for disaster. Don't put your dog in situations where she's tempted to chew and otherwise destroy inappropriate items.

But suppose she sneaks off to chew things? Try tethering her to you (see chapter 11, "Crate Training and Housetraining Your Dog"). She'll be forced to follow you around and pay attention to you—and won't be able to sneak off and chew something without your knowledge. While she is sitting around, give her something appropriate to chew. If she chews something inappropriate, offer to "Trade" with an appropriate item. Correct her with a "No!" and give her the acceptable item to chew instead. Putting things that your dog likes to chew out of reach is another option, as is making the items less palatable. You can use bitter agents, such as bitter apple spray, on inappropriate items that your dog normally chews.

How long does it take before your dog becomes completely reliable? Some relearn their behavior in a month or two, but many take longer. Some can never be trustworthy or may be trustworthy only while you're around. But by preventing the destructive behavior or eliminating the temptation, you should be able to reduce the amount of destructiveness.

Raiding

Some dogs love raiding counters, tables, and trash for edible tidbits. Some are sneaky and some are brash, but regardless of the method, raiding is a tough habit to break. If your dog gets away with it once, all the scolding in the world won't matter because your dog has hit the jackpot.

Start by assessing what you keep on your counters and where you keep your trash. Keep the trash behind closed doors where your dog can't get to it and keep food in cabinets with childproof latches (available at any hardware store). If your dog has learned to open the refrigerator (don't laugh—some dogs are quite capable!), you can purchase a childproof strap for it.

Keep your food out of your dog's reach. Many people find their conventional and microwave ovens a safe haven for dinner plates. If you have a confirmed counter raider

and have to have a lot of food out (for a party, for example), you should crate your dog so she can't get into trouble. You can also purchase static mats to help train your dog to stay off the counters while you aren't watching. These give a mild, unpleasant shock similar to what you get when you shuffle your feet across a carpet and touch metal. (I've shocked myself with them, so I know.) These mats are useful for keeping a determined dog off counters when you can't watch her.

Pennies in a Pop Can and the Squirt Bottle Method

One method for correcting a dog is to get several empty, clean soda pop cans, put a few pennies in each of them, and crumple them enough so the pennies don't come out. When shaken or thrown, they make a loud, unpleasant rattling sound most dogs don't like.

When you catch your dog doing something bad, toss a pop can in her direction (but do not hit her!). Don't let her see where it comes from. The more secretive, the better, so that the dog associates the correction with someplace above and not with you. You may need to toss several cans to make your point before you have to pick them up, so the more you have available, the more effective this trick is.

Another thing you can try is the squirt bottle method. Fill a clean squirt bottle with water, and when you catch your dog, squirt her with the water (on her rear end). Most dogs hate this and quickly stop what they're doing when it happens.

Digging

Digging is natural for many dogs, including those with terrier and northern breed backgrounds. Dogs dig for a number of reasons: to bury things, to unbury things, to dig cooling holes and dens, and for the sheer pleasure of digging. It's a tough habit to break.

Most dogs hate digging where their feces are buried, so backfilling the holes with your dog's feces and covering them with a layer of dirt will stop her from digging in those places. If your dog digs when you're not at home, you may have to keep her inside or put her in a dig-proof kennel run. If she digs when you're home, you can try the pennies in a pop can method or squirt bottle method (described in "Pennies in a Pop Can and the Squirt Bottle Method," above).

You may be able to train your dog to dig in one place by rewarding and praising her when she digs in the right place and correcting her when she digs in an inappropriate place.

Excessive Barking

Most dogs bark. Some dogs emit other vocalizations in lieu of barking, but most make some sort of noise. Dogs bark for a variety of reasons. Or they bark for no reason. In any case, too much barking will get you in trouble with your neighbors, as well as the local animal control and local ordinances.

Dogs are often encouraged to bark from the beginning. The dog sees someone down the street and barks. Her owner says, "Oh what a good dog!" and Princess gets rewarded. Or maybe, the owner doesn't praise her, but the person sees Princess and acts fearful. Princess thinks, "I'm big and tough now—I'll bark!" Either way, the barking is reinforced.

Princess quickly becomes an idiot barker. She barks at squirrels. She barks at leaves blowing in the wind. She barks at the moon. You've seen Princess, haven't you? She just likes barking. She's like someone who talks too much—they like hearing the sound of their own voice.

Whether you were the cause of your dog's barking or not, how do you shut her up? First of all, you shouldn't leave her outside all day while you're gone or all night while you sleep. (And trust me, owners of big-mouth dogs can sleep through anything, including dogs' barking!) Keep her inside. Your neighbors will thank you.

But suppose your dog is barking indoors or barking outside when you're home? Try the pennies in a pop can method. You can also use a squirt gun or squirt bottle. Get one of those super soaker toys if your dog is large or if your yard is big. A blast from a squirt gun usually silences a dog.

What if your dog barks or whines inside and you have an apartment? You can purchase a citronella collar that is activated by barking. In the collar is a tiny canister of citronella that sprays under the chin when the dog barks. Citronella is a strong scent, and most dogs hate it. A couple of whiffs, and your dog will associate barking with getting sprayed by citronella under the chin.

What about shock collars for barking? Don't use them. Think of how it would feel being shocked on the neck every time you spoke. Some shock collars can actually pierce and burn the dog's neck—very unpleasant, to say the least. If you're forced into considering these collars, consult with a professional trainer or behaviorist who can make recommendations or even supervise retraining.

Fear of Thunder or Other Loud Noises

Dogs who are afraid of thunder may have been encouraged by their former owners through coddling ("oh, poor thing!") or may simply be afraid. Although not a scientific observation, I've noticed that most dogs who are afraid of thunder or other loud noises are born this way, and the problem actually becomes worse with age. Again, though it's not a scientific fact, I've observed that shepherds and shepherd mixes seem to have an especially bad time with thunder.

You won't be able to easily correct this problem through training or desensitization. The best thing is to crate your dog during thunderstorms or around times when there are fireworks, such as the Fourth of July and New Year's Eve. Provide a safe environment for your dog, where she can't accidentally hurt herself or escape. Some medications are available through your veterinarian that might help lessen her panic.

Getting on Furniture

If you're a person who doesn't want your dog on the furniture, you should train her to stay off the furniture and enforce this rule all the time. This will require your dog to be crated when you're not home. If there's a particular piece of furniture your dog constantly climbs on, consider using an electronic static mat (you'll have to remove it for guests, or they may get a nasty surprise).

You can also use passive mats, made of hard plastic with bumps (similar to office mats for people to roll their chairs across). You can get an office mat and cut it to fit your couch, turning the bumps upward to make an unpleasant surface for the dog.

You can also keep an eye on your dog, and if she tries to get up on a couch, toss a pop can with pennies in it to surprise her off the couch.

Houdini Dogs

More clever than the average house dog, a Houdini dog finds challenge in steel bars and diabolical fences. If you watch a Houdini dog at work, you'll actually see her study the layout of the pen or fence to see if there is some way she can outwit it.

These clever canines are made, not born, but there appears to be a tendency in certain breeds to escape. Usually clever hound mixes, like Basenjis, and northern breeds, such as Samoyed and Siberian mixes, will be more inclined to escape-artist behavior, but any dog is capable. Owners create Houdini dogs by giving them inferior barriers. The dog figures out how to get out, and the owner puts up a slightly stronger barrier. The dog soon learns that with a little extra effort, she can get out.

How do you stop a Houdini dog? Well, if yours is just starting, you're in luck! Put up fencing that she can't dig under, climb over, or jump over. Keep her crated inside when you're gone. You can stop the Houdini in her tracks.

But what if your dog is a practiced adult Houdini? Think warfare: How is she going to break out of this? Look at your fence and your yard. You may have to build a special kennel with a top so your dog can't climb out. You may have to clip the latch so she can't undo it. You must watch an adult Houdini constantly. Otherwise, she'll be rewarded with her escape. Eventually, once she learns she can't escape, she might give up.

Regardless of which type of Houdini you have, exercise (both mental and physical) will go a long way in preventing escapes. Bored dogs become Houdinis; tired dogs have no energy to escape.

Jumping Up

Your dog may be enthusiastic when she greets you, but not everyone likes being jumped up on and kissed. There are times when jumping up isn't appropriate: when you have guests over, when you're wearing good clothes, or when there are children whom your dog can accidentally knock down.

An old trick was to put your knee up when a dog jumped. The problem with this tactic is that quite often the dog would simply bounce off and jump again. A better solution is to teach your dog to sit when she is greeting people. When your dog jumps up, tell her, "No! Off!" and put her feet on the ground. ("Off" is the command for four paws on the ground, remember?) Then tell her to sit. Don't pet her until she sits. Then, praise her quietly: "Good dog, what a good dog." If she jumps up, stop petting and put her in a sit.

If you stay consistent with this training, she will eventually learn that to receive a petting, she must sit nicely for people.

Separation Anxiety

Some dogs become frantic with their owners' leaving and turn to destructive behavior and whining when their owners leave. Sometimes the owner causes this behavior by making a big deal out of leaving the house. The owner returns to find the dog upset and coddles her when she returns. ("Did you miss Mommy?")

Part of the destructive behavior might be due to boredom and opportunity. You're gone, and you've just left your entire home as your dog's playground. Crate her when you leave, and don't make a big deal out of leaving or returning. This will help some forms of separation anxiety.

However, like fear of thunder and other loud noises, separation anxiety can be ingrained. First, crate your dog to be sure she can't be destructive while you're gone. If she whines or cries, a citronella bark collar may help curb her barking. (See "Excessive Barking," earlier in this chapter.) In some instances, your veterinarian may be able to help your dog's anxiety with certain medications.

What If It Doesn't Work Out? Options for Dog Owners

You and your dog aren't working out. In fact, you're not seeing eye-to-eye on anything. You're at wit's end. You're about ready to get rid of the dog.

First, stop and take a deep breath. Figure out what the dog is doing that has brought you to these desperate measures:

- If the dog is dangerous—that is, aggressive toward people and genuinely dangerous—have a veterinarian evaluate her. After that, have a behaviorist evaluate her to see if she can be retrained. If you're scared that the dog is putting you or your family in danger, euthanize the dog. This sounds harsh, but it may be necessary. No matter what you've done or haven't done, if the dog is a danger to your family, you shouldn't own her. And you shouldn't hand the dog off to other people who may become seriously injured.
- If the dog is doing something intolerable, such as chewing or house-soiling (and the root of the problem is not a biological problem), try

the methods described in this chapter for changing the behavior and seek a dog behaviorist who can help you retrain your dog.

- If your dog can't be retrained easily (few cannot), keep a level of control over the dog so that she can't exhibit the behavior. Crate her when you can't watch her or tether her (see chapter 11), keep her inside during the day so she can't bark, and so on.
- If you haven't yet taken your dog to obedience classes, do so. This will help strengthen your bond and will focus your dog on you. A lot of problems occur because of the lack of a bond.
- Exercise your dog! Give your dog a job to do. Most dogs are badly behaved out of boredom.
- Your are your dog's last hope. Train her and give her every chance to be the dog you want her to be.

The truth is, there aren't too many options when it comes to rehoming your pet. If she's badly behaved with you, she is most likely to be badly behaved with other people. She may end up being handed off from home to home until someone dumps her in a shelter. Unless the problem is biological, chances are the problem was caused by lack of training or by permissiveness. Unless you can figure out what you did wrong, you may very well have the same problem with the next dog.

If, for any reason, you need to place your dog in another home and you got her from a breeder, contact her breeder first. A reputable breeder should take the dog back under any circumstances. If the breeder doesn't take back the dog or if you've lost contact with the breeder, the next step is to contact breed rescue. Be aware that breed rescues are often run by volunteers and often do not have enough foster homes for pets, so you may have to keep your dog while they find a suitable place. Talk to your vet, who might be able to help you find a home for your dog. Some vets can place dogs.

Be cautious about placing your dog with someone you don't know. Some unscrupulous people look for free pets to sell to research or for dog fighting. Put a price tag on your dog to deter those who would be looking for free pets for nefarious purposes.

The last place to take a dog might be a shelter, but be aware that once you take a dog to the shelter, she may be put down right away. Don't kid yourself and think that your dog will find the perfect home. More likely in overcrowded shelters, she will die alone and frightened in a strange place. If at all possible, try to work out the problems you have before resorting to a shelter. Shelters are not necessarily bad places, but they should be the last place for your dog when you think you have no other options.

Finally, never dump a dog. That includes in the country because your dog is likely to die of starvation, get shot by a rancher or farmer for attacking farm animals or wildlife, or be killed by predators. In the city, dogs who are dumped end up posing a threat to people and other animals and live a terrible existence, eating out of trash cans and killing people's pets. Bring your dog to a shelter before you do that!

What You Now Know...

- ━ Bad behavior doesn't happen overnight. It usually occurs because of permissiveness and lack of training, with the pet owner allowing the behavior to worsen until it becomes intolerable.

- ━ You should always have your dog's health checked by a vet when she is displaying a behavior problem. Many medical conditions can lead to bad behavior.

- ━ There are no quick fixes for bad behavior. If you're committed to your dog, you're going to have to work through the behavior.

- ━ Train your dog to be the dog you want her to be; don't hand her off for someone else to try to retrain. Otherwise, your dog will likely go from owner to owner until she is dumped in a shelter.

Chapter 14

Teaching Tricks

What's Inside...

🦴 Learn how trick training will help you bond with your dog.

🦴 Learn how to make up new tricks.

🦴 Teach your dog fun tricks to impress your friends.

Trick training is more than just fun and frivolity. It's a great way for you and your kids to interact with and bond with your dog. Obedience is great, but if you *really* want to impress people with how smart your dog is (and we both know he's the smartest), show them a few tricks. It isn't a surprise that the talk-show host David Letterman has "stupid pet tricks"—people love to see dogs perform even frivolous tricks.

How does this help you bond with your dog? Spending time with your dog and working with him builds a greater bond than just cuddling and petting. Dogs are working animals—like people, they need a job to do, or they get bored. And when they get bored, they usually decide to do things that are natural to them—usually chewing and other destructive behavior. So give your dog a job by teaching tricks—and have fun with it.

This chapter explains how to teach several easy tricks to your dog by using a clicker or positive reinforcement (see chapter 12, "The Basics of Training," for more info on these training methods). Teaching tricks is where clicker training is especially fun and easy to use.

Deciding What Tricks to Teach

What kind of tricks do you want to teach your dog? You're limited only by your imagination and what you can teach him. Before trying to teach your dog a trick, first decide if it's something your dog can do. For example, you may be trying to teach your dog something he can't do because of his health. Arthritis and joint problems might be an issue, for example. Next, consider whether it's a good idea to teach your dog this trick. Teaching your dog to dial the phone may not be a good idea, nor would getting items from the refrigerator! Think the trick through, and think about whether your dog will take it to a level you don't want.

Creating Your Own Tricks

Creating your own tricks is limited only by your imagination and your dog's ability to do the trick. Some tricks are easy for a dog to learn. The best way to teach an easy trick is to click and treat when you see your dog do the behavior, such as clicking and treating to teach your dog to bark on command. But if you're trying to teach something that's not a normal behavior, you may have to lure your dog into it. For example, in teaching your dog to beg, you have to use a treat to get the behavior you're looking for.

When creating a more complex trick, consider what you want your dog to do and break it up into smaller tasks. For example, teaching your dog to drop to the ground and roll over and "play dead" when you say "Bang!" requires your dog to do three things: lie down, roll over on his back, and stay. You must first teach your dog how to do each of these things and then put them together to make them into the full trick.

This is where the clicker comes in handy. Start first with the easiest trick, maybe "Down." Click and treat for a quick "Down." Then, as your dog drops down, add "Roll over." In this way, you're chaining two behaviors together. Finally, have your dog stay belly up until you release him. Put the cue word "Bang!" with the chain of behaviors, and you've now got a theatrical performance. Of course, your dog must first learn each trick completely before progressing to the next stage.

Simple Tricks

The following are a number of fun tricks you can teach your dog.

"Give Me Five"

This is one of the easiest tricks to teach, especially if you've been teaching your dog with the clicker, as discussed in chapter 12. Work with him on "Paw it," using your hand as the target. If you've been using a target stick, lay the target stick on your hand and let him paw your hand, and click and treat. Then fade the stick. Start low, if necessary, and tell him, "Paw it." Click and treat when your dog touches your hand with his paw. Slowly raise your hand a little at a time and tell your dog to paw it. Click and treat. Once you have your hand in the "high five" position and your dog is slapping it without hesitation, add the cue words "Give me five." Practice with the cue words until your dog is doing the trick reliably.

"Wave"

"Wave" is a silly trick, but it's another remarkably easy command to teach. Hold the target stick a bit higher than you might to get your dog to paw something and tell him "Paw it." Click and treat. Do this a few times and raise the target stick to a point where your dog has to raise his paw. Click and treat each time.

Once you have the wave at a high enough level, begin to use the cue word "Wave." Click and treat each time the dog waves. Practice several times so your dog knows what "Wave" means. Then start fading the target stick.

"Speak"

"Speak" is an easy command to teach if your dog barks. (Most do!) In fact, you'll probably have more trouble shutting him up than getting him to speak! Start with the clicker and click and treat whenever your dog barks. He may be surprised and try to bark again. Click and treat. As your dog continues to bark for a treat, add a cue word, such as "Speak."

You can also teach your dog to speak by telling him "Speak" when he barks and praising him (and giving him a treat).

The opposite is "Quiet"—not a trick, but a command. After you teach your dog to speak, click and treat; when the dog is busy eating the treat, say "Quiet" before your dog can bark, and then click and treat. Practice "Quiet" with "Speak" to teach your dog to be quiet on command, too.

"Beg"

Beg is also an easy enough trick to teach. You'll need to practice the "Beg" command with a lure. Start by holding a treat over your dog's nose. See if he'll raise himself up into begging position. Click and treat (or praise him and give him the tidbit). Practice this several times and add the word "Beg." You'll have a begging dog in no time.

More Difficult Tricks

The following tricks are more like games.

"Go Find *Someone*" (Hide and Seek)

Hide and Seek is a great game to play with the kids (be sure they're old enough so they won't get knocked down in the enthusiasm!). Have your dog sit first and give one of the kids a treat. Have the child stay in the dog's view. Tell your dog, "Go find *Mary*." (Substitute the child's name.) If the dog is confused, have the child call the dog and then click and have the child treat. Work with the dog on this several times. Eventually get him to go to the child with the use of her name, without her saying anything.

Now, let's say you have another child, Scott. Give him treats. Tell your dog, "Go find Scott." Your dog may run to Mary, but Mary doesn't have the treats. Have Scott call the dog; click and have Scott treat the dog when he comes to him. Practice with Scott for a while.

Next, you need to differentiate between the two children. Have the children in two different places and tell your dog, "Go find Mary" or "Go find Scott." Click and treat when your dog goes to the correct child.

Once your dog has figured out who is who, try having the kids "hide" in the open in the next room. Tell him, "Go find Mary." He should start looking for Mary in the next room. If he doesn't, try leading him to the doorway and then click and have Mary treat him when he discovers her.

As your dog gets better at finding your kids, have your kids "hide" in the open in different rooms until your dog is good at locating them throughout the house. Then, you can start having them hide for real for a truly fun game of Hide and Seek.

"Bow"

A fun trick to teach your dog is to take a bow. You can click and treat when he does a play bow or you can use the target stick to lure him into the position. Start by moving the target stick just low enough so your dog must lower his head to touch it. Click and treat. Continue a few times until he understands that he must lower his head to get the click.

Now, lower the target stick and bring it toward him so that he has to lower his front end just a bit to touch it. Click and treat. If he moves, don't click—try to get him to lower his front end. By shaping his behavior a little at a time, you can get him to bow.

Next, add a cue word such as "Bow." Click and treat for each bow your dog takes.

Another way to teach your dog to bow is to lure him into position. Show him the treat and then slowly bring the treat from his nose toward his chest. Say "Bow." (Don't let him lie down—you want him to bow.) Either click and treat or give him lots of praise and treats. Practice this a few times, and you'll be having your dog take a bow in no time.

"Fetch"

Some dogs (like retrievers) fetch things naturally. However, some dogs won't fetch anything, no matter how hard you try. Nevertheless, you can try training your dog to fetch something with either positive training or the clicker. Find a toy or another item you want your dog to fetch. Good toys for fetch include Frisbees or soft flying discs, hard rubber toys, rope toys, stuffed toys, and tennis balls.

Show your dog the object and get him interested in it. If it's a tennis ball, try bouncing it along the ground and see if he runs after it. Give him praise or click and treat when he pays attention to it. Or if you're using a soft flying disc, try rolling it along the ground or putting food in it. Praise your dog or click and treat whenever he shows interest. Let him play with it for a while.

Now toss the object a short distance. If your dog has been enjoying the object, he'll go after it. (If he doesn't, bring him over to the toy and play with him and the toy a bit before you

 toss it again.) After your dog picks it up, call him to you. Click and treat or praise him when he comes with the toy. If he drops the toy before he comes to you, go with him to get the toy and then tease him with the toy so he takes it.

When your dog brings you the toy, offer a "Trade" with a yummy treat, so you're not playing tug-of-war or making him feel like he must guard it. Then, after he gives you the toy, play with him a bit and toss it again. Add the word "Fetch," and he'll be fetching in no time.

"Roll Over"

Most dogs roll over for a tummy rub. If your dog likes his tummy rubbed, you can pair it with the words "Roll over," and he'll start doing it in no time.

You can also click and treat when you catch your dog rolling over. He may be surprised and may try it again, or you may have to wait until the next time he does it.

Another method you can try is to have your dog lie down and use a target stick. Tell your dog to "Nose it" and move the stick so that he will have to roll over to follow it. Click and treat. Do this several times. Add the cue words "Roll over" when he is rolling over, and then slowly fade the target stick.

What You Now Know . . .

- Teach tricks that will not hurt your dog or cause bad behavior.
- You can impress your friends and delight your family by teaching your dog a few simple tricks.
- Most dogs love doing tricks. It helps create a bond between you and your dog.

Chapter 15

Your Dog as Part of the Family

What's Inside . . .

- Learn what kinds of identification are available for your dog to keep her safe.
- Learn about traveling with your dog.
- Learn about dogs in the workplace.
- Learn how to care for your dog when you go on vacation.
- Learn how to choose a pet sitter or a kennel.

Do you consider your dog part of the family? If so, you're in good company! According to the American Pet Association's statistics, more than 15 million people in the United States consider their dogs their best friends, and more than 13 million *more* people consider their dogs as important to them as their spouse or their kids. That's a lot of people—it's over half of the nearly 45 million dog owners as of 2003.

Did you know that almost 10 million people throw birthday parties for their dogs? Or that 32 million dogs receive Christmas presents each year? There's no doubt that dogs are here to stay as companion animals, and you're not strange or odd if you feel that your pup is an important family member. Let's look at some of the ways you can protect your new family member and include her in your life.

Identification

Before you start having fun with your dog, you need to take the time to have identification put on her. The more stuff you do with your dog, the more fun you'll have, but there is an increased risk of losing your dog.

Your dog should have two forms of ID—tags and a permanent form, either microchip or tattoos. She needs tags because not everyone knows to look for permanent ID; she should have permanent ID because she may lose her collar and tags.

There are pluses and minuses to all types of identification. Tags, which are the cheapest and easiest to use, can be removed from the dog or lost. Many people don't know to check for tattoos or microchips. If someone does find a tattoo, he or she might not know how to use it. Even if a person does know to check for microchips, scanners aren't cheap, and many scanners don't work with all possible microchips. There is no standard for microchips at this time, although the AKC has introduced the Home Again chip and the registration Companion Animal Recovery (which is available to mixed breeds as well as purebreds). You can get more info at www.akccar.org.

Not all shelters have scanners for microchips, although Home Again and other microchip manufacturers have offered microchip scanners for free or at low cost to shelters.

Tags

Tags are a cheap form of identification. Most tags cost between $4 and $8, although they can cost between $10 and $20; the more expensive tags may be gold plated or have a blessing from Saint Francis on them. Tags are easy to get. Many pet supply stores have tag-engraving machines that engrave a tag for under $10 right there as you watch. Your vet probably has mail-in forms for tags, and you can purchase tags through pet supply mail-order catalogs and online—even on eBay. I've even gotten some tags free with purchases of pet supplies. Some malls have tag engraving machines for pet and luggage tags.

There's no reason your dog should be without tags. Make two tags—one for her to wear and one as a spare. When you travel or go on vacation, have a separate tag made, with your cell phone number and the place where you will be plus dates. Every day, lost dogs turn up at shelters with collars but without tags.

Tattoos

But what if your dog loses her collar or tags? Luckily, you can use tattoos, a form of permanent identification that you can have on your dog.

Tattoos are a visible form of identification that's permanently marked into the skin. Unlike human tattoos, dog tattoos are not painful, but getting them can be distressing because the markers buzz loudly. Tattoos are put in two locations on a dog's body: inside the ears or on the inside of the thigh. Inside the ears is a poor choice—dog thieves will often lop off an ear to remove the identification. Tattoos are generally painless, but they are noisy, and most dogs hate having it done. They are less expensive than microchips, and easier for people to find. You must choose a unique number for your dog. However, those numbers must be registered with an ID registry in order to provide any help. There have been instances of tattooed dogs that weren't registered with a national registry, so the tattoo was in effect useless. See the "Animal Registry and Recovery Services" sidebar on page 193.

You can get tattoos done at a vet clinic, through a breed club, or from a groomer. Both NDR and Tattoo-A-Pet can refer you to tattooists in your area. Tattoos cost anywhere from $5 to $25, plus registration fee.

Microchips

A microchip is about the size of a grain of rice and is inserted under the skin, usually between the dog's shoulder blades. A microchip is encased in plastic, and it is activated only when a scanner is passed over it. You must have a vet or a shelter insert a microchip, which takes only a few seconds and causes very little discomfort. When the scanner is passed over it, it reads the microchip similarly to how a bar code reader scans groceries. Whoever reads the scanned number must contact the registry to look up the dog in the database. Microchips cost anywhere from $25 to $50, plus registration fee.

Traveling Together

If your dog is a member of the family, why shouldn't you bring her along on vacation? There are plenty of good reasons to have your dog with you when you go on vacation, and if you do a bit of preparation, things will go smoothly. Traveling with your pet can be pleasurable or a nightmare, depending on your planning and your pet.

Animal Registry and Recovery Services

The following are microchip and tattoo registry and recovery services. You can usually get a list of people in your area who offer tattoos or microchips (note that almost all vets offer microchips), and you can register your dog there.

AKC Companion Animal Recovery
5580 Centerview Drive, Suite 250
Raleigh, NC 27606-3389
800/252-7894
www.akccar.org

National Dog Registry
Box 116
Woodstock, NY 12498
800/637-3647
www.natldogregistry.com

Tattoo-A-Pet
6571 S.W. 20th Court
Ft. Lauderdale, FL 33317
800/828-8667
www.tattoo-a-pet.com

But before you start packing, start thinking. Taking a vacation with a dog requires a lot more time and preparation than just jumping in the car and going somewhere. Not all pets are good travelers, and many pets get carsick or behave inappropriately in new surroundings. In some cases, it's better to board your dog than subject her to the stress of a trip.

Likewise, some places—overseas trips, trips where you will be in museums all day—are poor choices to bring your dog. Before you decide to take your dog with you, find out if there are places where you can take your dog and facilities such as boarding kennels and emergency veterinarians in the area where you're traveling. What are you going to do while you're visiting? Is your dog going to be cooped up in her crate all day in the hotel room, or are you going to be going places where dogs are allowed?

Some dogs shouldn't travel unless you have no other choice. Young puppies, elderly dogs, and untrained dogs should not join you on vacation. With them, you should always hire a pet sitter or use a boarding kennel. Away from home, basic obedience commands—sit, down, come, and so on—aren't optional, they're imperative.

Make sure your dog is up-to-date on all her vaccinations, including rabies. If you're traveling in Lyme disease country or places where your dog might be exposed to *Giardia* (rural towns with limited water treatment), ask your vet if a Lyme disease or a *Giardia* vaccine is appropriate. Your vet can also advise you on what other vaccinations might be appropriate for your dog.

Travel Preparations

Before you head on out on a grand adventure—even before you pack—consider your dog. You will have to make reservations in hotels that allow pets. And just because a hotel allows pets doesn't mean it will allow your dog. Sad, but true—many hotels and motels have size restrictions. Some say cats and dogs under a certain weight are okay—as if a larger dog might do more damage! Some charge an extra fee to have a dog in the room. Some want a refundable security deposit. (For more info on accommodations that allow dogs, see the section "Staying in Hotels or Motels with Your Dog," later in this chapter.)

Whatever you do, don't think you can just sneak your dog in. Most motel owners are pretty savvy about what goes on. At the same time every year, I stay at a little motel in Utah with my dogs. The woman the last time mentioned, "Oh, you're the folks who stay every year one night." They remembered me and my dogs. Hopefully we've made a good impression because we always try to be quiet and we always try to pick up after the dogs. If you try to sneak in your dog, you might find an extra bill tagged to your room charge—or worse, find out you've been evicted. Not the kind of vacation you had in mind, was it?

Also, consider the type of vacation you're having. Some places are naturally conducive to dogs; others are not. Large cities with attractions where dogs aren't allowed may not be fun for your dog at all. Even some places that you would think would be perfect to bring your dog may not allow dogs or may severely restrict them. One such place is national parks. Many national and other parks do not allow dogs in the backcountry, although they will allow dogs on major logging roads and other areas. Some parks allow dogs in camping areas but not on trails or in any other areas of the park. Check with the park before discovering that your best friend isn't welcome or will not have a fun time.

When you take your dog on vacation with you, you'll naturally be bringing food along for her, but you may want to also bring bottled water. Some dogs' stomachs and intestines are sensitive to water from different sources and may have digestive upsets if you try to give them water from a tap away from home. In rural areas, it's a good idea to bring your own water anyway. Some places are on well water, or their treatment facilities can't screen out microorganisms such as *Giardia* (which causes severe diarrhea and dehydration). Plan on bringing enough food and water for a day or two longer than your vacation, in case of unforeseen delays.

Health Certificates

When you travel across state lines or into another country, you'll need your pet's health certificate, dated no more than ten days before the time you travel. You can obtain one of these certificates from your veterinarian, usually at a cost of no more than $25. If you travel by plane, you must have one of these certificates to transport your dog; it usually remains affixed to the dog's crate.

Have copies of your dog's health certificate and vaccination certificates with you at all times. This means you should make a copy to keep with you if your dog travels by plane and the original certificate is on her crate.

Airline Travel

Airline travel presents obstacles for those flying with dogs. When you're planning to take your dog on a flight with you, be certain to contact the airline well ahead of purchasing your tickets to find out what its (and the FAA's) latest rules and regulations are regarding transporting dogs. Some airlines will not transport dogs at all, and others may have size or temperature restrictions. A few will let you take a small dog on the plane with you if she will fit under the seat; some will let dogs travel with the luggage in the cargo area of the plane.

Assuming that you can fly with your dog, be certain that you arrive several hours ahead of your flight to get through security and get your dog ready for loading onto the airplane. The airline may require food and water dishes, but if your dog chews plastic (many do!), you can clip a small stainless steel bucket (available through pet supply catalogs) with a double snap to the inside of the crate as a water bowl. Prepackage all dog food and tape that to the top of the crate.

You should also have a package with all paperwork, stating where your dog is going, your home address and phone number, your cell phone number, any emergency numbers, and any specific instructions, in case you get separated from your dog. Include copies of all health records and vaccinations. I usually include a nice note to the handler: "Hi! My name is Rover, and I'm an Australian Shepherd mix. I'm very important to my owner. I'm very friendly, but I'm a little sleepy right now because my owner gave me some tranquilizers from the vet. My owner is Maggie Bonham, from 12345 Street Name Way, Denver, Colorado 80123, 555/123-4567. I'm flying UA 123 to SLC. She'll be staying at the Radisson Hotel, phone number . . ." It's a little chatty, but it gives the baggage handler some information and also shows that you care enough to give instructions on how to care for your dog.

I've used several different airlines to transport dogs over the years and each time, I've been pleased. Most airlines are keenly aware that your dog is your baby and are willing to accommodate you. I know that there have been horror stories, but they have thankfully not been my experience. Even so, it's best to plan a flight without any connections to avoid possible hassles.

Car Travel

Some dogs do remarkably well in the car. Others would rather have their toenails pulled out with a pair of pliers. If your dog is used to traveling to fun places in the car, you'll have few problems getting her ready for a big trip. If your dog hates riding in the car, perhaps you should rethink bringing her along unless you have no choice. In that case, talk to your veterinarian about possible sedatives and keep your dog in a crate.

When you travel with your dog by car, you should have your dog either in a crate or wearing a seat harness restraint. Both of these will minimize injury in case of an accident or if you have to stop suddenly. They're also useful in keeping your dog out of your lap while you're driving. Check on your dog frequently if you use a crate, especially in the summertime. Be sure that your dog is sufficiently cool and there is sufficient airflow through the crate to avoid the dangers of overheating.

It's important to think about the temperature inside your car. In warm weather, temperatures inside a parked car can soar to dangerous levels in a short time, even with the windows down. Be sure that your car's air conditioner is in good working order and make sure that the air around your dog's crate isn't blocked. Likewise, be sure that the sun doesn't hit your dog's crate while you're driving. Never leave a dog alone inside a parked car, even with the windows cracked, during summer. Even in a relatively short time (ten minutes or less), the car can heat up to fatal temperatures. When you get out of the car, your dog should get out, too.

One useful device is a portable fan that runs on batteries. These are great to clip onto your dog's crate and will help keep her cool in hot weather. In very hot weather, I like to freeze

---

Car Traveling Checklist

- ☐ Health certificates and vaccination certificates
- ☐ Phone numbers for emergency veterinarians in the area where you'll be traveling
- ☐ Dog first aid kit
- ☐ Enough food and water for your trip plus two days
- ☐ Travel crate
- ☐ Extra leash
- ☐ Paper towels and plastic bags
- ☐ Spot cleaner (enzymatic cleaner)
- ☐ Bags for picking up pet waste
- ☐ Treats
- ☐ Toys
- ☐ Portable cooling fans (battery powered)
- ☐ Dog's medication
- ☐ A collar with ID tags for both your destination and your home

---

two-liter soda bottles filled with water. You can put one or more in your dog's crate, and as the ice melts, you can then use the cold water for her to drink. Both fans and frozen bottles of water are great while you are in the car with your dog.

Cold weather, too, can be dangerous if your dog has a thin coat. In this case, keeping your dog warm is important. Keep her on a warm blanket. Dog coats or sweaters are not silly if your dog lacks enough fur to stay warm.

Plan to drive no more than four hours between stops, and plan to stop more frequently if your dog is elderly or is a puppy. Highway rest areas frequently have places to exercise dogs, but do so only on leash. Many dogs who are normally reliable off leash may not be in strange surroundings. Be a responsible owner and pick up after your dog when she defecates.

Going for a Ride

If you've socialized your dog to the car, car rides should be very enjoyable—especially if you go to fun places. Regardless of where you go, always prepare to carry your dog *inside* the car, preferably in a crate or belted in with her own safety harness. (You can purchase them at pet supply stores.)

Never carry your dog in the back of an open pickup bed. Dogs regularly get tossed out when the owner has to stop suddenly or swerve to avoid an accident. In some states, it's illegal to carry a dog in an open pickup bed.

I'll stress the dangers of leaving a dog in a car once again. Even if it's not that warm out, a car can heat up quickly *even with the windows down*. Your dog can suffer from heat prostration in a very short amount of time, which is why you must never leave your dog in the car in the summertime, even for a little bit. The dog must go with you.

Staying in Hotels or Motels with Your Dog

It seems that the travel industry has discovered pets. In their brochures and at their Web sites, most hotel and motel chains state whether their properties allow pets and what is available for them. In its tour books that are available to members, AAA also lists which hotels and motels allow pets. One word of caution, though: Don't always rely on books and brochures because the establishment's ownership may have changed and the new owners may not allow dogs or may have certain restrictions. Always call and ask when booking your accommodations.

Some hotels really like pets and cater to our four-footed companions. These hotels will offer services for your pup, including doggy room service and walks. For more information on pet-friendly hotels, visit www.petswelcome.com.

When you take your dog to a hotel or motel, choose a first-floor room, with a door that goes outside, if possible, so you can take your dog outside quickly if she needs to eliminate. Plus it's easier to not have to drag her crate into an elevator. Also, if you choose a hotel that offers room service, you won't have to go out to eat.

Pet Travel Resources

For online information on pet-friendly hotels, visit www.petswelcome.com. The following books also list hotels and motels that accept pets:

Pets on the Go: The Definitive Pet Accommodation and Vacation Guide by Dawn Habgood and Robert Habgood (Dawbert Press).

Traveling with Your Pet—The AAA PetBook, 2nd ed. by Cynthia Psarakis, ed. (AAA).

Great Vacations for You and Your Dog, 6th ed., by Martin Management Books (Martin Management Books).

The Portable petswelcome.com: The Complete Guide to Traveling with Your Pet by Fred N. Grayson and Chris Kingsley (Howell Book House).

Mobil Travel Guide: On the Road with Your Pet (Mobil Travel Guide).

It's important to show good manners with your dog when you travel. Sadly, many people abuse their welcome, causing hotels and motels that once accepted dogs to stop doing so. Always be mindful of the hotel's hospitality. The following are good rules for traveling:

- Always inform the hotel/motel that you have a dog.
- Never leave your dog alone in your room. A crated dog may howl or bark and disturb guests. A loose dog may destroy things or soil the carpet—as well as howl or bark.
- Ask at the front desk where you can exercise your dog. Bring a plastic bag or pooper scoop and pick up feces.
- Don't bathe, brush, or groom your dog in a hotel room.
- Don't let your dog sleep in the bed with you. (The next person may not like dog hair on the blankets and bedspread.) If your dog can't sleep except on a bed, bring an extra blanket or towel and lay it across the bed to keep the fur off.
- Put your dog's dishes in the bathroom or anywhere else where there is a tiled or linoleum floor. Dogs sometimes spill food and water when eating or drinking.
- Do not let your dog off leash to run.
- Keep your dog quiet.
- Use a lint brush or dog-hair roller to remove any dog hair from the furniture and carpet.
- Leave the room in good shape.

At Work

Did you know that you can take your dog to work? Pet Sitters International has sponsored a Take Your Dog to Work Day every year for the past seven years. They've teamed up with Iams Dog Food to promote Take Your Dog to Work Day on the last Friday of June. (Check out Pet Sitters International's Web site, at www.petsit.com, for more information about Take Your Dog to Work Day.)

You have probably seen plenty of dogs at different workplaces. Dogs sometimes hang out in retail shops to greet shoppers and meet people. I've seen dogs at travel agencies, in classrooms, at bookstores, in libraries, in pet supply stores, in hotels, at hospitals, at radio stations, in hair styling salons, and in other places where dogs aren't usually considered welcome. Some dogs are in unlikely places as well, such as aboard airplanes and ships. As a writer, I'm used to having dogs around when I work. Unfortunately, the appearance of dogs at work is more of an exception rather than the rule, but this is slowly changing.

There are reasons for not having dogs at work, such as a dog can be a distraction, or the clients of the shop may not like dogs, or the health department has excluded dogs from the shop because it carries food or is a restaurant, or someone is allergic to dogs. Whatever the reason, it's a tough sale to bring a dog into the work environment, especially if you work in corporate America.

Before you decide to take your dog to work, you must take the following into consideration:

- Your dog must be obedience trained and must be well-behaved. No exceptions. You're inviting disaster otherwise.
- Your dog must get along with other people, children, and even other animals.
- You must work for yourself or you must have gotten approval of the boss (and company) beforehand.
- You must have enough liability insurance in case your dog hurts someone either through a bite or knocking them over.
- You must have prepared adequately for what you're going to do with your dog while you actually work. Does your dog nap? Does she like to greet people? Do you have water, food, and a crate set up in case you can't watch your dog?

If you're able to bring the dog along to your job, start bringing her during a slow time and give your dog time to adjust to the new surroundings. The excitement of the new place may be a bit overwhelming at first, but eventually it'll become old hat, and your dog will get used to it.

All I Got Was This Lousy T-Shirt

There are times when you don't want to bring your dog with you when you travel. Maybe you're going someplace that doesn't allow dogs or maybe you're on a business trip. Or maybe your dog doesn't travel well. Whatever the reason, you might decide to board your dog at a kennel or hire a pet sitter.

Boarding Your Dog at a Kennel

There are several types of boarding facilities for dogs:

- **Boarding kennel:** This is a standard boarding kennel. It keeps dogs in pens and may or may not provide individualized attention.
- **Doggy day care, pet hotels, or pet spas:** These are usually associated with training schools, but they may be anywhere. Dogs are usually played with and given exercise. Depending on the size of the kennel, your dog may get to see the same people each day. Dogs usually come home relaxed and aren't as stressed out.
- **Training facilities boarding kennel:** This type of kennel is usually associated with a trainer or training facilities. Trainers may—at an additional cost—socialize or train your dog while you are gone.
- **Veterinary boarding facilities:** These facilities are usually run adjacent to veterinary practices. The vet is on call twenty-four hours a day.

Costs for boarding facilities vary widely, depending on the services offered. Some, for a fee, will perform on-site grooming or exit baths before you pick up your dog. Some provide training, games, snack breaks, and socialization time.

Ask your vet, trainer, or other dog owners whom they recommend to board dogs. Contact the American Boarding Kennel Association at 719/591-1113 (www.abka.com) for kennels in your area if you have no other recommendations.

Call each kennel and ask the questions in the worksheet "Finding a Kennel: Interview Questions," below, to help narrow down your search.

Finding a Kennel: Interview Questions

What hours can I come by and drop off or pick up my pet?

_____

_____

Can I provide my dog's own food?

_____

_____

Do you provide indoor-outdoor, strictly indoor, or strictly outdoor runs?

_____

_____

Do you have an on-call vet?

_____

_____

Do you have grooming available?

_____

_____

continues

How much do you charge per dog per day? Do you offer a discount for multiple dogs? If you care for more than one of my dogs, will they share a run?

_____

_____

Is there someone on-site at all times?

_____

_____

Is there supervised exercise time or playtime?

_____

_____

What disinfectants do you use and how often do you clean the kennels?

_____

_____

What additional services do you provide? How much do those services cost?

_____

_____

What vaccinations are required and how recent do they need to be?

_____

_____

Whom do you contact in emergencies?

_____

_____

 Once you have found a few kennels in your area that fit your criteria, make an appointment with them for an inspection. If the staff is reluctant to allow you to tour the entire facility, you should probably consider another kennel.

Contact the boarding facility well ahead of time. Most good boarding facilities fill up quickly—during peak times, small facilities and even larger ones may be full weeks or months in advance. If you own multiple dogs, this may present a special challenge if the facility is small.

Hiring a Pet Sitter

If you have multiple dogs or if your dog does not do well in a boarding kennel, consider hiring a pet sitter. All pet sitters will come to your house and feed and water your dog as well as walk and exercise her. Some will bring in the mail and newspapers, water plants, feed other pets, and make the home look lived-in while you are gone. A pet sitter can be anyone from a bonded and insured service to the neighbor kid next door. Whomever you choose as a pet sitter, remember that you are giving the person full run of your house.

Ask your vet, dog trainer, and other pet-owning friends who does pet sitting in your area. Quite often vets and trainers know someone who is looking to add to their income through pet sitting. Some may even be trainers or vet techs! You can contact the National Association of Professional Pet Sitters at 800/286-PETS (www.petsitters.org) or Pet Sitters International at 336/983-9222 (www.petsit.com) for a list of professional pet sitters. Be certain any professional pet sitter is bonded, licensed, and insured, and ask for references and a copy of their contract.

Questions to Ask a Pet Sitter

Are you bonded and insured?

_____

_____

Do you belong to either the National Association of Professional Pet Sitters or Pet Sitters International?

_____

_____

continues

Do you have a contract? May I see it?

_____

_____

What kind of pets do you take care of?

_____

_____

How many times do you visit?

_____

_____

What services do you provide?

_____

_____

Do you stay in the house to make it look lived-in?

_____

_____

Will you water plants (or perform other housekeeping functions)?

_____

_____

What do you do in case of an emergency?

_____

_____

Do you have references? May I contact them?

_____

_____

Once you settle on a sitter, have the person come over and meet your dog. Have the sitter walk and play with your dog. The interaction is very important—you want someone your dog likes and who is not afraid of your dog.

What about relatives, neighbors, and friends? Would they make good pet sitters? It depends. If the person you have in mind is dog savvy and knows how to take care of your dog, then by all means, have that person be your pet sitter. However, friends and relatives, no matter how well-intentioned they are, may not be smart when it comes to dogs. You can come home to a trashed house because your relative thought that keeping your dog crated or confined would be cruel. Your friend might let your dog off the leash, thinking she would come back. There are many reasons to use friends and relatives, and twice that many not to. Even if you make yourself clear, leave written instructions, and insist they follow them, sometimes they will do the exact opposite.

Regardless of whom you use as a pet sitter, always leave your vet's phone number and emergency number handy. Post an itinerary of your trip with numbers where they can contact you, should a problem arise. Clearly write out instructions for care. If your dog requires medication, put the information on the instruction sheet. Then, take a big permanent marker and mark the precise dosage on each pill bottle. If you have multiple dogs, be certain to put the correct dog's name on the bottle as well. I've provided a handy "Pet Sitter Information Sheet" in the appendix for your use.

What You Now Know . . .

- Be sure your dog has ID, both permanent and tags.
- There are several things to consider when planning to travel with your dog.
- You can have a lot of fun with your dog at work and on vacation.
- Some dogs go to work with their owners. You can try this out during Take Your Dog to Work Day.
- Your dog can go with you on vacation, you can board her, or you can hire a pet sitter.

Appendix

Useful
Resources

How to Use This Appendix

This appendix provides resources you can use to track various aspects related to your dog—from vaccination records to training records to emergency preparedness measures. Label a three-ring binder "Dog Records" and make as many copies of the forms in this appendix as you need. As you fill out the forms, place them in your three-ring binder for reference.

Important Phone Numbers

Contact	Name	Telephone Number
Primary veterinarian		
Primary veterinarian's on-call number		
Secondary veterinarian		
Emergency clinic		
Alternate emergency clinic		
Local poison control hotline		
ASPCA 24-hour poison control hotline ($50/case)	—	888/426-4435
Groomer		
Pet sitter		
Boarding kennel		

Vaccination Records

Puppy

Age	Vaccination Type	Date	Next Vaccination Due Date
8–10 weeks			
10–12 weeks			
12–14 weeks			
15–18 weeks	Rabies		

1 Year

Vaccination Type	Date	Next Vaccination Due Date
Rabies		

2 Years

Vaccination Type	Date	Next Vaccination Due Date

3 Years

Vaccination Type	Date	Next Vaccination Due Date
Rabies		

4 Years

Vaccination Type	Date	Next Vaccination Due Date

5 Years

Vaccination Type	Date	Next Vaccination Due Date

6 Years

Vaccination Type	Date	Next Vaccination Due Date
Rabies		

7 Years

Vaccination Type	Date	Next Vaccination Due Date

8 Years

Vaccination Type	Date	Next Vaccination Due Date

9 Years

Vaccination Type	Date	Next Vaccination Due Date
Rabies		

10 Years

Vaccination Type	Date	Next Vaccination Due Date

After 10 Years

Vaccination Type	Date	Next Vaccination Due Date

Veterinary Record

Dewormings

Date	Type	Next Fecal Exam Date

Veterinarian Visits

Date	Reason

Medications

Medication	Dosage per Day	Condition	Directions (Take with Food, Store in Refrigerator, etc.)

Surgeries

Date	Reason

Heartworm Tests and Preventives

Year: _____

Heartworm Test Date	Results

Preventive Given	Date
Month 1	
Month 2	
Month 3	
Month 4	
Month 5	
Month 6	
Month 7	
Month 8	
Month 9	
Month 10	
Month 11	
Month 12	

Chore Chart

Use this chart to divvy up chores. Under the day of the week, insert a checkmark when the task is completed.

Daily Chores	Whose Turn?	Mon.	Tues.	Wed.	Thurs.	Fri.	Sat.	Sun.
Take dog out (and in) in the morning								
Feed dog breakfast and check water								
Morning walk								
Take dog out (and in) at noon								
Feed dog lunch and check water								
Take dog out (and in) midafternoon								
Exercise/play with dog								
Training (15 minutes)								
Afternoon walk								
Feed dog dinner and check water								
Exercise/play with dog								
Take dog out (and in) before bedtime								
Tuck dog into his crate								
Weekly Chores	**Whose Turn?**	**Mon.**	**Tues.**	**Wed.**	**Thurs.**	**Fri.**	**Sat.**	**Sun.**
Brush and examine dog for abnormalities								
Clip dog's toenails								
Bathe dog (may do less often than weekly)								
Take dog to training class								

Daily Crate-Training Chart

Use this chart to divvy up crate-training responsibilities. Under the day of the week, insert a checkmark when the task is completed.

Duty	Whose Turn?	Mon.	Tues.	Wed.	Thurs.	Fri.	Sat.	Sun.
Take dog out first thing in the morning								
Take dog out after breakfast								
Take dog out before going to work/school								
Put dog in crate before leaving for work/school								
Take dog out at lunchtime								
Take dog out after lunch								
Put dog in crate before returning to work/school								
Take dog out after work/school								
Take dog out after dinner								
Take dog out after playtime								
Take dog out before bedtime								
Put dog in crate before bedtime								
Take dog out if whining at night								

Disaster Preparedness Checklist

☐ Pet first-aid kit

☐ Enough pet food and potable water for three days

☐ Copies of your pet's health records and vaccination records

☐ Pet's medication

☐ Photos of your pet, in case he gets lost

☐ Bowls, leashes, and can opener

☐ Travel crates

☐ Hotel contact #1 _____

☐ Hotel contact #2 _____

☐ Hotel contact #3 _____

☐ Hotel contact #4 _____

☐ Hotel contact #5 _____

☐ Emergency vet #1 _____

☐ Emergency vet #2 _____

☐ Emergency vet #3 _____

☐ Emergency vet #4 _____

☐ Boarding kennel #1 _____

☐ Boarding kennel #2 _____

☐ Boarding kennel #3 _____

☐ Boarding kennel #4 _____

☐ _____

☐ _____

☐ _____

☐ _____

☐ _____

☐ _____

☐ _____

☐ _____

☐ _____

☐ _____

Pet Sitter Information Sheet

Pet Sitter's Name:

Dates on Vacation:

Pet's Name	Species (Dog, Cat, etc.)

Contact Information	Telephone Number
Your Cell Phone	
Veterinarian	
Emergency Veterinarian	
Emergency Contact	

Hotel Name/Number	Dates There

Visitation Instructions

Visit _____ times each day   Walk _____ times each day

Instructions:

Feeding Instructions

Feed _____ cups of food to _____ (name) at _____ (times)

Feed _____ cups of food to _____ (name) at _____ (times)

Feed _____ cups of food to _____ (name) at _____ (times)

Feed _____ cups of food to _____ (name) at _____ (times)

Special Feeding Instructions:

Medications

Pet's Name	Medication	How Often	Possible Adverse Reactions to Watch For (Note Symptoms)

Vaccination Records

Pet's Name	Date of Last Rabies Vaccination

Special Instructions:

Kennel Information Sheet

Pet's Name	Species (Dog, Cat, etc.)

Contact Information	Telephone Number
Your Cell Phone	
Veterinarian	
Emergency Veterinarian	
Emergency Contact	

Hotel Name	Dates There

Feeding Instructions

Feed _____ cups of food to _____ (name) at _____ (times)

Feed _____ cups of food to _____ (name) at _____ (times)

Feed _____ cups of food to _____ (name) at _____ (times)

Feed _____ cups of food to _____ (name) at _____ (times)

Special Feeding Instructions:

Medications

Pet's Name	Medication	How Often	Possible Adverse Reactions to Watch For (Note Symptoms)

Vaccination Records

Pet's Name	Date of Last Rabies Vaccination

Special Instructions:

Index